The Power
of Life Lessons

The Power of Life Lessons

How to Learn Your Lessons and Create the Life You Want

Linda Gannaway, Ed.D.

KEATON
Publishing

Copyright © 2017 Linda Gannaway

All rights reserved.

Published by Keaton Publishing, a division of TCS Communications, LLC, Fresno, California

The author gratefully acknowledges those who granted permission to use copyrighted and previously published material: (1) George M. Gazda, William C. Childers, and Richard P. Walters for use of the Sensory Modality Checklist (copyright © 1982); (2) Richard Niolon for use of the List of Feelings Words (2008); and (3) Joe Henderson for use of material from *Did I Win? A Farewell to George Sheehan* (copyright © 1995). Each of these individuals holds the copyright or publishing rights. See the Notes section for additional information.

The purpose of this book is to help you learn your life lessons and create the life you want. It is based on the author's education, experiences, and insights, along with the lessons she has learned from life.

The author's personal stories in this book are true. The stories about other people are used to describe situations the author has encountered; however, circumstances have been changed to protect anonymity and in some cases, composites are used. Any resemblance to actual identities is unintentional.

You should use the book as a general guide and resource, but as with all books of this kind, it cannot address the individual situations of readers. It is not intended to be, nor should it be, relied on or construed as medical, health, nutritional, psychological, financial, legal, or any other kind of professional advice, service, or therapy. As noted several times in the book, you should consult a competent professional in the appropriate area for any individual advice or treatment you need.

The results you get from reading and doing the activities in the book may be different from the results others achieve. All information and references in the book are believed to be accurate at the time of publishing but may change over time. There may also be typographical and other errors in the text.

The author and publisher are not liable or responsible for any loss or damage caused, or alleged to have been caused, directly or indirectly, by the information and activities contained or referenced in this book, or your application of them.

ISBN-13: 978-0998506609
ISBN-10: 0998506605
ISBN-13: 978-0998506692 (ebook)
Library of Congress Control Number: 2016910732

Cataloging and publication information is available at the back of this book.

Cover design: Kathi Dunn, www.Dunn-Design.com

First edition

To my parents, Sarah and Jim Gannaway.
My deepest thanks for your faith, values, and unconditional love.

"Education is not the filling of a pail, but the lighting of a fire."

—William Butler Yeats

Contents

Chapter 1: Things Happen for a Reason 1
The Story Behind the Story and What's Inside this Book

- Here's How Life Lessons Empower Us 2
- Creating the Life You Want 3
- How to Use This Book 5
- No Regrets. 5

Chapter 2: Adventures in the School of Life 7
Understanding Our Journey through Life from a Bird's-eye View

- My Adventures in School 10
- How We Make Progress 12
- School Rules 16
- Using Intention 22

Chapter 3: All about Life Lessons 29
A Closer Look at What We All Need to Figure Out

- Characteristics of Life Lessons 31
- Types of Lessons 37
- How to Identify Your Life Lessons 41

Chapter 4: Finding Our Teachers 45
Discovering Who and What Can Teach Us What We Need to Learn

External Teachers

- Experiences 47
- People 49
- Coincidences 51
- Places 55
- Animals 58
- Time 60

Chapter 5: Discovering Our Internal Teachers 65
Exploring the Messages from Within

    Internal Teachers

- Bodies 65
- Thoughts. 69
- Behaviors 72
- Emotions 76
- Addictions. 82
- Dreams 88

Chapter 6: Intuition, the Ultimate Teacher 93
Tapping Into the Wisdom of Your Natural Instincts

- How Is Intuition Helpful? 94
- How Does Your Intuition Communicate? 96
- A Lesson on Listening 101
- Listen, Trust, Act 102

Chapter 7: The How-Tos of Learning 109
Applying a Step-by-Step Learning Guide

- A Model for Learning 109
- Three Steps to Competence 113
- Your Learning Style 117

Chapter 8: Turning Obstacles into Teachers. 123
How to Identify Obstacles and Accept the Gifts of Their Instructions

- Hazardous Zones 125
- Time Management 131
- Procrastination 139
- Limiting Beliefs 148

Chapter 9: Continuing to Grow 161
Developing a Lifestyle that Increases Your Learning Curve

- Managing Stress 162
- Increasing Your Energy 174
- Clearing the Clutter 185
- Becoming a Growth Seeker 194

Chapter 10: Doing What You Came Here to Do 201
Discovering Your Purpose and Accomplishing Your Goals

- Finding Your Purpose 201
- Setting and Achieving Goals 211
- Learning to Shine. 221

Chapter 11: Teaching What You Learn 229
Sharing with Others for the Benefit of All

- The Paybacks of Giving 229
- Finding Your Spot 234
- Continuing to Shine 235

Appendices
- Appendix A: List of Feelings Words 241
- Appendix B: Inner Guide Imagery Exercise 243
- Appendix C: Sensory Modality Checklist 245
- Appendix D: Thought-Stopping Form 249
- Appendix E: Goal-Setting Form 251
- Appendix F: Goal-Setting Imagery Exercise. 253

Notes 255

Index 263

Acknowledgments 273

Invitation 275
- An Invitation to Book Clubs and Other Groups 275

About the Author 277

Chapter 1
Things Happen for a Reason

The thought exploded in my head like an amped-up firecracker, leaving three words permanently etched in my brain: "Student of Life."

It came from nowhere and with absolutely no warning. I had just finished a relaxing run with my dog at a local park. As the sun started to set, we took a little time to rest on a small knoll. Sitting in the cool grass of early evening, I silently observed the surrounding trees. Then it hit me. I can't tell you how, but I instantly knew the words referred to a book—one I was supposed to write.

I'd never planned to write a book, but it felt next to impossible to ignore such a dramatic experience. I didn't have to work the following summer, so I took that time to write a first draft. Thoughts flowed out of me as if I were taking dictation. Words appeared on my computer screen before I consciously thought about them. Although I took good care of myself during that time, swimming most mornings and watching my diet, I didn't want to eat or sleep—just write. After two months of nearly nonstop typing, I completed a three-hundred-page manuscript. Then almost as if nothing had happened, I went back to work, and my life returned to normal.

Wondering whether there was any truth to what I'd written, I started using the material in my own life, testing the ideas and applying the self-help techniques. My learning curve accelerated. I no longer got stuck in my usual places, I could navigate through difficult situations with a lot less stress, and I actually enjoyed some of the circumstances at work that used to make me squeeze the arms of my chair.

After several years of personal testing, I became convinced that the material was solid, and I couldn't wait to share it with others. As a counselor on a university campus, I introduced parts of the book into my counseling sessions with students. Without exception, they found it helpful. After that, I developed thirty hours of course instruction and taught graduate classes on the book, again with positive results.

One of my students worked in a state prison with inmates who would soon be released. He started using the material from my class to help them make the transition back into their communities. I felt thrilled when he told me that and saw it as a more-than-obvious sign I needed to edit the book and get it out there.

Things happen for a reason. It wasn't by chance that I had that experience in the park or that I wrote this book. I later realized the book is part of my mission and purpose in life.

When I talk about this material with groups of people, I always know it's anything but coincidental as to who shows up. There is always some basis for why they come, even though it may not be clear at the time or may seem trivial until later. The same applies to you with this book. Look for reasons you're reading it—and why you're reading it now.

Here's How Life Lessons Empower Us

As I've studied life lessons over the past thirty-some-odd years, I've been continually astonished by the fact that they can help us make improvements in our lives, regardless of our current situation and no matter where we start. So if you're struggling just to get by right now or have some nagging problems, life lessons can help. If you're doing okay but want to do better, life lessons can teach you how. Even if you're already wildly successful, you can use the information from your life lessons to reach new levels and find even more success.

Growth and progress are unlimited. Our lives can always get more productive, abundant, purposeful, enjoyable, and just plain fun. We can always take the next steps to improve our lives and the lives of others. Life lessons show us the way. By definition, they provide the "practical wisdom" that helps us reach our goals faster and easier.

While we're here on planet Earth, we have certain types of lessons to learn, which include **common** and **unique** lessons. Common lessons apply to all of us. Everyone needs to master them. Like how to be independent, how to be happy, how to love and be loved, and how to find meaning in our lives.

And because each of us is unique, every single one of us also has unique, individual, and personal lessons to master during our earthly journey. Just as every grain of sand is different from all the rest, every one of us is different and special in our own way. Each of us has a uniquely distinct path to walk through life. That means every one of us has our own individual lessons to learn, along with an ideal time frame for learning them. These include lessons on relationships, jobs, finances, and health.

Throughout this book, I share lots of my own personal stories and the lessons I've learned from them. I also include some of the lessons I've learned from my students and other teachers in my life. However, the book will not tell you what lessons *you* should learn. That's because I don't know what lessons you need to learn. Each of us needs to figure those out for ourselves.

You're already learning life lessons or else you wouldn't have gotten this far. But you may be learning them more by happenstance or trial and error. The key is to make your learning more conscious and deliberate. Then, the more you practice, the more accurate and automatic your learning becomes.

So instead of telling you what lessons to learn, I will encourage you to identify your own lessons and give you tools to be successful in learning them—descriptions, examples, strategies, and activities. These tools are written in a workbook-type format to make it easy for you to apply what you're reading to your personal life. The book takes you through a step-by-step process of learning the lessons that are meaningful and relevant for you—now. And yes, even in those problem areas where you may have been stuck for years.

Creating the Life You Want

In the following pages, you'll find information that will help you see life from a bird's-eye perspective, as if you temporarily rise above day-to-day living to see the big picture of your life. Fly above the daily grind for a view of "*Aha*, so that is what's happening." We all want to make sense of our world. It's empowering to know how everything fits together.

Keep reading and you'll also discover the teachers in your life, both ***external teachers*** (like people, problems, coincidences, and animals) and ***internal teachers*** (like our bodies, thoughts, behaviors, emotions, addictions, and dreams).

Problems usually show up in our lives as unwelcome external challenges, but they're actually incredibly valuable teachers. The same applies to our addictions. They can cause serious setbacks until we realize they're internal teachers desperately trying to help us learn what they have to offer. In chapter 5, I share the multitude of lessons I learned from admitting I was a workaholic, addressing the underlying causes, and then figuring out how to create boundaries and balance around my work.

Our internal teachers also include intuition. It's that gut feeling where you "just know." All of us are intuitive, even if we think we aren't. Chapter 6 includes a simple guide for getting in touch with your intuition and starting to trust the astounding wisdom it has to offer.

When you get better at identifying your life lessons and teachers, you start to accelerate your growth and success. You also start to figure out how to respond to adversity in all its myriad forms, like hardships, sidetracks, and wake-up calls. They all have lessons to help us move forward. Wiser. Stronger. More resilient. More capable of handling even greater challenges in the future. That's growth.

We'll also take a look at how to create a lifestyle that increases your learning curve. Lifestyle issues usually include improving your sleep, diet, and exercise, as well as plugging your "energy leaks"—things like unfinished projects, people you need to thank or apologize to, physical clutter, and the mental clutter of our limiting beliefs. For instance, you'll discover how childhood experiences impact you today and how to change deep-seated beliefs that may have kept you repeating dysfunctional patterns for years.

A life well lived includes doing what we came here to do. That means learning the common and unique lessons that allow us to achieve our dreams, fulfill our purpose, develop our talents, and share them with the world. So at some point, all of us need to identify our purpose in life.

Many people naturally follow the path of fulfilling their purpose, sometimes without knowing it. Others need to be more focused on discovering what that is. We all need practical skills on how to turn our purpose and dreams into realistic goals that we can accomplish without major stress. Chapter 10 provides tried-and-true strategies for setting and achieving your goals.

People often tell me that time is their biggest obstacle in achieving their goals. They say things like "I don't have time to do all the things I *need* to do, much less the things I *want* to do." This book includes several sections on how to improve your skills with time management and procrastination. As a recovering procrastinator, I'll share my firsthand insights into our needless delays. We tap into a tremendous source of power when we control the way we use our time.

Another major obstacle? Stress. Even though stress is inevitable, it's possible to learn how to keep it at healthy levels, at least for the most part. Each of us has an optimal stress zone—the place where stress becomes positive energy and helps us accomplish our goals. It's where stress propels us forward rather than slowing us down. That's the zone to aim for. I'll teach you how to do that.

It's not a coincidence that we're here on Earth—and that we're here now. We're all here for a reason. Each of us has a unique gift to give, talents to share, and a way to make things better. By honoring our own uniqueness, showing up every day as our authentic selves and doing the best we can, we not only improve our lives but also contribute to others. Everyone has a light to shine. Each of us can make a difference.

How to Use This Book

I've written this book with the same format I used in teaching university classes on this material. That's why I suggest you read the book from front to back. However, if you're currently struggling with a particular issue like procrastination, feel free to turn to that chapter and start there.

Also, if you notice you have a special interest or curiosity about a certain topic in the book, you might want to check that out first. It could be your intuition nudging you in a specific direction. If you feel more energy when you read a given section, pay particular attention to that energy and the section that sparked it.

Throughout the book, I introduce an idea and give an example, usually a personal example. Then I provide activities to help you think of one or more examples from your life related to that same idea. For instance, in one of the sections on teachers, I'll describe how my mom was a significant teacher in my life and taught me a valuable lesson when she said, "Each of us is responsible for our own happiness." Then you'll have a chance to do the activities at the end of the section. In that case, it's to identify someone who's been an influential teacher in your life and look at a lesson they helped you learn.

The activities are designed to help you learn the important lessons in your own life. Because I don't know what those lessons are, I encourage you to take the time to actually do the activities. They provide time-tested methods to help you discover and master your own lessons. Maybe you can meet with a friend, do them together, and compare your responses. Or perhaps you can share what you learn with a family member or someone you trust. The point is to find ways to get actively involved with the material; that will make all the difference in how much you get out of your reading.

No Regrets

One of the things I emphasize throughout the book is how to make decisions now to keep from ending up with major regrets at the end of your life. Most people find it's not the things they did but rather what they *didn't do* that they regret the most. That's all the more reason for us to manage our time, accomplish our goals, create the life we want, and do what we came here to do.

We're only here for a little while. Life lessons can help us make the most of it.

Let's get started.

Chapter 2
Adventures in the School of Life

"You'll be laid off in July."

I said those words to myself out loud, over and over, as if repeating them would break through my disbelief and make them more real. But with each repetition, I felt even more anxious and sick to my stomach. And the whole ordeal still seemed unbelievable. I was clearly struggling to accept such horrible news.

After I read and reread the layoff letter from my employer, I kept asking myself, "How could this happen?" I'd worked in a university counseling center for ten years where I tried to give my best, did more than was expected, knew I was helping students, and felt I earned my promotions, only to find out none of that mattered in a budget crunch. Along with six other counselors, I lost my job.

Rumblings about layoffs circulated for at least a year before the fact, so it wasn't like I had no warning. But you always hope that somehow you won't end up on the cut list. This time, I did.

In looking back on that experience, part of me already understood it was time to move on and do something different. Months before the layoffs, I'd be sitting in a staff meeting, paying attention and even chiming in, when out of nowhere, a calm but firm voice inside my head would say, "You're not supposed to be here."

What? I loved my job, thoroughly enjoyed the students I got to work with, and every single person on our staff seemed like family to me. But I knew that voice belonged to my intuition, and I knew my intuition was always, always right.

When I was completely honest with myself, I had to admit I felt burned out. Counseling the down-and-disheartened, hour after hour, day after day, can drain you dry no matter how much you enjoy it. Twice in the year before the cuts, I got up in the morning, got ready for work, drove to within two or three blocks of the campus, and then turned around, drove home, and called in sick, when my only illness was my inability to face that particular day on the job. Whoa. Instead of sick days, we called them mental health days. But I taught classes on stress management, and I knew those two days were a serious sign of burnout.

Employee layoffs at a state university were rare—and newsworthy. Not long after the cuts were announced, an appointment was made for those of us who were affected to go to the unemployment office, all at the same time. There to meet us on the sidewalk of the busy nearby street was a video crew from a local television station. I felt mortified! I assumed that at least some of the people who saw me on TV would think I got laid off because I was a bad employee. The situation seemed awful enough, but the news coverage and my assumption made it even worse.

There's always a reason why things happen. Not only can I be loyal to a fault, but I probably never would have left a job I liked so much, even if I felt burned out, and even if it were time, unless I got the boot. So the Universe (Divine Energy, Spirit, God, Creator, Life, etc.) stepped in. This power greater than we are found a way to force me to leave. And despite my fear and resistance, that turned out to be perfect. After going on unemployment and searching for a job with an anxiety-fueled mania, I got hired back by the same university, only this time I worked in the athletics department. That position presented a completely different set of challenges, which was exactly what I needed right then.

What happens when life throws you a curve ball? Or puts a huge problem right in your lap so it's impossible to ignore? In my case, it meant I'd been at a job a long time, maybe too long, and it was time for a change.

This book gives you tools for how to deal with those kinds of whammies, delays, and detours. It provides strategies and techniques to help you learn your lessons and make progress in your life, regardless of where you start. Whether you're currently stuck in a standstill, doing okay but inching along at half speed, or you're already extremely successful and going lickety-split, life lessons can make your life better.

When you look at your own life, can you see places where you seem stuck? Maybe you've hit a plateau in your career and don't know how to take it to the next level. Perhaps you're living a ho-hum life and long for more excitement and fulfillment. Many people hold a secret passion, which they would love to turn into a business or share with the world, but it remains trapped inside their hearts and minds. Every single one of us has a natural talent that yearns for expression throughout our entire lives.

Perhaps you're one of many who are worried about the economy, politics, or the environment. You're concerned for yourself, your children or grandchildren, and future generations. You want to make a difference, but you're not sure where to start or how to go about it. You might be struggling to keep up with the day-to-day responsibilities you've already assumed, so how could you possibly take on more? And yet a part of you wants to do more. Maybe *needs* to do more. Something is missing from your life. An aliveness. A passionate cause. A way to offer your unique gifts. A way to live without regrets.

During our time here on Earth, we have dreams to achieve, a purpose to fulfill, and this phenomenal, lifelong opportunity to develop our talents and potential. Learning our lessons in life allows us to keep making progress and eventually accomplish what's ours to do.

I worked at various universities for more than twenty-five years, and throughout that time, I heard students, faculty, and staff share their concerns about being unhappy despite their outward success. They talked about trying over and over to achieve their goals, but they found that obstacles kept getting in the way. Some had been going along fine but suddenly ran into a roadblock. Others wrestled with the same problems for years. Many of us experience the issues they struggled with, so they might sound familiar. Are you:

- stressed out as you try to accomplish everything you *need* to do?
- frustrated by too little time to do the things you *want* to do?
- feeling trapped in an unsatisfying or unhealthy job, even after trying a number of different strategies to improve the situation?
- unhappy in a relationship with a spouse, partner, friend, or family member but not sure how to make things better?
- unable to lose weight despite your best efforts and multiple attempts over several years?
- frustrated with your inability to start an exercise program and stick with it?

People who struggle with these issues have one thing in common: they need to learn at least one lesson in order to get unstuck and get on their way.

All of our problems, unfulfilled yearnings, and unexpressed talents contain lessons on how to resolve them. They are our teachers in disguise. If we focus on following the instructions they provide, we begin to see how the Universe uses our problems and heartfelt desires to get our attention, teach us our lessons, and help us move on.

Part of our inherent nature is to continually stretch and grow, to constantly become more of who we have the potential to be. Life will go to unbelievable lengths and find infinite ways to support us in this ever-evolving process. This "support" includes periodically throwing challenges onto our path to make sure we stay sharp and don't get complacent. The process continues regardless of our age. Children have certain lessons they need to learn to become independent and able to function on their own. Adults must master a whole host of lessons all the way through their lives. Our learning never ends.

Life lessons have the ability to guide you through your experiences in such a way that by the time you get to the end of your life, you have no major regrets. The research on regrets reveals some surprises. When people on their deathbeds were asked about their biggest regrets, it wasn't what they did or the mistakes they'd made. Instead, they most regretted what they *didn't do*. And although this may make you think about things like driving a fancy car, skydiving, or traveling the world, those weren't among their regrets. In one study, people said their biggest regret was that they hadn't been more true to themselves. Other top regrets included wishing they had developed better relationships with themselves and others.

In the following pages, you will be encouraged to identify what's important to you, what you want to accomplish, and what would feel unfinished if you didn't get it done. You'll also find lots of techniques on creative goal setting, time management, and how to get the most mileage out of the time you have.

My Adventures in School

I clearly remember one of the first times I consciously applied some of the techniques in my own life that you will read about in this book. I was working as an academic advisor in a university athletics program. One of my coworkers got another job and left our office on short notice, just when we needed to do academic advising with over five hundred student-athletes for the following semester. Our staff had to find a way to advise all those students by working more than our usually heavy loads. The task felt overwhelming and seemed almost impossible, but we simply had to buckle down and get it done.

I somehow got it that—like it or not—I had just been enrolled in a class in the school of life on stress management. It was a metaphorical class but one based on real-life circumstances. My normal reaction would have been to feel some resentment for this major imposition but to still slug through, doing a good job, all the while counting down the days until the advising was over. But instead, I decided to take it on as my personal challenge to try to get an A in that class. Not just an A but an A-plus.

In the fleeting moment when I made that mental shift, the entire scenario changed. I felt a burst of energy and eagerness to do my absolute best to pass that class with the highest possible grade. And the only way to do that was to give it my best shot, bring every bit of enthusiasm I could muster, use all the stress management techniques I could think of, and most of all, give the student-athletes a fun, quality experience.

When that marathon advising ordeal ended, I still felt energized instead of drained like I would have if I'd approached it in my usual way. I felt stronger and more confident about my ability to get through the next tough time that would inevitably come along. And I knew without a doubt that I earned the highest grade, because I gave it my all.

I believe the Universe uses the challenges in our lives to help us learn valuable, in-the-trenches, real-life lessons. Our job is to master the lessons contained in those experiences well enough to pass the tests that life presents. Once this happens, the problem or challenging situation goes away, and we get to move forward, hopefully more skilled, knowledgeable, and courageous. That's how we grow and develop our potential. Embracing everything we face, including the difficult times, with enthusiasm and determination to do A-level work can provide the focus, passion, and aliveness that make life fun, rewarding, deeply meaningful, and inherently rich. It causes us to do—and be—our best.

Getting laid off taught me one of my more important life lessons: **move from victim to student.** I felt victimized when I lost my job. We all feel like victims at different times in our lives. My emotions around all of that included pretty intense betrayal, anger, sadness, and fear. I needed to express those feelings, because I didn't want them to become emotional baggage I carried from then on. But after that, instinct kicked in, and my inner voice told me in no uncertain terms, "You can't just sit here. Figure out what you need to learn. Get out of your victim position and on with your life." In other words, become a student of life—now.

I'm a student at my innermost core, at a level that's bone deep. Learning has always been intrinsically fun for me. I don't think it's a coincidence that I stayed in school long enough to get my doctorate in education, an Ed.D. in counseling, worked at several different universities, became the director of a university learning center, and ended up writing a book on learning life's lessons. It wasn't until I started writing the book that I felt I was finally doing at least part of what I came here to do. I also believe that every other thing I've done in my life was exactly what I was supposed to be doing at the time. You're always on your path, whether you're aware of it or not.

In between getting my master's degree in counseling and my doctoral program, I continued taking the courses needed to become an educational examiner in Arkansas, where I lived at the time. That meant I could do testing with students in the public schools. Working through a federal grant, teachers in grades one through twelve sent students to me who were struggling in their classrooms. I gave them intelligence and achievement tests, and my colleague administered auditory and language assessments. Together we analyzed students' learning difficulties, wrote comprehensive reports of their strengths and weaknesses, and provided strategies to their teachers and parents on how they could improve.

Although I only worked at that job for two years, the experience proved invaluable. It gave me a hands-on, in-depth understanding of exactly how we learn and how we get stuck in the learning process. I dissected learning disabilities on a daily basis and developed a special place in my heart for anyone with those challenges.

One day I was driving home from work, and I asked myself, "So what are you actually measuring with these IQ tests?" That's when I came up with my own definition of intelligence, which is "the ability to identify and appropriately use relevant information."

I believe we can all improve our learning. We can get better at identifying and using the information that's relevant to whatever we're dealing with at the time. That means we all have the potential to become better students of life. This book includes the concepts and tools I developed as an educational examiner, along with other techniques I've used throughout my career to help people learn, grow, and succeed.

How We Make Progress

Imagine you're an eagle and can soar above the terrain of life. You can look down and see the cycle of birth and death. You observe how people are born, grow, have babies, become old, and eventually die. You notice how some of the people learn their life lessons easily and quickly, how some struggle, and how others die without learning their lessons or doing what was theirs to do.

Now imagine that you can look down on your own life. You observe your patterns, tendencies, and ruts, and you can be objective about what's working and what's not. Looking at life from this meta-level can give us perspective. It can help us more clearly see how to move forward and prevent us from sliding off to the side of the road as we travel.

When I looked at my own life from this strategic distance, and when I reflected on the lives of the thousands of people I've worked with over the years, here's what I saw:

> *Life is a school for learning lessons. Once you learn your lessons, you get to move on to the next class, where there are more lessons to learn. If you don't master your lessons well enough to pass the tests that life presents, you have to repeat the class until you get it right. And if you're really slow, you will get a wake-up call.*

This simple metaphor helps us understand our progress through life. It also provides a road map to point us in the right direction when we're sidelined by life's inevitable obstacles, as well as our own missteps and unsuccessful attempts.

Sometimes when I get stuck, it feels like I'm having to repeat the third grade for about the fifth time. That's when I take a step back, look at my situation as if I'm a detached observer, and use the concept that my life actually is a school. We're all enrolled in various metaphorical classes, like the stress management class I found myself in at work that I described earlier. Once we learn the lessons in our current classroom well enough to pass the tests that life will regularly put on our path, we graduate and get to move on to the next classroom, where more lessons wait for us.

But what happens if we don't learn our lessons and don't pass the tests? Then we have to stay and repeat the class until we get it right. We struggle, going through the same material, and have to keep dealing with the same problem or situation over and over. In this part of our life, it's like being Bill Murray in the classic movie *Groundhog Day,* where we get stuck in a time warp and live every day as the same day. We stay stuck—*until* we master the lesson well enough to pass the tests that life presents. And if it takes us too long to learn the lesson, the Universe will give us a wake-up call, which is a more urgent message to pay attention, master the material, pass the exams, and move on.

For example, let's say we're all involuntarily enrolled in mandatory classes on personal health. We need to learn certain lessons in order to stay healthy enough to function, and if we don't, our bodies won't support us. I rarely get sick, but when I do, it's almost always because I've been cutting corners with my health. Usually it's that I try to cram too much into my schedule, don't sleep enough, get run down, and eventually catch a cold or the flu or whatever bug is going around at the time. It's like my body starts talking and says, "If you won't slow down and take care of me, then I will stop you in your tracks and make sure you get the message." That's an example of a wake-up call.

After going through this scenario over and over, repeating the class on sleep I don't know how many times, I finally learned the lesson on how I can't get too sleep deprived or else I'll get sick. It sounds so simple, but it took me years to finally get it right. That doesn't mean I won't ever get sick in the future, but it won't be because I intentionally cut my sleep short. Like it or not, getting my z's has to be a priority for me.

Although sleep is only one of the classes included in the lessons on personal health, it's one of the most fundamental. When I worked as a personal counselor in university counseling centers, students came in who hadn't slept for several nights in a row, often after breaking up with a boyfriend or girlfriend. They looked like they had serious mental health issues. However, after a couple of nights of good sleep, they might still be stressed or grieving, but they wouldn't show any signs of mental illness, because they didn't have those kinds of problems. They just needed some sleep.

Short-term sleep loss can have major consequences, including impaired memory, loss of concentration, poor judgment, and difficulty making decisions. And long-term sleep deprivation wreaks havoc on our bodies. Recent studies indicate that chronic lack of sleep can lead to risks for developing conditions like obesity, diabetes, high blood pressure, and heart disease, just to name a few. If you haven't already graduated from the class on sleep, now may be the time to enroll and aim for that A. Each of us has different sleep requirements. Figuring out how much you need—and getting it—is a prerequisite for doing and being your best. The quality and amount of sleep we get affects every single thing we do.

In looking back on why it took me so long to learn the lesson about sleep, part of it was that even though I knew I need to average around seven hours each night, I didn't *want* to believe that. I tried to ignore and deny it, refusing to accept what my body needed. Seeing that stubborn streak in me was an eye opener, so now I'm on the lookout for that stubbornness when I get stuck in other classes.

In the school of life, I'm currently enrolled in a variety of classes, which include how to market a self-help book, how to intensify my workouts at the gym (without getting injured), how to declutter my life, and how to balance my personal relationships with work, family, and "me" time.

When I look down the road, I can see that I will perpetually remain enrolled in classes on personal health. Sleep is only one of the subjects covered.

Over years of trial and error, I've found that in order to do and be my best, I need four pieces in place: sleep, exercise, meditation, and a healthy diet. I'm constantly learning new lessons in those areas in a comprehensive class I call "Optimal Health."

Somewhere along the line, I got it that making my health a priority gives me my best shot at completing whatever I'm here to do. It takes time and energy to live a healthy lifestyle, but boy, is it worth it in terms of how you feel and what you get to do. This is especially the case as I get older. Now it takes a more deliberate effort than when I could slide by and get away with all kinds of unhealthy transgressions simply because of my youth.

Using the metaphor of life as a school can make it easier to put some distance between us and our problems. It can help us identify ways we've been successful in the past and draw from those experiences when we step into unfamiliar territory. The metaphor also gives us a blueprint, a form of hope to hold on to in those more extreme circumstances when the path gets dark, our bodies get tired, our minds get confused, and the light of our spirits burns low. We all go there at one time or another.

Seeing life as a school for learning implies that each of our classes is temporary, and if we feel like we're stuck in a class and can't get out, we can cling to the belief that "this too shall pass." The only constant in life is change, and recognizing the short-lived nature of life's difficult or painful circumstances reminds us to work like crazy and do whatever it takes to pass the tests that will allow us to move on. It's motivating. On a personal level, the metaphor also makes me more aware of the temporary nature of some of the blessings in my life, knowing they could disappear in an instant, and to enjoy and appreciate the good things while they're here—and while I'm here.

---

1. *Activities*

Think about your life and identify at least three metaphorical classes you're currently enrolled in. These are the parts of your life where you're learning new lessons, and they might include classes on your relationships, job, finances, sports, hobbies, personal health, or other areas. Write down at least three classes.

    1. Three (or more) classes I'm currently enrolled in are:

Then ask yourself,

    2. Which classes am I doing well in?

3. What class or classes am I struggling in?

Throughout this book, I will recommend different activities to help you apply the material in your personal life. I encourage you to do all the activities and actually write down your responses. Writing them down will increase your learning curve. Doing the activities with one or more other people who are reading this book will also help. I suggest you find one place where you keep all of your written responses, whether that's a notebook, hard-copy file, or some type of digital storage. There's not enough space to write all your responses in this book.

School Rules

Just like in other types of schools, certain rules apply in the school of life. Although many of us don't like rules, it's helpful to at least know what they are, because that gives us a better chance of passing our classes faster, with less effort and stress. Some of the following are similar to those included in Cherie Carter-Scott's book *If Life Is a Game, These Are the Rules*.

I always went over these rules in the university classes I taught on learning life's lessons, and the students in the classes usually found that one or two of the rules had special meaning for them. As you read through this list, make a mental note of any of the rules that stand out for you.

1. We are all enrolled in a year-round school called life, and classes are held every day. Some days we learn more than others, but every day we are given opportunities to learn.

Have you ever stopped to think about how many things you're learning at any given time? These might include sports or hobbies, technology skills, self-improvement, finances, religion or spirituality, cooking, house repairs, different aspects of your job, and relationships with family members, coworkers, and friends. This list comprises the metaphorical classes you're enrolled in, and each class usually includes a number of lessons you need to learn. The process of learning is so constant and feels so normal that we often don't realize how automatically it happens every day.

I've heard it said that planet Earth is especially conducive to learning, because the consequences of our actions come quickly in our school. We're in a great place to learn our lessons, and because every moment brings opportunities to learn, it makes sense to focus on getting better at it.

2. There are no coincidences. Everything that happens in our lives has

meaning and purpose. Some events are more meaningful than others, but nothing occurs by accident or chance.

What if—just what if—nothing is coincidental, and everything that happens to us is orchestrated to support our learning? This kind of extreme optimism can cause us to give up our judgments about what's "bad" in our lives and to simply embrace what "is." If we can change our thinking about the events in our lives, seeing them as messages and instructions on how to learn our lessons, we no longer ignore, resist, or resent reality. We stop arguing with life and feeling like it's our opponent. It may sound radical, but this kind of optimistic attitude and thought process can supercharge our progress in school.

Jack Canfield, author of *The Success Principles* and *Chicken Soup* books, described it well when he referred to this attitude as characteristic of someone who's an ***inverse paranoid***. Instead of thinking the world is plotting against you, imagine that the world is actually conspiring to help you along. Rather than getting mad when things don't go your way, see it as a chance to learn something important. Everything has a meaning and purpose to support our learning and growth. Interpreting our lives this way can prevent needless suffering and open up a world of possibilities we've never even thought of.

3. With every experience, the Universe gives us information to help us learn our lessons. There will also be tests to see if we can apply what we learn in our day-to-day lives.

This school rule relates to the previous one, but it also includes the part about how life tests us to make sure we've learned our lessons. In the school of life, a lesson is never fully learned until we pass the tests and prove we can apply the lesson in our day-to-day lives. Passing the tests means developing enough competence that we can pass the tests with accuracy and consistency.

For example, I set a goal to get in better shape, which meant going to the gym at least twice a week and doing at least three hours of weekly exercise. Essentially, I voluntarily enrolled in a metaphorical class on exercise. It took a long, long time, but now I hit the gym regardless of whether I feel like it, have pressing deadlines, am running late, or whatever else might serve as an excuse not to go. I've passed the tests on regular exercise. It's automatic, and I don't even have to think about it. Chapter 7 describes the details of this process.

4. As soon as we learn whatever is expected in our class well enough to pass the tests, we are promoted to the next class, where there are more lessons to learn.

Just like in the other schools, we have to pass our exams in the school of life before we can graduate to the next class. Our learning continues throughout our lifetimes, and the list of possible classes to take is endless.

My parents used to live in a retirement home in another state that had rooms available for visitors to rent, just like you would rent a hotel room. I visited my folks often and stayed in a visitor's room, which meant I got to know many of the residents quite well. During our many discussions, I marveled at how much they were still learning about life, and these were people who were well into their nineties. Learning. Never. Ends.

5. If we don't learn our lessons well enough to pass the tests, we must repeat the class until we get it right.

This is another way of saying we must pass the tests that life presents, but it's also more than that. We must stay in the same classroom and go back over the material until we develop the competency to prove we're ready to move on. We start going through our personal *Groundhog Day* experience.

Have you ever felt like you just couldn't learn something? Maybe it was a new skill at work, or perhaps it had more to do with your personal life. I learned early on that if I exercise regularly, I feel better than when I don't, but it took me literally years to consistently act on that awareness. I would exercise for a while, and then something would happen—I'd travel, or get sick, or get extra busy, or the weather would be lousy—and my exercise routine would be the first thing to go. I must have repeated that metaphorical class at least twenty times. After a while, you start to feel incompetent, if not downright inadequate. Some classes are harder to pass than others. Some take more tries to get it right.

6. If we have to repeat a class and are held back in school, we may experience it as punitive. In this school, however, there is no punishment—only consequences for our own behavior. The Universe never punishes, only teaches.

I mentally beat up on myself when I kept failing the class on regular exercise. I'd silently say to myself, "You know you need to exercise. What's so hard about making that a priority? Why can't you get your act together and make it happen? You know you'd feel better." The tone of my inner voice felt like a scolding.

Sometimes when we fail one of our classes and have to enroll again, it feels like we're being punished, like life isn't fair or it's too hard. Or maybe we take on that punitive attitude internally and punish ourselves with our thoughts and self-talk the way I did. Regardless, when we have to repeat a class, it simply means we're not ready to pass the tests and move on. It's not a punishment. We just need to double down and get smarter about how to master the material. This topic is addressed in depth in chapter 8, "Turning Obstacles into Teachers."

7. The natural flow or sequence through school is one where we as students become increasingly aware and more and more competent. This growth continues into old age. Although we may get into classes that are painful and difficult, the progression of growth generally leads to greater enjoyment of ourselves and of life.

The energy of our lives is like a river, constantly flowing forward as we continually grow and evolve. Sometimes we're in still, calm waters, enjoying the scenery and the moment. At other times, the river turns into the white water of rapids and falls, and we must work hard to keep from going under. This may mean developing new navigation skills or simply focusing on applying the skills we already know in order to make it through. The treacherous, more challenging parts of the journey help us become more competent, and they're interspersed with the smoother sections of the river that allow us to catch our breath, reflect on what we've learned, and integrate our learning into a deeper foundation of knowledge and abilities.

Studies on happiness show that older people report being more happy and satisfied with themselves and their lives. They've had years of white-water experiences to help them get there. Although it may not happen until long after the fact, I always try to express my gratitude for the tough times in my own life, because they eventually offer the gifts of greater awareness and a deeper ability to feel contentment and joy.

8. If we remain too long in any one classroom, not learning our lessons, we are in effect resisting the natural flow, and the Universe will try even harder to get our attention and help us move on. Our messages and instructions become louder and stronger and are sometimes referred to as "wake-up calls."

Imagine you're floating down the river of life but get stuck and don't continue moving forward. Maybe you decide you like it where you are and don't *want* to keep going. Or perhaps you get caught in white water and can't figure out how to get past it and move downstream. Whether our stagnation is voluntary or involuntary, it's not going with the natural flow of life and will eventually have consequences we probably won't experience as positive.

Wake-up calls alert us that something is wrong and send a warning that we need to pay attention and deal with whatever is keeping us stuck. I received a wake-up call every time I got sick from too little sleep. At a more extreme level, they happen with unfortunate regularity when people get lured into addictions. We're all familiar with the predictable pattern of addictive drug use, which results in shattered lives. If we look back at those situations, we can see that the Universe tried over and over to teach the lessons that would get the person back on the right track. We can only hope that our own wake-up calls serve their purpose and that we make the midcourse corrections that will prevent us from hitting rock bottom.

9. Each of us is here for a reason; there is something we came here to do. We have lessons to learn and a purpose to fulfill.
It's not an accident that you showed up here on Earth. We are all here by divine design, individually selected to occupy a unique place in the mosaic of the time we're here. We all came for a reason, and that reason fits in perfectly with the issues and circumstances that happen concurrently with our life spans. Learning our lessons helps us take the greatest advantage of the time we're given and gives us the strongest chance of fulfilling our purpose.

It's also not a coincidence that you came here *when* you did. I'm a baby boomer, born into the generation of hippies and freethinkers. And although my earlier boomer experiences were relatively tame and watered down, I still grew up in a culture that questioned the norms and values that had gone unchallenged for generations. I'm glad. Now that questioning is part of me. It's contributed to who I am and where I am.

All of us are born into the generation that can best support us in learning our lessons and completing our purpose. The Universe is astoundingly efficient in that way, not missing any opportunities to help us do what is ours to do.

10. We will be provided with all the time, resources, and support we need to successfully complete our classes and fulfill our purpose. As students, it is up to us to take advantage of what is offered.
When I was younger, I was perpetually swamped, always on the go, constantly running as if life were a sprint instead of a marathon. Although it felt like I was making progress in my life—setting goals and reaching them—I didn't give much thought to the ultimate purpose of my life or the reason I was here. If I had, I would never have thought there would be enough time to fulfill that purpose, because I couldn't fathom how my future would change.

In looking back now, I can see that I was "practicing" the skills I would need to fulfill my purpose every step of the way. The Universe was actually preparing me for what I now refer to as a calling, a desire so deep and strong that it's bigger than I am. And lo and behold, almost as soon as I got clear about my purpose, time opened up in my life, giving me the perfect opportunity to complete my purpose, if—and only if—I don't mess around. This pattern in my life isn't unique. If we stay diligent in our studies in the school of life, utilizing the resources the Universe provides, at least part of our lifetime will allow us to do what we came here to do.

11. Everyone has at least one unique talent to develop and gift to give. Part of our purpose for being here is to develop our talents and make a contribution through our gifts. By doing what we love and are naturally good at, we access more of our potential, which benefits us and others.

As we go through life, we develop certain skills. We may or may not enjoy the times when we use these skills. For example, most of us learn how to drive a car, but we might like driving or might not. These learned skills are different from our natural, God-given talent, the seed planted inside each of us that naturally wants to grow and thrive. Developing our talent and sharing it with others causes us to access more of our potential and brings an immense sense of fulfillment.

I became Lauren's academic advisor when she was recruited for the women's swimming team at the university where I worked. Lauren learned to swim as a young child, enjoyed it, and eventually got good enough to earn a full scholarship that paid for her college education. But after years of looking at the bottom of a pool and getting up most mornings for practice at six o'clock, the enjoyment faded, and she saw her swimming as more of a job, a way to pay for school.

Swimming was a learned skill for Lauren, but her real dream was to become a veterinarian. That seed began to sprout early on, when she would try to doctor her family's dogs and cats. Her natural affinity with animals was mutual; they seemed to sense her caring and wanted to be around her. Working with animals made Lauren happier than any other potential career, and lots of animals would get her help because she eventually went to vet school and developed her natural talent.

12. We can make greater progress through school if we align ourselves with the Creative Force in the Universe and become co-creators of our lives. This means going with the natural flow and living in balance and harmony with the laws of nature and our authentic selves.

I stumbled across a book years ago, and the title has stayed with me ever since: *Don't Push the River: It Flows by Itself*. I feel like I'm trying to push the river when my off-kilter thoughts cause me to strike out on my own, separating me from nature (like when I don't take care of my body), or when I'm trying to be someone I'm not. The results of that pushing take different forms, but I never experience them as positive.

Conversely, when we're going with the natural flow of life, living in harmony with the laws of nature and being true to ourselves, the river of life can take us to the heights of bliss. I can't count the number of people I know who have found that nurturing and caring for others is who they are. It's the role that's most authentic for them. Their caregiving assumes many forms, from caring for immediate family members to helping others through their jobs, which often include teaching, counseling, and medical professions. These people's lives seem to flow from one loving, caring moment to the next, and the progress they make in the school of life is nothing short of extraordinary.

---

2. *Activities*

1. *Take a few minutes right now and look back over the school rules.*

2. *Ask yourself: Which rule has special meaning for me? Why is it meaningful?*

Write down the rule you selected, along with the reason you chose it. Then keep your written responses in the same place as the other activities we'll do throughout this book.

Using Intention

Learning our lessons in life can be exhilarating when things go well. We speed through our classes, ace the tests that show up on our paths, and continually get to explore exciting new territory. Life is good. But even the smartest among us can succumb to the occasional hard teacher or get into a class where we have no aptitude or prior experience. That's when all our smarts and resourcefulness may fail us, and we fall into a quagmire of setbacks that can shackle our self-confidence and shove us into the slow lane.

Intention has the potential to accelerate our progress in both cases. Whether we're already shining A students or struggling just to pass our classes, using intention is analogous to zipping into the fast lane and staying there.

Just to clarify, however, the goal of life is not to always go fast. Life is not a race. Sometimes the goal is to linger in still waters, savoring the moment.

Some of the most accomplished and productive people I know never seem to rush or hurry. They're just masters at time management and have learned to keep their attention focused in the here and now. We can all learn to separate ourselves from the rush of the world and find our own rhythm and pace, one that is comfortable and natural for us.

However, this type of preference for a less hurried or rapid speed is different from getting stuck in school. When we get stuck, we don't feel like we have a *choice* to move forward. We have to repeat the class we're enrolled in, going over and over the same material, because we can't seem to learn the lessons well enough to pass the real-life tests. Normal progression through school is one of more steady learning and growth, of consistently moving forward. And intention can help us achieve this.

So what is intention, and why is it so powerful? The dictionary definition of intention refers to a determination to create a certain result or outcome. It's both a sharp mental clarity and an emotional attitude that makes us 100 percent focused on accomplishing a goal or purpose. It's when every thought, feeling, and cell in our body aligns and says, "Yes, let's do this—no matter what it takes."

We see the visible results of the power of intention in the sports world on a regular basis, and we seem to never tire of the replays of determined athletes who accomplish what look like impossible feats through their well-honed mental focus. It's in the football pass that gets caught by the receiver in the middle of a pack of opponents after the quarterback "saw" the catch happen in his head before the ball left his hands. Intention shines through when the golf ball lips the cup and magically falls in after the golfer visualizes a successful putt. We marvel at the long shot in basketball that hits the backboard at just the right angle to send it swishing through the basket to win the game, despite the pressure of the buzzer signaling the end of final play. That's no surprise to the player who visually rehearsed that shot over and over before the game ever began.

In our own lives, the power of intention may not be as obvious, but that doesn't mean the same mental focus isn't creating mini-miracles on a daily basis. One place I see this happen in my own life is in completing some task within a limited amount of time, when I would swear on the front end there's no way I can get it done.

Case in point: I used to regularly fly back to Arkansas to visit my then ninety-two-year-old father who lived in a retirement home. I had asked him to move closer to me, but he didn't want to move. So in addition to calling him every day, VS (my sister) and I took turns traveling to see him. Our trips invariably became packed with visiting with our dad, doctor appointments, banking, unexpected shopping, and meetings with various staff where he lived in an effort to make up for our long-distance caretaking. When our planes landed, we knew we only had so much time to get everything done, so our focus and determination started out exceptionally strong.

I don't know how to explain the number of times during those trips when coincidences became a normal part of my day, and everything on my to-do list got accomplished, other than to attribute it to intention. The same held true for my sister when she was there. For example, just when I thought I wouldn't have time to catch up with my dad's nurse about a brand-new medical issue, I'd run into her in the hall. She might mention something about needing to get my father's telephone checked, and right after that, I'd *happen* to see the maintenance man as I was heading into another meeting. I would discover that my dad needed some new clothes, and the first store I'd go into had exactly what I was looking for—on sale.

Although I was usually tired after my visits, during the time I was there, I had all the energy I needed and then some, to the point that it was almost a high. It made me wonder what it would be like to live every part of my life without one iota of resistance, with every thought, feeling, and action perfectly lined up to accomplish my goals. So that every day was guided and fueled by the power of intention.

During the time I worked in college athletics, part of my job as an academic advisor was to ensure that the student-athletes maintained their academic eligibility to play. With some athletes, I only needed to complete a quick review of their coursework to see that they were fine. With others, especially those who wanted to change their majors or students who transferred in from out of state, finding a way to keep them in the major they wanted and still stay eligible was often more difficult.

Out of sheer necessity, our office staff developed an informal motto around getting the athletes eligible—*whatever it takes*. Keep working on solutions, within the academic rules and what was in the student's best interest, and find a way to make it happen. If the athletes also added their intention and effort, we could almost always pull it off. That's when I learned about the value of "whatever it takes." Whatever it takes to get a student eligible. Whatever it takes to learn my lessons and move on. Having that attitude at the beginning of a goal can make all the difference in whether or not we succeed.

Intention requires effort on our part to get all our internal resources aligned and commit to a whatever-it-takes attitude. But our individual effort is only one part of the formula. The other factor involved in the astounding, almost unbelievable results of using intention has the potential to create a much greater impact, and that's the contribution from the Universe. When we get crystal clear about a goal, it's as if all of life says "Yes," and we tap into a reservoir of energy that's been waiting for us all along. That invisible energy kicks in and takes care of the details we can't control. It smooths out the path and leads us smack dab into the results we want. The help we get from this unseen force is described ever so eloquently in one of my favorite quotes by Johann Wolfgang von Goethe, a German writer, which says:

> *Until one is committed, there is hesitancy, the chance to draw back, always ineffectiveness. Concerning all acts of initiative and creation, there is one elementary truth the ignorance of which kills countless ideas and splendid plans: that the moment one definitely commits oneself, then Providence moves too. All sorts of things occur to help one that would never otherwise have occurred. A whole stream of events issues from the decision, raising in one's favor all manner of unforeseen incidents, meetings and material assistance which no man could have dreamed would have come his way. Whatever you can do or dream you can, begin it. Boldness has genius, power and magic in it. Begin it now.*

Knowing about our own extraordinary performance abilities (when parts of us aren't dragging our feet) and understanding how the Universe will jump in to support our strong intentions gives us a major leg up on learning our lessons in life. We can use that power of intention to learn our lessons faster, with less stress, with less experimenting for the right answers through trial and error, and with a whole lot more fun.

When I first started using intention, and for a long time after that, I felt like it was hard work and that it was *supposed* to be hard. Like I had to muscle my way forward, stay constantly focused on my goal, and almost force my goal into existence. But somewhere along the line, I noticed a shift. Yes, I had to do my part. But I started getting swept up in the energy of the goal, and it started happening with far less effort on my part. So instead of working like a dog to *make* it happen, after I set my intention, I could start to *let* it happen through me.

Here's an analogy. I love to dance. I took dancing lessons for many years, and now I dance around my house pretty much every day just because I enjoy it. Sometimes **I dance to the music**. I consciously move my body to the beat. Sometimes **I am the music**, and I get swept up in merging with that energy. And on really exquisite days, **the music dances me**. I'm not thinking about dancing, or anything else. My body moves to the beat as if propelled by the music itself.

That's often how it's become when I use intention. The thought of the goal, my intention, and the energy that comes from Providence when I commit to that goal propel me forward. The steps to my goal become like the dance. I merge with intention. And intention dances me.

Sometimes it's difficult for us to realize that we don't have to know exactly *how* we're going to fulfill our intention. It's hard to believe that once we know *what* we intend to have happen, we can trust the Universe to fill in the details on how we're going to get there. In fact, sometimes our specific plans for reaching our intention actually get in the way and slow us down. It's often better to go with the flow and let it happen rather than working hard to make it happen.

It's also possible that the Universe and your subconscious will create something better than your intention. The power of your intention can draw from all the resources the Universe has available, and you may get to experience something beyond your grandest dreams. As you will see in chapter 10, these same possibilities apply to our goal-setting as well. With some intentions and some goals, we don't have to plan out the steps of how we're going to reach them. Once we know where we want to go, "all Providence moves" to help us get there. That's what happened during my trips to visit my dad.

If you want more information on this somewhat magical process, I suggest you read the late Wayne Dyer's book, *The Power of Intention*.

Let's say you want to become the best you can be at your job. What would that look like? You would be the person who leaves no stone unturned in searching for solutions to each problem, the person who develops a resiliency to setbacks and failures that keeps you moving toward your goals, regardless of what appear to be the odds of success. You would think, act, and feel like you were absolutely and undividedly committed, without one ounce of holding back.

Once you set an intention, it helps to find a picture of the end result of what it will look like when you accomplish that intention. If your intention is to be great at your job, maybe you would see yourself getting a promotion and moving to another office. The more specific the picture, the better. You could even imagine your name on the new office door. Now imagine that your outcome might turn out to be even better than what you imagined. And that working hard at your job seemed easy and fun.

If your intention is to go to Hawaii, you could find a picture that would show happy people on a Hawaiian beach. You could even cut out a photo of yourself and insert it in the picture. And then put the picture where you will see it often—maybe on your refrigerator or above your desk. When we get a clear picture of our intentions, we get an additional boost, because our subconscious minds go to work figuring out how to make them happen.

Adding other senses also helps. For example, imagine you're already in Hawaii. Notice the vast expanse of the ocean's perfectly flat horizon. Feel the warm sun on your skin. Hear the sound of seagulls. Smell the wet sand. Taste the salty ocean breeze. If you get all your senses involved, it makes it even more real. Always allow for the possibility that your intention might turn out to be better than what you imagine.

And what would it look like if you became a better student in the school of life? See yourself easily moving through your metaphorical classes, enjoying yourself, the people around you, and life in general. When you figure out how to be a better student of life, the possibilities for your future become endless. It can start with intention. The rest of this book gives you the tools and strategies to succeed.

Do you know what you want to accomplish? Do you have short-term and long-term goals for your life? Chapter 10 includes exercises to help you get focused and motivated. For now, tuck the power of intention into your pocket of possible resources and know that Providence is waiting to help with your success whenever you're ready.

---

3. Activities

1. *Reflect back on your own experiences and identify a time when you thought there was no way you could accomplish some task or goal, and yet you managed to pull it off.*

    - *What's one goal or task you thought was impossible but succeeded in doing anyway?*
    - *Did you have a strong intention to get it done?*
    - *Did you get unforeseen help from the Universe to support your efforts?*
    - *Did you have a picture in your head about what it would look like when you succeeded?*

2. *Imagine that you decide to focus your intention on becoming the best student of life you can possibly be. Becoming better students of life means we need to start doing the things we know work for*

us and stop doing the things we know don't work. Write down your answers to these questions:

- *What's one activity I could <u>start</u> doing, that I'm not currently doing, that would make my life significantly better?*
- *Picture that. What would it look like if I started doing that activity?*
- *What's one activity I could <u>stop</u> doing, that I'm currently doing, that would significantly improve my life?*
- *Again, get a picture of what that would look like. What would it look like if I stopped doing that activity?*

If you feel curious or excited about the possibilities that intention might bring into your future, it's a sign that part of you is eager to explore new classes in the school of life. Let's start by learning more about life lessons in this next chapter.

Chapter 3
All about Life Lessons

Not long after I retired from my final university position, I joined a gym and started taking a Pilates class, which is similar to yoga. Almost all the people in the class were quite a bit younger than I was—by decades. I've always been coordinated and good in sports, so I figured that after a while, I would take my usual place as one of the better students in the class. But four months went by, and I finally realized that wasn't going to happen. I could go to the gym every day, but I would probably never be as good at Pilates as many of the others who were there.

That's when I relearned the lesson about how getting older means I'm in different classrooms in the school of life. My previous lessons around anything athletic usually focused on how to improve my strength and skills. But now I'm learning that even if I do that, it doesn't mean I'll naturally end up near the top of the class. My current challenge is to accept my new position and realize I don't *need* to be at the top. Because this change is taking some getting used to, I periodically remind myself that it's okay by saying things to myself like "I'm in class to focus on taking care of my body, to make sure I feel good enough to do all the other things I want to do in my life." That helps.

But here's the deal. No matter how old you are, your life lessons will change because of your age and experience. Whether you're a teenager, young adult, middle-aged, or older, your chronological age shifts your priorities and the tasks you face, which means different lessons pop up on your path.

The field of developmental psychology studies the changes we encounter during our life span, including various social, emotional, and cognitive stages of change. For example, children learn about trust from the people around them; adolescents focus much of their energy on learning social skills so they can fit in with their peers; young adults deal with intimacy issues as they consider marriage and children; and throughout adulthood, we grapple with intellectual concerns such as mortality and the meaning of life. All these stages bring different lessons to learn. How well we succeed in mastering these lessons determines the course of our future development. Many of us know people who act much younger than their chronological age. This often happens because they weren't able to learn the lessons from an earlier period in life.

We all need to learn **common lessons**. The tasks identified by developmental psychologists represent lessons we all have in common; all of us need to learn them. Other lessons are unique to us as individuals. No two personal histories or series of life experiences are identical, which means some lessons apply only to certain individuals and only need to be learned by them. Every single one of us has lessons only we need to learn. These are our **unique lessons**.

So what are these creatures called life lessons, and how can we turn them into the kinds of friends that become our trusted, welcome, and worthwhile companions through life? Life lessons are guides or instructions on how to traverse the next section of our journey, how to keep moving in the right direction, stay on track, and continue to grow. I like one of the dictionary definitions, which refers to them as "practical wisdom." They're the concepts we learn that make an impact on our subsequent choices and behaviors, which then determine how our future unfolds.

Just as with any new person we meet, life lessons can become friends and allies, or they can end up being obstacles and adversaries, especially if we try to ignore or resist their advice. Sometimes learning a lesson becomes so excruciating that the lesson feels like an outright enemy. But if we can hang in there and see it through to the final stage of learning, our lessons offer the gift of freedom to move forward into more advanced classrooms and new adventures in life. Learning our lessons also offers the gift of increased self-esteem for struggling, successfully making it through, and passing the tests that life requires of us.

Math is not my strongest suit, and I'll never forget taking a statistics class in graduate school that almost did me in. I worked harder in that class than any other and finally managed to pull off a B. But I was so proud of that grade! Understanding regression analysis wasn't exactly what I'd call practical wisdom, but the experience of feeling mentally slow and dense, digging in, floundering even more, and finally figuring it out gave me a renewed sense of self-confidence about my ability to face other challenges and make it through. That's the kind of life lesson worth learning.

Some lessons we learn with the first message or set of instructions. Others take years, perhaps a lifetime, for us to finally get them right. Some we never learn. Our hardest lessons are often the ones that help us grow the most.

So if the Universe is trying to help us move through this metaphoric school of life, how does this happen? How do we receive our instructions? And how can we understand those instructions in terms of lessons? Let's start answering these questions by first examining both the obvious and more subtle nuances of our lessons in life.

Characteristics of Life Lessons

Although our life lessons are often clear and direct, they can also be elusive and fleeting, remaining concealed and hidden from our day-to-day awareness. For example, recurring dreams are often messages from our subconscious inner world about lessons we need to learn. We have to deliberately interpret those dreams to understand their meaning. Most of us also have recurring problems that keep happening in our lives, in our external environment. Those problems contain lessons, and the problems usually won't go away until we learn our lessons well enough to pass the real-life tests.

As a freshman in college, I became enamored with psychology with the first class I took, changed my major to psych, and started a lifelong fascination with the study of human behavior. I distinctly remember when we learned about the stimulus-response pattern. I also recall the exact *aha* moment when I realized that life lessons have some of the same characteristics as a stimulus. They're both events that cause something else to happen. Understanding the characteristics of life lessons can make them easier to identify, so here's what to look for.

1. Frequency

How often we get instructions about a particular life lesson can vary along a scale of frequency ranging from never to all the time, with different rates in between. It's important to note that we are referring to the number of times we're *aware* that we're getting instructions. No doubt, the Universe tries to deliver innumerable messages that go unnoticed and slip right past us, but all we have to go on is our conscious perception of frequency.

For example, the first time someone recommends that I read a certain book, I make a mental note. The second time the book is suggested, I wonder if I need to put it on my reading list. By the third time that same book is recommended, I ask myself, "Could it be a coincidence that someone told me that three different times?" and promise to at least skim through it. Every single time, I find something valuable in that book that helps me with one or more lessons.

2. Intensity

In general, instructions about lessons start out relatively quiet and subtle, more like whispers, hints, and nudges. Maybe a slight tap on the shoulder. If we miss our cue—moreover, if we miss it multiple times—our instructions may become louder and more intense, similar to someone pushing you or shouting in your ear. If we still don't get it, if somehow we aren't aware that someone is shoving or yelling right at us, we may get a wake-up call. Here the experience is more akin to hitting a cement wall or running off the road, and it can range from close calls and near disasters to an actual crash that stops you altogether. For some of us, at certain times, it seems like that is what it takes for life to finally get our attention.

Let's go back to the example of the lesson about sleep when it comes to taking care of our bodies. How many of us have learned that lesson the hard way? We ignore the messages we get from our bodies telling us we need more rest. We can usually get away with this for short periods of time. Our bodies then start to protest more loudly. Maybe we get headaches, the sniffles, or a sore throat, yet we still don't respond. Finally, it may take some type of full-blown, serious illness to wake us up to the fact that we can't keep running around, constantly sleep deprived. Not all illnesses are the result of this process, but when they are, we can sometimes look back and see the signs we either missed along the way or chose to ignore.

3. Urgency

Life lessons also fall along a continuum of urgency. Some lessons need to be addressed right away. If you have a medical emergency, you need to act on that message immediately. We can take our time with some other instructions, because they can be delayed without negative consequences. Maybe you have gotten the message that you need to clean your closets, but doing it later would be just fine. Exactly how we define urgency depends on our personal perception. What is urgent for one person may not be for another.

And what's not compelling for you may be urgent for the Universe. Sometimes we meander through life not paying attention, and all of a sudden we get a wake-up call, which is a definite sign of urgency. A fairly common example is when you are driving along in your car, thinking about who knows what or doing something in addition to driving, and suddenly you barely miss having an accident. That's when you realize someone was watching out for you, because the Universe just managed to get your attention *and* protect you from harm. This type of wake-up call is sometimes referred to as **divine protection** or a **divine intervention**. These lessons need to be learned right then, immediately, on the spot, so the Universe doesn't have to repeat itself with a potentially different outcome. For example, we hear stories all the time about tragedies that occurred because of texting and driving, yet this habit remains epidemic.

4. Importance

Lessons and instructions can also be placed on a scale of importance. How important is it for you to pay attention to certain messages or instructions you get in the school of life? How important is it for you to follow up on those instructions? Here again, the determination of importance is personal. One person might place job and career lessons at the top of the list, whereas another might put family and personal relationships as number one. In general, we will be more sensitive to instructions that relate to what we value as important.

A second but certainly no less significant aspect of importance has more to do with major versus minor lessons, those that are large in contrast with smaller ones. How important is it to your overall growth for you to learn a particular lesson? There's a quote by Robert Service that says, "It isn't the mountain ahead that wears you out; it's the grain of sand in your shoe." Some of life's lessons are major in that once learned, they allow us to move forward in the school of life at a much less stressful, if not always faster, pace. People who are successfully recovering from an addiction or some type of debilitating physical or mental illness may understand this on a very personal level.

5. Timing

In terms of which lessons we learn when, it seems the Universe has this extraordinary internal clock, which is personalized and individually synchronized for each of us, a clock that somehow knows exactly when we are ready. The hints and instructions and opportunities will keep appearing on our path until we develop whatever competency is required and can successfully apply the teaching.

When I was in college and living in the dorms, my roommate and several of our friends would go to meals together at the campus dining hall, come back from lunch or dinner, smoke cigarettes, and play bridge. That's when my smoking began, and despite feeling guilty, knowing it was wrong, worrying about my health, and making several short-lived attempts to stop, I found it too difficult to quit over the next several years. Then I got sick. Really sick.

I'm usually healthy and never sick for more than a couple of days, but this particular respiratory infection lasted an entire week, and it scared me. I honestly thought it was a direct and explicit message from The Almighty that

I was supposed to stop smoking right then, and that if I didn't, I would get cancer.

In looking back at that experience, I can see the perfection in the timing of my illness and the alarming message that went along with it. By that time I had finished school, was in a good job, didn't have a lot of stress in my life, and wasn't around other people who smoked. I knew that kind of fear doesn't come along very often and that it was actually a gift. Who knows if I would have gotten cancer, but I accepted the gift, and despite numerous urges and temptations after that, I never picked up another cigarette. It was the perfect time for me to quit, and in some uncanny way, life seemed to know that. My guilt and fear had escalated over time, giving me numerous and blatantly obvious opportunities to learn the lesson, which I usually tried hard to ignore. But they culminated when a solid week of illness held my feet to the fire until I finally made the commitment to stop. You repeat the class until you get it right.

6. Relativity

The concept of relativity can be difficult to grasp, but once you understand it, learning can actually get easier. Many of our life lessons are relative to the situation. In other words, the appropriateness of the lesson *depends*. It may depend on people, places, events, timing, and any number of other contextual factors. Many of us struggle with the concept of relativity. Probably most of us would like to think that once we learn a lesson—once we get it down—it will apply across the board, at all times, forever. But life is more complex than that.

Think for a moment about how you decide what clothes to wear. You don't wear the same clothes to work or to a job that you would wear to a formal affair. You probably wear different clothes to exercise than you would to paint your kitchen. You decide what to wear based on the occasion or context, and therefore, *it depends* on what you're planning to do.

Here's another example. Let's say that you are working on the lesson about trust, specifically trusting other people. Some of us want to deal with trust in an either/or, all-or-none way. Either we are going to trust other people, or we're not. We need to either open up and take risks by trusting others, or we need to remember that people aren't trustworthy and to stay withdrawn and protected.

From a relative perspective, the issue of trust *depends*. It depends on who the person is that you are considering trusting, it depends on what you might trust that person with, it depends on whether the person has a track record of trustworthiness with you, and it depends on what type of relationship you have in the first place. It depends. One lesson about trust might apply in one situation with one particular person, and a different lesson about trust might apply in another circumstance with someone else. Accepting that complexity gives us the chance to make better decisions. Sometimes, in order to move on to the next classroom, we need to deal with life lessons on a relative, case-by-case *it depends* basis.

Over my many years of working in higher education, I often served on search committees for hiring new employees. Those searches usually involved bringing our top three or four candidates to campus for personal interviews. We would often include at least one question that presented a common dilemma involved in doing the job and ask the candidates what they would do in that situation. I was always impressed when I heard candidates answer with "It depends." They would go on to mention several contextual factors that would influence their decisions, and that alone told me they had some solid work experience. Their responses also told me that they could think in relative terms. I wanted to hire people who would be able to make decisions based on thinking through the circumstances rather than blindly following a policy or common professional practice. The most qualified candidates usually didn't give "always" or "never" answers. They had already learned the lesson about "it depends."

⁓

As a college counselor, I've worked with hundreds of students who were experiencing recurring problems, issues that kept surfacing in their lives. One student I remember in particular, Jessica, was a sophomore who seemed to always end up in bad relationships with her boyfriends. Jessica had good insight. "I know I pick men who don't want to get too close, and it never works out," she told me one day. "I'm so tired of breaking up and having to start over with someone new." Jessica understood her problem and could see how she kept choosing men who were emotionally distant in the same ways her father was, yet she couldn't seem to *do* anything different. Her insight wasn't enough.

In this case, indications of a lesson that needed to be learned had occurred **frequently** in Jessica's life. Many of those situations had the characteristic of **intensity** because of the pain she experienced when the relationship ended. Learning the lesson had a great deal of **importance** because she eventually wanted to get married. And Jessica felt the **timing** was right for her to figure out whatever would allow her to finally enjoy a healthy, committed relationship.

Problems that stem from our family of origin are sometimes layered and complicated. Successfully resolving those problems usually means learning many new lessons that are more appropriate for where we are as adults. With Jessica, she had to grieve for the father she never had before she could begin to change her pattern. She then needed to let go of the baggage she was carrying from her childhood—the feelings and beliefs about men and about herself—that she kept taking with her into every new relationship. Once she did that, she was eager to learn new behavioral skills about how to take better care of herself in relationships and how to interact with her boyfriend in healthier ways.

After Jessica graduated, she stayed in school to get her master's degree, so I worked with her off and on over a number of years. The last time I saw her, she had been in a relationship for over a year with someone very different from her father, and she felt things were going pretty well. "We sometimes argue over little things, but it doesn't make him want to leave," she said. The relationship was still challenging for her, but for the most part, she was pleased with the ways she was handling those challenges. She had learned her lessons well enough to move into the next classroom, where there were more lessons to learn. Jessica wasn't stuck anymore. She had the courage to face what was hidden from her awareness, the feelings and beliefs that lay buried in her subconscious, and by doing that, she earned her promotion to the next class in the school of life.

---

4. <u>Activities</u>

As you were reading through the characteristics of life lessons, did any examples from your own life come to mind? If not, think of a personal example right now—a lesson you've already learned. Write it down, and then ask yourself:

- Did I need to get <u>frequent</u> messages about that lesson, or did I learn it right away?
- Were the instructions <u>intense</u>, or were they more like a hint or a gentle nudge?
- On a scale of one to five, how <u>urgent</u> was it for me to learn that lesson?
- On a scale of one to five, how <u>important</u> was it for me to learn that lesson?

- *How did the <u>timing</u> of when I learned that lesson make it easier or harder to learn it?*
- *What about the characteristic of <u>relativity</u>? Does the lesson apply all the time, across the board? Or does it depend? Do I need to modify it based on what it's about, where I am, or who I'm with?*

Identifying life lessons you've already learned—and the ways you received your instructions—can help you be on the lookout for new lessons that life is trying to help you master. The more we pay attention in school, the better we get at recognizing our instructions the first time or two they're offered.

Types of Lessons

Have you ever felt like you came to the wrong conclusion about an experience? Maybe you misjudged a situation, which caused you to make a mistake down the road. Or perhaps you misread a person's intentions, and the person ended up hurting you. Maybe you looked at so-and-so and thought that person had it all together, so you tried to imitate that person, and you sacrificed your uniqueness and authenticity along the way.

Life lessons follow a similar pattern. Our goal is to learn lessons that are life affirming, growth producing, and carry us further down the river of life. However, sometimes we get confused or off base in our thinking, and we come to the wrong conclusions. We learn lessons that instead stunt our growth and cause us to get hung up in the mental debris of a bad call. This is similar to getting stuck in the river, wedged in between logs along the side, caught on a submerged tree, or going round and round in a pool of swirling water.

Our lessons can fall into one of two categories: **growth producing** and **limiting**. Limiting lessons either limit our growth or are downright harmful. An example of a limiting lesson is thinking your uniqueness is odd, even embarrassing, when it's actually what makes you special. We learn harmful lessons when we decide that numbing our feelings with food, alcohol, drugs, shopping, and other unhealthy escapes will somehow make things better.

The lessons we're focused on throughout this book fall into the first category. They're called life lessons because they affirm, nourish, and promote life. They support our growth, help us pass our classes in the school of life, and lead us down a path where we can develop our talents and do whatever we're here to do. They're the practical wisdom that keeps us moving forward and headed the right way. It may sound straightforward, but despite our best efforts, we often learn lessons or make decisions that sideline us temporarily or take us in limiting or harmful directions. We may fail to learn from our experiences, or we learn the wrong things.

We also need to distinguish life lessons from facts or information. If you learn a fact of history, that's not a life lesson. However, if you take that fact and use it to develop some kind of practical wisdom for your own life, then it becomes one. That's what happened to me in my statistics class. I learned information about statistics, but I learned a life lesson when I realized that if I dig deep and keep moving forward in difficult situations, I eventually become more resilient and better able to handle the next rough spot that will invariably come along.

Our growth-producing life lessons come in two different types: **changing** and **permanent**. We live in a physical world which is constantly in a state of flux. Our bodies transform daily, our thoughts come and go, and our relationships evolve over time. Seasons change into seasons which change into other seasons in an endless continuum. The cliché that what's here today will be gone tomorrow is absolutely true in our physical reality.

It's sometimes easier to grasp this concept of constant change when we consider factual information. Most of us know that whatever we learn about technology today will probably be obsolete by next month, if it's not already. But how many of us have been brought up short by believing that the job we've held for fifteen years will always be there? How many of us have been caught off guard when a long-term relationship ended, and we never thought that would happen? Or that our health would ever become a major concern? We take certain things for granted and assume they're never going to change.

In the last section, we looked at the relative characteristic of life lessons, where the lesson applies only in certain situations or contexts. *It depends* on external circumstances. Changing lessons are different. They change *over time,* from when you're a child, to an adolescent, to an adult, and throughout your adult life.

Let's examine what changing lessons mean to us as students of life, because they have the potential to cause massive confusion and keep us repeating the same class again and again. That's because changing lessons require us to **unlearn** them, let them go, and then learn a completely different lesson instead. We need to voluntarily give up lessons that maybe we fought hard to learn in the first place, that we may have learned with enormous pain, effort, and struggle through horrendous circumstances. They might have been what gave us our best shot at making it safely and sanely through whatever was going on in our lives at the time. We're grateful for those lessons, and we're scared to give them up. But what we learned in the second grade may not work when we're in the tenth grade.

Many people learned invaluable lessons about how to survive as children in the midst of dysfunctional and destructive family dynamics. But what they learned as children about how to stay safe may need to be unlearned as they get older. Continuing to act out of a survival mentality jeopardizes the quality of their lives as adults when they're in different life situations and have more resources and options than what they experienced growing up.

Often some of our toughest lessons as adults have to do with changing lessons, with unlearning and letting go of what we learned during an earlier time in our lives so we can live fuller and healthier lives in the present. That was the case in the previous example about Jessica, who needed to let go of many of the lessons she learned from her father before she could experience a healthy adult relationship with her boyfriend. We'll explore this more in chapter 8 on dealing with obstacles.

In addition to changing lessons, we have **permanent** lessons. These apply no matter what the circumstances, no matter what we're doing, no matter who we are with, and regardless of where we are in our lives. They go beyond the circumstances of our physical world.

For example, some people adhere to lessons like "Do the right thing" or "Take the high road," which is always their approach every time, over time, without exception. The details of how that plays out will change, but they may believe and use those lessons throughout their lives.

As a child, I adhered to a lesson that said, "Always do your best." It went along with the adage, "If something is worth doing, it's worth doing well." I wouldn't call myself a perfectionistic or overachieving kid, but I tried to be good, follow the rules, and generally please the people around me. I thought I would live the rest of my life according to that lesson.

Flash forward thirty years, and I was in a relationship with a partner who had a different take on life. He worked hard and did his best at what he saw as priorities, but he also had this funny, fun-loving streak and a laid-back attitude that provided a welcome counterbalance to my super-conscientious and sometimes overly serious approach.

So we bought this house together and added an enclosed courtyard, which tended to trap the leaves from the surrounding trees. One day I was out in the courtyard sweeping the leaves—doing my best, of course—which meant making sure I swept up every single leaf. We had invited another couple over for dinner that night, so I wanted it even more clean than usual. Watching me work so hard to ensure that it ended up looking close to immaculate, my partner said to me, "Why are you busting your butt to sweep the courtyard?"

"Because I want it to look nice."

"It's just going to get dirty again the next time the wind blows," he replied matter-of-factly.

Of course, I already knew this, but something about *how* he said it rocked my belief system in a way I never would have expected. His comment forced me to examine whether my lesson of "Always do your best" needed to be revised. And it did. That day, in the courtyard, with the impending fall of more leaves, I learned the lesson about "good enough."

I realized that some things in life aren't worth the time and effort it takes to do your best. If something isn't a priority for me, maybe I don't need to give it my all. Or perhaps because of the nature of the task, it doesn't make sense to give it 100 percent, like sweeping the courtyard. Maybe it's okay to do a "good enough" job and let that be just fine; maybe I don't need to *always* do my best.

So what started out as one permanent lesson has now evolved into two. "Do your best" on what you consider priorities and things where doing less wouldn't be acceptable, either because of your values and standards or because of the kind of task it is. Then accept "good enough" on most of what's left. Of course, I never had enough time to do my best at everything anyway, but I always felt like I *should*. I said to myself, "What I'm doing isn't enough. I should do more, and I should do it better."

Now this distinction keeps me from feeling guilty when I choose to give any given project less than my best. Especially when I'm overloaded with priorities, it's a relief to deliberately place certain responsibilities into the good enough category and not feel bad. Making conscious decisions between the two approaches provides practical wisdom as I move forward, giving me more time and energy to accomplish what's truly important and to experience the things I enjoy.

One of the morals of this story is to be extra careful about adopting any rigid life lessons that include absolutes like *always* or *never*. Although like mine, those lessons may be well intended, they often result in consequences that are limiting or even harmful. I went through a lot of unnecessary guilt and self-created stress during the time I tried to always do my best, and I wouldn't wish that on anyone. So throughout this book, when I mention doing your best, I'm referring to doing quality, A-level work on the priorities that are most important to you—not necessarily on everything. We'll cover this more in chapter 8.

How to Identify Your Life Lessons

If we're going to get better as students of life, then learning how to identify our life lessons becomes essential. Recognizing our lessons allows us to pass our classes the first time instead of having to repeat them, and it opens the door for us to explore the enticing new chapters in our lives that are inherent at more advanced levels. Try these strategies for improving your skills.

1. Pay attention in class.

For years, I taught study skills classes to college freshmen. I always found it interesting to note how many ways they could find to keep from paying attention in class. These included talking to the person sitting next to them, snoozing, doing homework for another class, and playing on their cell phones or laptops. One of the topics we covered was how to improve your memory. Their distracted behaviors became teachable moments to emphasize the fact that we don't remember information that never gets recorded in our brains to start with. I could be giving them the answers to the next test, but if they were texting a friend and never heard me, they would completely miss out.

Similarly, if we're constantly distracted from the here and now by our own busyness, digital devices, stress, mental chaos, frazzled emotions, or whatever else, it will be hard to learn our lessons, or even know the Universe is trying to teach us something. So the first thing we need to do is ***pay attention in class***. We need to wake up to what is happening in our lives, notice the coincidences, open our minds to a possible reason or purpose for what's going on around us, and ask ourselves if there's a lesson embedded in what we're dealing with. If you currently have any problems in your life, it means you need to learn one or more lessons to resolve those problems, so those are obvious ones to look for.

2. Use intention.

Tapping into the power of intention can become an especially effective tool in helping us identify life lessons. Make a 100 percent commitment to becoming a better student of life, which includes getting faster at recognizing lessons the first time they appear on your path. Using intention is like flipping on a switch inside, a switch which signifies that all systems are on "go." We're mentally clear, emotionally invested, and doggedly determined to succeed with a whatever-it-takes attitude. According to Goethe, that's when Providence jumps in, and "all sorts of things occur to help one that would never otherwise have occurred." Try it. It can turn even the most arduous task into an ace in the hole. The difference between giving 99 percent and a flat-out, no-holds-barred effort can be as wide as the Grand Canyon in terms of our results.

3. Remember what you already know.

Here's another tip for identifying your lessons: remember what you already know. For example, you already know about the characteristics of life lessons, which provide name tags for our faithful friends each time they show up. Their name tags say the following:

- **Frequency:** If something repeatedly comes into your awareness, pay attention. The Universe may be trying to teach you a lesson. For instance, I always read a book after three people recommend it.

- **Intensity:** Our instructions range from a fleeting thought or quiet internal voice to full-blown wake-up calls. Learn to listen to the hints, nudges, and shoulder taps before they escalate in intensity.

- **Urgency:** All of us need to constantly scan our horizons for any signs of an urgent lesson. For example, if a serious health issue shows up, move health lessons to the top of your list.

- **Importance:** We're more likely to pay attention to lessons about things that are important to us and less likely to pay attention to things we see as less important. That's one way we miss our cues, so stay vigilant.

- **Timing:** Look for those ideal times to knuckle down and learn a lesson. The right timing may reveal itself through necessity, or you may get a choice about when to make learning a particular lesson a priority.

- **Relativity:** Some lessons change according to the situation. The appropriateness of the lesson is relative; *it depends* on the context, like people and places. For example, you can't trust everyone, so only share secrets with people who are trustworthy.

If we learn to recognize our friends by their characteristics sooner rather than later, then life doesn't have to smack us on the forehead with a two by four to get our attention. The goal is to avoid those unruly wake-up calls.

4. Learn from the past.

Another technique for getting better at identifying our lessons today is to look backward, identify lessons we learned in the past, and figure out how we knew we needed to learn them.

5. *Activities*

Right now, ask yourself the following questions:

- *What's one important life lesson I've learned so far?*
- *How did I know I needed to learn that?*
- *What's another life lesson I've already learned?*
- *Who or what told me or showed me I needed to learn it?*

This activity can be repeated any number of times, helping us see the lessons we already have under our belts.

Recognizing the lessons we've already learned can be validating. It shows us we're already learning lessons or else we wouldn't have made this much progress in our lives. It's also helpful to look for any patterns in how the Universe got our attention, so we knew there was a lesson to learn.

Identifying previous lessons can help us better see the ones in our current classrooms. We can also look ahead and anticipate lessons and tests that are coming our way in the future. For example, most people learn enough lessons around time management to keep from being late when paying their income taxes. However, if they look down the road and see that their taxes will take extra time next year, they can anticipate what lessons they will need to use to pass the real-life test by still meeting the filing deadline.

5. Practice, practice, practice.

Mastering any new skill means we need to practice—a lot. We have to practice identifying life lessons if we want to get good at it. Try these suggestions.

6. *Activities*

1. *Take a few minutes at the end of the day and ask yourself these questions:*
   - *Did I learn any new life lessons today?*
   - *Did I relearn any lessons I already knew?*

2. *Identify any problem areas in your life and ask:*
   - *What could those problems be trying to teach me? If nothing comes to mind, guess.*

> *3. If you made a mistake or feel stuck in some part of your life, then ask:*
>
> - *What lesson or lessons do I need to learn? Guess if you have to.*

The more we practice identifying lessons on a regular basis, the more we increase our chances of passing our classes the first time we enroll.

6. Ask for help and support.

Talk to your friends, family, and coworkers. Ask for their support in your learning process. Ask them about a problem you're having by saying something like "What do you think I need to learn to resolve that?" Ask the Universe for help in improving your skills. Ask for lessons that will help you identify your lessons. Pray if you're the praying type. Look for other resources that might be helpful, such as books, seminars, and other types of training. There are many sources of available support. If you make a sincere effort to receive that support, and if you keep taking the next step, and the next and the next, the Universe will eventually respond and provide what you need.

7. Look at it another way.

Did you ever play with a kaleidoscope when you were a child? It's a toy that looks similar to a telescope. If so, you probably remember holding it up to the light and seeing intricate details of bright colors and fascinating designs. With only a fraction of a turn, the whole pattern changed into a totally different picture.

Another technique for identifying our lessons is to look at them from another angle. Let's slightly turn our kaleidoscopes and look at life lessons from the viewpoint of our teachers. The next chapter focuses on the teachers in our school.

Chapter 4
Finding Our Teachers

As I walked from the parking lot toward my office building, my head buzzed with nonstop thoughts about work. The obsessive thinking was just another symptom of my stress overload, but this particular morning, it consumed my mind more than usual.

The loud sound of "caw, caw" came from the crows that hung out in the redwood trees outside my office. It interrupted my barrage of thoughts and made me aware of just how lost I'd become in my ruminations. The crows kept at it. Suddenly, "caw, caw, caw" sounded like laughter, and the thought crossed my mind that the birds were laughing at me for being so caught up in my internal clamor. As my mind flashed back, it seemed like the only times I remembered the crows being so loud was when they interfered with the noise of my obsessing. What if they laughed at me each time I walked into work and was completely oblivious to my surroundings because of the incessant chatter in my head?

I chuckled to myself just thinking about the possibility that the crows were laughing *at me*. If so, the joke was *on me,* and I certainly deserved it. And if their laughter was a message that I needed to spend less time in my head worrying, it coincided with another lesson I was learning at the time: **lighten up and don't take yourself so seriously**. I could feel those awarenesses settle into my body in a way that told me all of that was true.

In the school of life, our teachers are anywhere and everywhere we need them to be, provided with the same sense of impeccable timing as our life lessons. As soon as we're ready to learn a lesson, the Universe jumps into action and sends the best teacher for the job. We may or may not like the teachers who appear in our lives, but they inevitably show up bearing the gifts of information we need to know.

Our teachers can be anyone and anything in our particular classes, those who can help us learn the lessons we're expected to master. One of the main reasons we get stuck in school is because we fail to recognize someone or something as a teacher who is trying to get our attention. We often can't identify the life lesson because we don't perceive the teacher as a teacher.

Teachers resemble life lessons in that they come in all different sizes, shapes, contexts, and degrees of clarity. Just like lessons, some teachers are hard and some are easy. But if you remember from actually being in school, the most difficult teachers, the ones who really made you work, often required you to learn the most. And you felt the greatest sense of accomplishment when you finally passed their classes. You knew you worked hard to earn that passing grade, knew you deserved it, and after all your efforts, you felt a healthy sense of pride, even if you kept it to yourself. Some of our hardest lessons, taught by our most difficult teachers, can give us the greatest value and mileage as we navigate through life.

In general, teachers fall into one of two categories: **external** and **internal**. External teachers are those outside of us, in our environment, and include life experiences, people, places, coincidences, animals, and time. Internal teachers are those inside us, including our bodies, thoughts, behaviors, emotions, addictions, dreams, and intuition.

In the previous example, the crows became my external teachers, pointing out the fact that I was way too far into my head again. My obsessive thoughts were internal teachers, telling me I'd gotten too stressed out. And that "settling" feeling in my body when I figured out the message was another internal teacher, my intuition, speaking through my body and confirming that my hypothesis was right.

Teachers may be as informal and happenstance as the passing message on a bumper sticker or billboard that tells you something you need to hear right then. They can be as formal as an acknowledged student-teacher relationship with a mentor, boss, hero, idol, role model, family member, or friend. Teaching styles may be as varied as the teachers themselves. Some teachers come right out and tell you, "This is what you need to know." Some tell you what to look for but don't actually give you the answer. Some help you learn where to find the answers, and some teach you one of the more powerful lessons—how to ask the right questions.

Everyone and everything in your life right now has at least the potential to be your teacher. That includes the people you enjoy being around, and perhaps especially those you don't. Paradoxically, it's often the people we perceive as adversaries or enemies, those thorns in our sides, who bring us some of our most valuable lessons. By the same token, those "I-wish-you-would-just-go-away" problems we experience usually reveal their silver lining after being resolved. And frequently those parts of ourselves that we dislike or fear the most shower us with some of our most beneficial gifts—*if* we can accept what they're trying to help us learn.

External Teachers

Because we're continuously enrolled in the metaphorical school of life, we constantly have teachers in our environment to help us learn what's expected in our classes. The following list isn't comprehensive, but it's a starting point for you to identify the external teachers who are currently in your life.

Experiences

We often hear it said that experience is the best teacher. Experience is one teacher among many, and if we learn how to extract the lessons from our experiences, they can become incredibly powerful catalysts for our progress and growth.

Our lifetimes consist of a long continuum of experiences that started out as "situations." As we go from one situation to another, we make choices and decisions, and as those situations play out, they become our life experiences. The key is to benefit from our experiences so that we emerge on the other side stronger and wiser and better able to have a "good" experience from our next situations. That means we need to maintain our vigilance and awareness of what's at stake in situations and do our best to learn from each and every one of them. And what's at stake is: (1) learning the right lesson or lessons, (2) missing the opportunity to figure out the important takeaways, or (3) sometimes getting confused or mixed up and learning, or trying to learn, the wrong lesson.

During my extensive career of working at various universities, I went through several years where I was on a one-year contract, which meant I never knew if I would have a job the next year. And I usually didn't find out until the end of my contract whether it would be renewed. I'm a planner, someone who loves security and knowing what's coming up in my future. With a one-year contract, I couldn't have any of that, and it made my anxiety escalate to more-than-uncomfortable levels.

I kept asking myself, "How can I find some degree of job security?" That's because I kept thinking, "If I just had a secure job, my life would be so much better, and I would be so much happier, or at least less anxious." I was convinced that the lesson I needed to learn was how to find a secure job.

Then one day, I'll never forget, I was in the grocery store, pushing my cart around the end of the produce aisle, when I heard a song from the piped-in store music. I noticed the song because it annoyed me. I had to stop and focus on why I suddenly felt irritated, and that's when I put the two together. The song was Bobby McFerrin's "Don't Worry, Be Happy," which is a delightful song with a compelling message. But I didn't want to hear someone telling me to be happy. After all, I had no job security, so how could I possibly feel happy?

That's when it hit me. *I was trying to learn the wrong lesson.* Although it made perfect sense for me to want and look for job security, on some level I knew that was an illusion. I also knew that no degree of job security would make me truly happy. Nope. I finally figured it out and declared to myself, "The lesson is to learn to be happy *regardless* of your circumstances." Oh! Now that *really* made sense. And from that day forward, I have worked hard to hold on to my happiness, sometimes in spite of whatever's going on in my life.

The years of being on a one-year job contract were tough on me. I wasn't in a relationship at the time, so there was no one else's income to fall back on. If I didn't work, I didn't eat, and I stressed and worried about money *a lot*. Looking back on those experiences, I wish I'd learned the lesson about happiness sooner than I did. I could have saved myself a lot of grief. By the same token, I'm extremely grateful to have finally figured that one out, because I have the rest of my life to reap the rewards of doing the things that make me happy in the good times, and perhaps especially during the bad.

Once I learned the happiness lesson in the job situation, it generalized to other parts of my life. I could look at other situations and immediately see the illusion of "I'll be happy when…": "I'll be happy when I reach a certain income level…when my relationship with so-and-so reaches a more even keel…when I go to the gym enough to get in better shape." The list could be endless, and for most of us, it usually is. But the silver lining of my "problem" of no job security now shines bright in my life. When I get caught up in thinking that a certain change will bring me happiness, I take a step back and make a conscious decision not to go down that road.

There's a quote by Vernon Sanders Law that says, "Experience is a hard teacher because she gives the test first, the lesson afterwards." If we're faced with a situation for the first time, sometimes this adage is true—we can't know the lesson until we reflect back on what we needed to learn. But many of our situations in life are repeats or at least similar to what we've experienced in the past. If we keep learning what we need to learn, life becomes more predictable, and we stand on a firm foundation of the knowledge we've accumulated in the past. That's exactly what happened after I learned the lesson on "I'll be happy when…"

For me to finally master that lesson, it took a precarious job experience to serve as an external teacher, accompanied by a particular song, another teacher in my environment. The third teacher was internal, my emotional irritation, telling me that the words to the song had hit a nerve. The Universe had given me lots of chances to learn the happiness lesson before that. Finally it sent three teachers to get my attention and figure out what had kept me stuck. I also think my previous years of unhappiness made me more receptive to coming up with a different solution. As a student, I felt more than ready, and lo and behold, three teachers appeared.

---

7. <u>Activities</u>

Our experiences in life can be powerful teachers. Write down at least two life lessons your experiences have taught you.

- *One lesson I have learned from my life experiences is*
- *Another lesson I have learned from my experiences is*

People

Have you ever been reading along, and something the author says jumps out of the material and hits you as if it were personally meant for you? Or maybe you overhear snippets of a conversation, and one comment sticks in your head, giving you a message about a lesson you need to learn. I often will suddenly hear words to songs I've known for years in a completely different way, one that helps reinforce something I'm trying to learn right then. Or one time my supervisor at work told me something negative about my leadership style on a performance evaluation, and it turned out to be exactly the feedback I needed to learn a crucial lesson in another area of my life.

The Universe definitely speaks through people in helping us figure out the lessons we need to learn right then, whether they be authors, strangers, songwriters, supervisors, or anyone else handpicked to deliver the message. We often recognize people as our teachers; maybe that's because people actually are our teachers when we formally attend school. Family members, friends, lovers, coworkers, neighbors—anyone can be our teacher. In fact, every person who ever has been, is, or will be in our lives has the potential to help us learn something.

Our family members are some of our most significant teachers, exerting a powerful influence on how far we go in the school of life. Most experts agree that what we learn during our first five years has critical, long-term effects on our overall growth and development. Within that period, we learn attitudes, beliefs, values, prejudices, habits, and traditions. We learn lessons about love and whether or not we're lovable and acceptable. We learn about trust—trusting ourselves, trusting others, and, more generally, whether the world is a safe place to be. There are lessons about intimacy, boundaries, and how to deal with conflict—basically how to relate to ourselves and others. These lessons include how we relate to our own feelings, our sense of personal power and potential. We learn how to take care of, or not take care of, ourselves and others. We learn how to survive in the world.

In any given relationship, we are both student and teacher at the same time. We can learn from the person we're with, and that person has the opportunity to learn from us. If nothing is coincidental in the school of life, that means all of us were born into families that could help us learn whatever lessons we came here to learn. At the same time, as children or siblings in that family, we become teachers to other family members based on what they need to learn. In our school, everyone and everything is interrelated and interdependent; we all need each other to make progress.

In general, whatever you learn in your family of origin becomes the blueprint for how you experience other relationships in your life. We are all drawn to what is familiar, and we tend to continually recreate in our adult lives the reality we experienced as children, because that's our "normal." This means we keep learning the same lessons from people—the good and bad, the healthy and the unhealthy. The pattern repeats over and over. The players may change, the scenes and locations may be different, but the lessons remain the same. Not always, but often. In the previous example, Jessica kept finding herself with men like her father, learning the same heartbreaking lessons with them that she did with him.

But here's the deal. When we're young children, we're trying to survive, to stay safe, to find love and acceptance. The lessons we learn about how to do that may be exactly right for what's going on around us. But then we grow up. The people and circumstances in our lives change, and we may need to **unlearn** our old lessons and then master completely different lessons than the ones that worked for us when we were younger.

One of the most common places I see people get stuck in the school of life is when they continue to use the same outdated lessons they learned as children. Those lessons may have been perfectly appropriate and even lifesaving back then, but today, as adults, those lessons make them miserable and hold them back. Those lessons become limiting beliefs, insidiously invisible, and they create a glass ceiling on who we allow ourselves to become. Examples of outgrown lessons include: "don't be selfish, don't express your feelings, don't *have* feelings, you should be ashamed of yourself, you're not enough just the way you are," and so many more that we often unconsciously adopt.

We'll look at how to identify and get past these old, limiting beliefs in chapter 8 on dealing with obstacles.

We also adopt lessons from our families that set the stage for us to live happy, healthy lives. I was incredibly fortunate to grow up with two parents who loved me unconditionally. The lessons they taught me were invaluable. For example, even though my dad ran a busy law practice and did a remarkable amount of community service, he always managed to spend lots of quality time with me and my two sisters. From that I learned that I have inherent worth.

And I'll never forget the day my mom taught me a significant lesson. She was driving, with just the two of us in the car, when she said, "Each of us is responsible for our own happiness." I didn't fully understand the meaning of her words, but I knew they were important. It wasn't until later that I realized the extent to which she followed her own advice and provided a shining example of a life filled with joy.

---

8. Activities

Think back on all people who have been your teachers—family members, friends, authors, role models—anyone who has made a difference in your life. Then ask yourself:

1. *Which three people have been the most important teachers in my life?*

2. *What's the most important life lesson each of these three people has helped me learn?*

I suggest you write down your teachers and the lessons you learned from them. And if it's appropriate and you haven't already, you might want to find a way to thank them for what they helped you learn.

Coincidences

I sat in my veterinarian's office with one of my pets, waiting on our appointment for a routine checkup. As I waited, I noticed a bright pink piggy bank sitting on the receptionist's counter with a sign next to it that said, "Donations." The sign had a picture of a dog and some text, but I didn't read it. Knowing that my vet did a lot of rescue work, I decided to contribute, comfortable in my assumption that it was a good cause.

Looking through my purse for money, I figured I would give a couple of dollars, maybe five max, so I surprised myself when I pulled out a twenty-dollar bill and slipped it into the then-happy pig. They called me back for the appointment right after that, so I stopped wondering about my atypical behavior.

However, the next time I went into my vet's office, I saw the same piggy bank, this time with a sign that said, "Thank you." I asked the receptionist what happened with the money, and she lit up as she told me the story. A couple saw someone throw a dog out of a car as they were driving behind it on the freeway. The couple stopped, got the dog, and brought it to my vet. He spent almost an entire weekend trying to save the dog as she teetered on the edge of death. Because of the number of broken bones, he enlisted the help of another vet who specialized in bone surgeries. Together, they saved the life of the little dog. The couple who brought in the dog decided to adopt it but couldn't afford any vet fees, so both vets waived the costs of their services. The money in the piggy bank went toward the antibiotics and other medications the dog needed when the couple took it home. The receptionist then said, "The donations came within five cents of paying for all the medications. Isn't that amazing?"

When I heard that the donations covered all the costs, almost to the penny, I immediately understood why I contributed more than usual, and I suddenly felt like I was part of a much greater connection to a worthy, compassionate cause.

Then I started thinking about this story. What were the odds that this kind couple would be driving directly behind the person who threw out the dog, or that they would take it to one of the only vets in town who would manage to save its life—for free? And how likely would it be that the donations would add up to almost exactly the cost of the medications the little dog would need to go home? Those kinds of coincidences defy all odds. They pull you up short and reveal a deeper thread of connection and purpose that runs invisibly throughout our lives and experiences. They showcase the handiwork of the Universe as it supports our pure intentions and heartfelt desires. I'm always astonished by the astronomical chances that coincidences reveal and have learned to see those as the Universe's way of saying, "Yes. Yes, this is right. Yes, that was what you were supposed to do. Yes, this is a sign to go in such-and-such direction as you continue on your journey through the school of life. And yes, I am one of your most intriguing teachers." Coincidences provide unique messages in more-than-unique ways if we can tune into what they have to offer.

According to the *Merriam-Webster* dictionary definition, coincidence means "the occurrence of events that happen at the same time by accident but seem to have some connection." A coincidence may look like a chance encounter, but the people who notice it may see it as personally meaningful, almost as if the Universe created just such an improbability to provide the exact information they need right then. The infinitesimal odds of certain events coming together at the same time reveal the extent to which the Universe will go to support us on our path.

Swiss psychiatrist Carl Jung saw coincidences as evidence of events that happen beyond the physical world and referred to them as **synchronicities**. Jung was one of the first theorists to pull away from the established thinking of logic and linear causality to explore the possibilities of a different source of orchestration for the events in people's lives. He opened the door to the concept that the seemingly random happenstances that sprinkle themselves into our daily living provide evidence of a deeper, greater good at work beneath it all.

Coincidences come in two different types: **minor** and **major**. Minor coincidences are noteworthy and certainly interesting, but they only make a small impact on our lives. Major coincidences, on the other hand, hold deep meaning and exert a powerful influence in one's life.

I'm always fascinated by how people meet their spouses, and I know a number of married couples whose initial meeting occurred through such minuscule odds that you have to believe part of the Universe's plan involves playing Cupid. The same goes for how people find their jobs. Often, their instructions on which direction to turn happen through one or more coincidences that land them in the perfect spot for their next career. Those are examples of major, highly meaningful coincidences, ones that change the course of people's lives, sometimes forever.

I remember the first time I became aware of coincidences in my own life. When I was in the ninth grade, our family took a vacation to Colorado. We stopped to have a picnic at one of the gorgeous camping areas near Estes Park, where we just *happened* to run into our neighbors who lived one house down from us in Arkansas. What were the odds? I thought about that experience the whole rest of the trip, marveling at how we didn't even know our neighbors were planning to travel that summer, then ended up at the same place at the same time thousands of miles away from home. I found it not only remarkable but somewhat startling. That coincidence didn't contain a lot of heavy meaning or alter the course of my life, so in that regard, it was relatively minor. However, it made a major impact on my thinking by introducing me to the enthralling world of bizarrely improbable events.

I've noticed that coincidences tend to happen more often when I set my intention on a good cause, like making a difference in someone else's life. For example, while working at various university jobs, I frequently had the opportunity to support students who were somehow stuck in the system. Maybe they missed an enrollment deadline and were scrambling to register for classes. Or perhaps they went through some personal crisis, ended up getting academically disqualified, and were trying to get back into school. Often, they landed in my office at the midnight hour, just before the final cutoff.

I can't tell you how many times those students were able to slide in under the wire and get into school because of a series of coincidences. For instance, every single staff person I called on their behalf would coincidentally be in the office and available to help out, which might lead us to the conclusion that, in several cases, the students had under thirty minutes to get across campus and turn in a form to meet the deadline—barely enough time to make it (if they hustled) and get the problem resolved. Astounding. After those experiences, I would sit back in my chair, look up, and say to the Universe, "Wow, thanks!"

Do you remember the Goethe quote about intention? One part says, "The moment one definitely commits oneself, then Providence moves too. All sorts of things occur to help one that would never otherwise have occurred. A whole stream of events issues from the decision, raising in one's favor all manner of unforeseen incidents, meetings, and material assistance which no man could have dreamed would have come his way." That's what we're talking about here.

Coincidences are evidence of Providence in action, and they happen in all of our lives. One of our assignments as students of life is to pay attention and learn to identify them as they are happening so we can pick up on the instructions they have to offer. Here's an easy one to put on your radar: notice the number of times when you need to talk to someone, and then you *happen* to run into the person, or that person *happens* to call you about something completely different. Then realize that the Universe, or Providence, is supporting your efforts.

The day of my grandfather's funeral started out dark and rather gloomy, with intermittent light rain throughout the morning. After the funeral, we went to the cemetery for a short, and thankfully dry, burial service. However, on the way home, the sun broke through, and a rainbow appeared in full display in the sky, as if to tell us, "All is well." The rainbow brought us such comfort, and I can't believe the timing of such a meaningful event was in any way coincidental.

9. *Activities*

Try these suggestions on how to fine-tune your awareness of coincidences and the instructions they offer.

1. Think back on your past and identify one coincidence you remember that happened in your life. Then ask:

   - *Was I aware of the coincidence when it happened, or did I recognize it after the fact?*
   - *Did the coincidence provide information or other resources I needed at the time? If so, what?*
   - *Was the coincidence highly meaningful, one that had a <u>major</u> influence on my life (like meeting my spouse or finding a job), or was it <u>minor</u> and less meaningful?*

2. Practice recognizing coincidences that occur around you in the present moment, as they unfold. You might even want to write them down. When we increase our awareness, we also increase our chances of learning the lessons these mysterious and delightful teachers have to offer.

Places

When I work with groups of people, I often include guided-imagery activities that focus on relaxation. Without exception, when I ask people to identify a physical place where they feel safe, calm, and relaxed, they immediately come up with one. Some people find that safe space in their own home, like in their bedroom, or underneath a tree in their backyard. For others, it's often a special place in nature, like at the beach, in the mountains, or beside a lake or stream.

Every place, each physical and geographic location has its own energy, its own vibrational field. Though most of us know a place we can go to feel calm and relaxed, we also know of places where we feel unsafe, places that feel dangerous and threatening, and that have "bad vibes." There's one shopping mall relatively close to where I live that has always felt creepy to me. I recently heard that someone was fatally shot there, so who knows what I might be picking up on? If we pay attention to how places affect us, to what reactions we have when we're there, we can learn valuable lessons not only about those places but also about ourselves, and use that information to our advantage. For example, one of the reasons I bought the house I'm in now was because of the positive energy I felt every time I went inside or even drove by. I knew before I ever moved into my house that it would be a peaceful place to write.

Places can have a significant impact on us, with or without our conscious awareness. In his book, *The Teachings of don Juan,* Carlos Castaneda tells a story about working with his teacher, don Juan Matus, a Yaqui Indian "Man of Knowledge." One night the two of them were on the front porch of a house when don Juan instructed Carlos to "find his spot." He said there was a physical place on that porch where he could sit without getting tired and where he would naturally feel happy and strong. Carlos spent hours walking, sitting, rolling, and feeling his way around the porch until he indeed found his "spot," the place that felt right for him.

Sometimes we will go somewhere and knowingly or unknowingly be drawn to our "spot." For example, have you ever gone into a restaurant and somehow known where you wanted to sit? Or perhaps gone in and the waiter or waitress tried to seat you one place, but it didn't feel right, and you asked to be seated somewhere else?

I used to attend a lot of weekly meetings with the same people, and I became more than a casual observer of where people sat. Within several weeks of starting to meet, people seemed to find their spots, and after that, they sat in the same place every time. I noticed that when I sat in my own spot, I felt more comfortable and empowered to contribute to the meeting, even when it meant bringing up uncomfortable topics.

If possible, my spot in a group of people means sitting where I can see everybody else, because I want to be able to observe everyone's verbal and nonverbal communication. Also, I used to work as a social worker for the state's child protective services and needed to go into homes where there was suspected child abuse or neglect. Naturally, parents become threatened when they think you might take their children away, and I never knew what I might run into when I made a house call. Sometimes I asked the police to meet me at the house, just in case the situation became volatile. But at the very least, I always made sure I stayed where nothing was between me and the door. If you need to go someplace that seems risky or has bad vibes, try to position yourself so you can see everything that's going on and can leave fast if you need to.

One place is so unique and such a powerful teacher that it deserves special mention. That place is nature. Whether it's in a forest, by the ocean, beside a lake or river, or just looking at the sky, nature has a way of silently speaking to us that quiets our minds, relaxes our bodies, inspires us with beauty, and refreshes our souls.

The very essence of nature is to give us gifts through the resources it provides. One of these gifts is the lessons we can learn. For example, a tree provides shade to anyone who needs it. The tree doesn't first ask about your ethnicity, income, religion, political affiliation, or any other characteristics. It just gives to all people alike, whenever there's a need. Sometimes when I get judgmental about people, which we all tend to do, it helps to remember the lesson about equality that I learned from the trees.

The number of lessons we can learn from nature seems endless. Finding simple ways to spend time outdoors on a regular basis, like gardening, walking your dog in a park, or enjoying a cool evening breeze, can help us take advantage of this ever-present teacher.

---

10. *Activities*

1. *Becoming more aware of the "vibes" of physical places helps us take in more information from our environment and from our own more subtle inner world, all of which can be used to our advantage. Try it. Notice where you feel comfortable and uncomfortable, and let those feelings teach you about places to stay and those to avoid.*

2. *Without giving it much thought, just off the top of your head, think of a place where you feel calm, safe, and relaxed. Got it?*

Imagery Activity to De-stress

If you need a quick stress break, imagine being in your safe place. You can do this with your eyes either open or closed.

Take a few deep breaths and see yourself in your safe place in your mind's eye—not as if you're looking at yourself on a stage—but see it as if you're in your own body, looking out of your own eyes. What do you see in this place? What are the objects, colors, and textures you're looking at? Listen for the sounds of your safe space. Hear those now. And allow yourself to tap into the feelings that are associated with being there, in the place where you feel comfortable and relaxed.

Then open your eyes and return to the present, knowing that your special place is always waiting there for you to visit in your imagination, whenever you need some peace and calm.

Animals

Although animals might be considered part of the world of nature, as teachers they deserve separate mention. Across different cultures, certain animals are often recognized for their special qualities. For example, eagles are known for their keen sight and vision; lions, tigers, and other large cats for their speed, strength, and grace; dogs for their loyalty and unconditional love. Even the smallest creatures can be our teachers. If you watch ants in the line of duty, you see that their persistence and steadfast determination is nothing short of heroic.

During a magazine interview, author James Redfield talked about how a bird was instrumental in receiving ideas on how to write his first book, *The Celestine Prophecy*, which became an international best seller. Redfield was staying in Sedona, Arizona, which is well known for its mystical powers. While sitting on a ridge, a crow came and circled close to his head, then flew back into a canyon. He thought this was interesting, but when it happened again the very same way, he decided to follow where the crow seemed to be leading him. Redfield was immediately drawn to sit in one spot where ideas flooded into his mind, ideas that helped shape his book. The bird was a teacher, leading him to the place where he could receive inspiration.

As we were growing up, my parents allowed my two sisters and me to have a long line of various pets, including dogs, parakeets, hamsters, turtles, fish, and occasionally chickens or ducks for Easter. I also rode horses for years—training, showing, and teaching riding—even after I left home for college. The lessons I learned from my connections with animals accumulated over time to include: an appreciation for their different personalities, their playfulness, and their lack of ego, how they accepted me no matter what, kept all my secrets, and sometimes became a treasured best friend. Today I live with a collection of rescue pets and am continually delighted by how much they enrich my life, relieve my stress, and make me laugh, every single day.

Did you know that just petting a dog can lower your blood pressure? That's according to the online Harvard Health Publications. Dogs teach us how to calm down, how to literally lower our heart rate, and how to live in the present moment, because that's where they live.

Although I'd never been a cat person, one time a brown, tabby stray cat adopted me, as cats are apt to do, so I named him Seva (pronounced *save-ah*), which means selfless service. In telling my mother about my new pet, I mentioned his name and added, "It's because I'm serving him by taking care of him." Without a second's hesitation, my then eighty-year-old mother, with her characteristic perceptiveness and wisdom, replied, "Do you think he's serving you with his unconditional love?" And of course, she was absolutely right. That was even before I found out he was the kind of cat who would come to me every time I called, just like a dog.

Seva preferred to remain mostly an outdoor cat, and he turned into the neighborhood peacemaker. After I got him neutered, he made friends with all the bully cats and won over everyone's affection, even those neighbors who weren't in the least bit cat friendly before meeting him. Having one cat sometimes attracts others, and it wasn't long before a stray kitten showed up and took to Seva as if he were her missing mother. Although I bought two cat beds for my patio, the kitten insisted on sleeping practically on top of Seva, which he tolerated, more or less, depending on how annoying she seemed to him at the time.

As the kitten became more bonded, Seva would periodically rebuff her affection, pinning her down by biting her on the back of the neck or trying to chase her away. When he turned on her like this, I noticed the kitten would freeze and crouch on the ground, as if to make herself defenseless. And it worked. He would immediately become more tolerant of her presence.

Seva came into my life at a time when I was going through a rough period at work. Administrative changes meant I had a new supervisor who had a different leadership style than what I was used to. Although I'd always enjoyed the relationships with my previous supervisors and received positive feedback on my job performance, suddenly it seemed that nothing I did was right or good enough. I felt like I was always in trouble. The situation got so bad that I finally went to talk with an employee relations counselor who helped me put things in perspective by saying, "Everyone has a difficult boss at least once in their career. The key is finding a way to relate to your boss that doesn't make him feel threatened."

The instant the counselor said that, I flashed back to watching the kitten interact with Seva. When she irritated him, and he reacted by turning on her, she froze and became submissive. *Aha.* I immediately knew that's what I needed to do with my new boss: take a step back from my usually assertive stance and become more passive, trying hard not to create any kind of a threat or even discomfort. Although my relationship with my supervisor didn't change overnight, it improved substantially, and I can thank a couple of stray cats for helping me learn that lesson sooner rather than later.

11. *Activities*

Think back throughout your life on the animals you have known or observed, both pets and other animals. Take a few minutes to identify some of the more important life lessons they have helped you learn. I encourage you to write them down.

- *One lesson I have learned from animals is*
- *Another lesson I have learned from animals is*
- *Other lessons include*

Time

I've taught time management for years—in college classes, at conferences, and while working with individuals on how to accomplish their goals. One day I asked myself, "I wonder why you keep teaching the same thing over and over and don't get bored?" Almost before I finished asking the question, my intuition replied, "Because the advice you give others is what *you* most need to hear." Oh.

It's not that I don't get a lot done. Other people often see me as more productive than most, although I'm not sure that's the case. However, I am keenly aware of how crucial it is to use my time focused on what's important, what's in keeping with my values, goals, and purpose in life. Because when that inevitable call comes and my time on this earthly plane is over, I definitely don't want to leave kicking myself for not using my allotted time to accomplish whatever I came here to do. Nope, I'd rather anticipate that possibility now and head it off at the pass.

After all the books and articles I've read on time management, after all the stories I've heard from other people about how they struggle to get more done, and after carefully observing my own relationship with time over the years, the time management technique that's become the most effective for me is seeing time as a teacher—a powerful, close-to-all-encompassing teacher—because we live our lives through the passage of time.

One of the most basic lessons time taught me has to do with self-esteem.

If we don't use our time the way we want or the way we plan, we often end up feeling bad about ourselves. After a while, bad feelings about ourselves result in low self-esteem, which affects every single thing we do.

Let's say you come home from work exhausted and need a little time to relax and decompress. But instead of doing something healthy, like exercising or connecting with your spouse, children, or pets, you plop down in front of the television for way too long, go to bed later than you'd planned, and end up feeling worse the next morning. Although some people use television as a healthy form of downtime, entertainment, education, or even as a reward, many others get caught in its distraction and experience it as a time waster.

How many of us have wasted hours or days, even weeks, glued to some electronic device that temporarily takes us out of life altogether and then regretted our indulgence and had to play catch-up after the fact? In our electronic culture, this is an increasingly common experience.

We all need healthy time-out periods from being focused and productive. Sometimes we plan those breaks, and sometimes they happen spontaneously. For example, I've had unexpected conversations with friends, family, and even strangers that threw me off my schedule, but those talks felt meaningful, and they left me feeling renewed.

However, we can undermine our self-worth when we unintentionally waste time, however we define that. When we tell ourselves we're not going to spend so much time on social media, for instance, but keep doing it anyway, it undermines our trust in ourselves. That often results in us having less confidence in our ability to accomplish future goals. Successfully managing time, or more accurately, managing ourselves in relationship to time, matters. It matters a lot.

I'm a recovering procrastinator. For years, I would procrastinate with the best of them, leaving things until the last minute and then swooping in to pull off close-to-miraculous feats in the final hour, meeting my deadlines (barely), and feeling like a hero—a stressed-out hero—but a hero nonetheless. It wasn't until I started teaching classes on procrastination that I took a step back and observed my own process. Wow. Did I get an eyeful, like how I enjoyed the suspense of whether or not I'd meet the deadline and how I became addicted to the adrenaline rush of my self-created drama.

Basic principles of psychology tell us that if we keep doing something over and over, it's because there's a reward or payoff involved. We're getting something out of it. A behavior that's not rewarded or reinforced will extinguish. We'll stop doing it. The payoffs for my procrastination included excitement, an energy high from the adrenaline, a sense of personal power, and an antidote for boredom in situations where it was just another mundane task. No wonder my procrastination lasted for years.

If you're a procrastinator, you're not alone. So many people get stuck in their procrastination and don't know how to untangle the reward system, much less find alternative, healthy ways to build those rewards into their lives. We'll look at techniques for stopping procrastination in chapter 8, "Turning Obstacles into Teachers."

Our efforts to get past procrastination frequently require us to learn complex lessons. In contrast, one of the simplest lessons for managing time is called **time on task**, which refers to the amount of time spent focusing on a task or goal. The nitty-gritty of accomplishing anything worthwhile almost always involves lots of time focused on your goal. As Thomas Edison said, "None of my inventions came by accident. What it boils down to is one per cent inspiration and ninety-nine per cent perspiration." That perspiration is what we mean by time on task.

Even though most people know they need to spend more time focused on their goals, for some, that becomes not only difficult but impossible to pull off. Entire lifetimes can drift away while we continue to say, "Someday I'm going to _____" (you can fill in the blank). But that someday never comes.

I clearly remember when I realized that at some point I would retire. For years my workaholic lifestyle shielded me from thinking like that; it's easy to get lulled into a perception that you'll work forever when you work so much. I was in my mid-thirties at the time—embarrassingly late to just be waking up to that eventuality—but I also felt surprisingly hopeful that if I were diligent in my savings plan, somehow it would be okay.

Because I love to learn, when faced with a new situation or daunting task, I usually jump into my student role and try to learn everything I can. So I started taking classes on retirement planning, and in my very first class, the instructor gave us a powerful quote that said, "Expenditures rise to the level of income." By that he meant that whatever you make, you'll spend—*unless* you pay yourself first by taking money off the top and putting it into savings. I decided to try it and asked my payroll office to deduct money from my monthly checks and deposit it in a retirement account. Because I made so little money at the time, I felt anxious and doubtful that I could live on the remaining amount, but to my astonishment, I had enough money to last to the end of the month—every month. My experience took on this supernatural aura. It almost seemed like magic.

In preparing for a time management talk several years later, that same quote came into my head, and I suddenly saw the parallels between money and time. That's when I remembered an adage called Parkinson's law which states, "Work expands so as to fill the time available for its completion." Another *aha* moment. That was the lesson I'd struggled to learn over and over, the same lesson I watched countless others wrestle with, sometimes for years.

Time doesn't just show up to give you the extra you need to accomplish a new goal. We're not *given* any more time. Instead, we have to take it off the top and *make* the time to make things happen. We have to schedule however much time we need to accomplish our goal and trust that all the other things in our lives will somehow get done. Or maybe we'll find that we don't need to do everything else, at least not right then. Making the time to work on our goal becomes our priority, and we fit everything else around that.

This single-minded focus on completing our goal takes us back into the almost mystical realm of the power of intention, similar to my somewhat magical experience with saving for retirement. If we become clear in our intention to accomplish a goal by a certain time, we mentally and behaviorally adjust to meet that deadline. And not only that, but as Goethe says in his famous quote, "The moment one definitely commits oneself, then Providence moves too. All sorts of things occur to help one that would never otherwise have occurred." In other words, the Universe steps in and says "Yes" to our efforts, and we're likely to get extra support along the way.

Most of the material on time management focuses on how to complete goals and get things done, because that's where most of us get stuck. However, another essential aspect of managing our time isn't about being productive; instead it's about taking time out to just *be*. People find different ways to take time out, like meditating; artistic or creative expression; becoming completely absorbed in a craft, physical activity, or sport; spending time with children or pets; or maybe by being in nature. Including these kinds of time-out activities balances the scales of work and our personal lives and can paradoxically make us more productive.

Never one who wanted to feel like a hypocrite, I try to practice what I preach about time management. Despite all my foiled attempts, I keep trying to learn the lessons that help me use my time to the best advantage, that get the most mileage for the lifetime spent. This doesn't mean becoming compulsively busy and workaholic but rather doing what's important and keeping my life in balance along the way. Something tells me that in the school of life, I will forever remain enrolled in a class on time management, and that every day, I will ask myself to make decisions about my use of time that honor and support the reason I'm here.

12. *Activities*

1. *If you're happy with the way you spend your time, congratulations! Effective time management can be a huge step toward accomplishing your goals and purpose in life.*

2. *If you're among the majority of us who want to improve our relationship with time, you can start by understanding that time is a teacher and ask yourself:*

   - *What lessons have I already learned about time?*
   - *What lessons do I still need to learn?*

Some people who struggle with time management simply need to learn new techniques and put them into practice. You can always try reading books, articles, and online material and see if they work for you. Other people have more deep-seated conflicts that prevent them from managing their time well. These usually include the long-term procrastinators who pay serious, negative consequences for their delays. We will cover this in more depth in chapter 8.

Chapter 5
Discovering Our Internal Teachers

In contrast to external teachers, our internal teachers are those inside of us, those parts of ourselves that offer invaluable instructions—if we can learn how to extract and accept their wisdom. Internal teachers include our bodies, thoughts, emotions, behaviors, addictions, dreams, and intuition. We open up to their instructions through self-awareness: listening to ourselves, observing ourselves, through self-discovery and self-reflection.

We all have the ability to be both a participant in our inner experiences and an observer, to do something and at the same time, watch ourselves do it. Although we can only focus on one perspective at a time, it's possible to learn how to increasingly shift our awareness into the observer perspective, monitoring ourselves as we are involved in any given activity. Practice observing your inner world, focusing your awareness on each of the following parts.

Bodies

What does it mean if you have ridges on your fingernails? Does it seem like your hair is falling out more lately, or is that normal? Why does your stomach get upset after you eat spicy food? Is that ache in your knee something serious, or did you overdo it when you worked out and just need to let it rest? All of these messages from our bodies tell us to pay attention, that we might need to address some specific concerns. If we learn to listen to the many voices of our bodies, we can figure out how to provide them with better care. Our bodies talk to us all the time, which can sometimes be inconvenient and maybe even annoying. But the problem isn't in their talking. Problems get created when we don't listen.

Most of us have issues with our bodies, things about them that make us self-conscious. But whether we like or dislike our bodies, they're ours to keep during this trip to Earth. Sometimes referred to as temples of worship or spirits in the flesh, our bodies provide a vehicle for our souls so we can move around on our journey through this lifetime. Just like cars are vehicles we use to get around some of the time, our bodies are the vehicles we use all the time.

In order to become good students of life, we need to get academically fit—sound in body, mind, and spirit. This means taking good care of our bodies so they can help us progress in school, to develop a healthy relationship with them and treat them with respect. The particular lessons we need to learn depend on where we're starting from. A continuum of lessons on self-care ranges from healing on one end—if we're injured, sick, or functioning below par—to those on peak fitness and optimal health on the other.

Years ago I attended a class called "Writing and the Body," which focused on improving your writing skills by incorporating the messages and energies from your body. At the end of the first class meeting, the instructor gave us a homework assignment: "Write a history of your body." That was it. No other instructions.

The assignment sounded simple enough, so that evening, I started in. I wrote in longhand. Pen to paper. Nonstop for almost an hour.

But *how* that happened surprised me. I meant to write about my body. Instead, my body took over. She wrote to me, or the part of me I think of as my mind. She told *me* about her history, rather than me (my mind) writing down what happened to her. I quickly resigned myself to letting my body tell her own story. In fact, it seemed like a good idea. Once she started, her messages poured out of my pen, like she had been waiting years for me to give her a voice and allow her to speak.

My history through her experiences started out pretty predictable—she was born; she felt the feelings of those around her; she enjoyed learning new skills like walking, running, and swimming; and she eventually grew into a teenager with hormones to navigate and more intense emotions to have to deal with. So far, so good.

But once my body began to write about being in college, her tone changed, and that's when she really opened up. She reminded me about the partying I'd done and how alcohol and cigarettes entered the scene.

Here's what she wrote: "In college. I'm 19. Why are you smoking? You know it makes me feel bad. OK. I'll forgive you."

But what really got to me was when she told me about how hard I pushed her in graduate school. Becoming stronger, she wrote: "I feel like you've been mean in the way you pushed me beyond fatigue to the point of exhaustion—often because of poor planning on your part—not stopping when I got tired, but instead forcing me to go on by doing lots of caffeine so you could accomplish whatever you wanted, totally disregarding what I was trying to tell you about how I needed to rest."

Wow. She was angry. With good reason. That *is* what happened.

She remembered it all, every time I smoked a cigarette, partied too hard, loaded up on caffeine, or cut my sleep short. Hearing things from her perspective touched me deeply, made me cry, and for the first time ever, I felt this empathy and compassion for my body as if she were a longtime friend I'd mistreated, never wanting to know how my actions affected her or made her feel.

After she expressed all the negative things she'd been holding in for decades, my body paused. Then she wrote about the good things I'd done for her and how much she appreciated those. She thanked me for usually trying to eat healthy and for being an athlete throughout my life. She reminded me of the times I would go home from work with the muscles in my neck and shoulders burning from too much tension and time at my desk. Then she thanked me for learning how to stretch out those muscles and for getting into a habit of stretching every day. I felt surprised by her long list of thanks.

That simple writing exercise became the starting point for developing a new relationship with my body. Before then, I wanted her to do what I wanted her to do and feel how I wanted her to feel. But with that one activity, I truly understood that she had her own emotions, needs, and limits. And I realized that by taking care of her and working together, she could help us both feel great and get even more things done.

Today I have a heightened sensitivity to the messages my body offers, and I try to act on those right away. I've learned that she's more than willing to offer her feedback—the positive and the negative—now that she knows I want her input. For example, when I'm exercising, my body tells me what kind of pain is okay and what kind of pain says, "Stop. Now." She tells me which foods agree with me and which ones don't, helping me fine-tune my diet in ways a nutritionist never could. She also tells me exactly when to stop eating, because she doesn't like to feel stuffed.

Fortunately for me and my body, I left the drinking and smoking behind. The caffeine has been a different story. But my body has helped me learn countless lessons about how to take care of her, how to avoid excesses and keep things in moderation. I'm astounded by her remarkable ability to heal and how forgiving she's been over all these years.

I don't think I'm nearly as generous and forgiving of other people as my body's been with me. Clearly, I still have lessons she can help me learn.

We live in a culture that overemphasizes the body and physical appearance. As a result, many people overidentify and think they *are* their bodies. But we are not our bodies. If we were, we wouldn't be able to separate ourselves and have a dialogue between the two parts. At the same time, we often mistreat our bodies to the point of abuse, acting as if their primary jobs are to make us look good and help us get what we want.

Our bodies are teachers—powerful teachers with the potential to help or hinder us on this journey through life. As vehicles for our souls, then just like a car, we need to keep them well maintained and running at maximum efficiency. When we take good care of our bodies, they can provide enjoyment, pleasure, and unlimited opportunities for expression and growth. If we aren't currently treating our bodies with love—helping them help us—then we still have lessons to learn.

---

13. *Activities*

1. *Ask yourself:*

   - *What's one lesson my body has helped me learn?*
   - *If other lessons come to mind, also jot those down:*

2. *Quite often our bodies won't talk to us directly unless we explicitly invite them to speak. Here are some questions you can ask your body to answer:*

   - *I like it when you...*
   - *I don't like it when you...*
   - *Please start...*
   - *Please stop...*

You can repeat these questions until your body no longer responds. If your body is willing to give you answers, thank it for sharing.

3. *You may want to ask your body to write you a letter the way I did in the homework assignment. Before you start, let your body know it has complete freedom to tell you whatever it wants and that your role is to just listen from a nonjudgmental place, simply accepting whatever your body says.*

Set aside at least an hour to do the letter writing. Pick a time and place where you won't be interrupted. If you think you might be upset by the things your body tells you, ask a friend or family member to join you. Better yet, do it together, and then share and discuss what you learn.

Thoughts

Just as we aren't our bodies, neither are we our thoughts, although many of us think we are. If you stop for a moment and observe your thoughts—watching them as if they are words moving across a television screen—you realize that someone besides your thoughts is doing the watching. That *someone* is our essence, consciousness, or soul, the spark of energy that remains a constant during the entire time we're living in our bodies.

Our consciousness is the witness to our entire lives. It watches what happens when you are a child, an adolescent, and an adult. It watched all the times when you got stuck and thought, "I'll never get through this." Our consciousness was also there to observe the times you thought, "I need to remember that somehow, I always made it through tough times in the past. Something always happened to help me get through."

Usually that spark of pure awareness remains hidden beneath the constant chatter of our thoughts as we go through our busy, overstimulated lives, but that doesn't mean it isn't present, waiting for us to throw open the door and welcome it into our world. Observing our thoughts gives us the opportunity to open that door.

When you start to witness your thoughts, you immediately notice their hyperactive nature and how they constantly switch from one subject to another. In some meditative practices, the mind is referred to as a drunken monkey because of this chronic tendency to jump from one topic to another in a random, tree-swinging frenzy of undisciplined thinking. The goal of meditation is to tame the monkey mind, which brings much-needed rest, creates a sense of peace, and improves focus and concentration for everything else you do in your life.

Our hyperactive, unruly thoughts can sometimes ramp up into high gear, causing out-of-control worrying and obsessing. My own thoughts often run at a frenetic pace, and once they latch onto a problem or even a potential problem, they sometimes don't want to let go. That means I tend to be a worrier.

I vividly remember when I first started worrying and couldn't stop. I was in junior high school, with all the accompanying hormones, popularity, and friendship issues that plague most teenagers. I would lie awake at night, worrying about one thing after another in an endless cycle of anxiety and insomnia. This pattern went on for months.

One night, out of desperation to get some sleep, I spontaneously imagined that a piece of black construction paper was about one inch away from my face, and I focused on carefully observing the paper as if it were completely real. If a thought came into my mind, I *saw* it as a written sentence shooting in from the outside edge of the paper. My goal was to mentally brush the sentence out of view as I continued to concentrate on the paper's blackness and texture. When I pushed the sentence away, it erased the thought from my mind, enough so that I didn't get involved in thinking about it anymore right then.

Years later, I realized this simple activity was like the classic insomnia technique of counting sheep as they jump over a fence—a monotonous, repetitive task that allows the brain to relax and eventually get bored enough to drift off to sleep. When I started learning meditation, I could see the similarities between the insomnia strategies and taking a witness position. My goal in meditation was to again observe the intrusive thoughts but not get drawn into their content.

Although our thoughts can cause problems—like when we worry too much or when they take a destructive bent—they're phenomenal teachers. Much of the time it's important to listen to the content of our thoughts, because they offer messages and instructions we need to hear. Many of our thoughts help us stay focused and productive, and we would wander way off our paths without them. They help us understand, process, and integrate lessons we learn from all of our other teachers. And as we learn to harness our thoughts and focus their content, they can become a tremendous power for good.

It's also important to realize that some of our thoughts are not at all true. They don't accurately reflect what's grounded in reality. They're just thoughts that come and go, like the wind. However, many of us respond to *all* of our thoughts as if they're gospel truth and then act accordingly, which sometimes causes us to make mistakes and head off in the wrong direction. For example, how many times have you misunderstood someone, acted as if your version of their communication was real, perhaps gotten mad or hurt, and then ended up making a mess in the relationship? It happens all the time. That's even more of a reason to keep a healthy, arm's-length distance from your thoughts, especially when they're upsetting, and to question their validity from the get-go.

Becoming an excellent student in life requires training our minds to pay attention in class, to study and concentrate on specific content. Just like we exercise and work out our bodies to stay in good physical shape, we can also do fitness training for our minds, which helps them get better at the laser-focused power of intention. Part of that training includes periodically taking a break from our thoughts, allowing the mind to rest and relax. That's why so many people have found that some type of meditation helps keep everything else flowing forward with greater ease and speed.

As we become more skilled at focusing, our thoughts become incredibly powerful tools in the creative process. There's a saying that "energy follows thought," which means that whatever we think about often manifests in the physical world. For example, if you think of yourself as courageous, your verbal and nonverbal behaviors usually reflect those thoughts. In other words, it becomes a self-fulfilling prophecy.

The self-fulfilling aspect of our thoughts makes it even more important that we monitor our thoughts and keep them productive. One of the more astounding lessons about thoughts is that you don't have to think about whatever comes into your mind. You don't have to let your mind be that drunken monkey, randomly jumping from one topic to another. You can learn to be purposeful in your thinking and *choose* what you want to focus on, knowing that the focus of your thoughts will likely become a reality in your life.

If you think about certain future goals—getting a mental picture of what you want and visualizing the desired outcome—you increase even more the probability those goals will materialize. That's why doing visualization with goal setting is so effective. We tend to create what we think about and see in our minds. We draw that goal toward us by our thoughts and intentions. Chapter 10 includes more detailed information on this process. It's exciting and incredibly empowering.

---

14. *Activities*

Meditation Exercises

Meditation is one of the fastest ways to make progress in the school of life. It's how we can welcome our soul into our awareness, giving it a chance to play a larger role in our lives. The many types of meditation allow us to pick and choose which ones work best for us. Here are several you can try.

> 1. *Set aside ten minutes in a place where you won't get interrupted. Sit in a comfortable position, close your eyes, and observe your thoughts. See them as if they are words or sentences mov-*

ing across a television or computer monitor. Do not get engaged with the thoughts, no matter how interesting or compelling they seem. Just let them flow across the screen, watching them come and go, as if they're part of a movie that's outside of you. That's it.

2. Here's another way to start getting into meditation. Sit with your eyes closed and simply listen to all the sounds around you for ten minutes. If that seems too long, do it for five minutes.

3. You can also sit for five to ten minutes and listen to your body. Notice all the physical sensations of your body, like the rhythm of your breathing, any warmth or coldness in your body, your posture, any pain or discomfort. Simply observe. Be a witness.

These simple activities can start to open you up to new energies, awarenesses, and possibilities. To get started, take time to practice observing your thoughts at least twice a week, and watch what happens. Then add more practice times until you're eventually meditating every day.

Some people find it exceptionally difficult to stay still long enough to meditate. If you're one of them, you can explore different types of meditation through books, classes, or online materials. Sometimes you need to try out several different types before finding one that works for you. Chapter 9 also contains movement meditation techniques.

Behaviors

I find myself standing over the kitchen sink, eating cottage cheese straight out of the container. I eat almost half of a brand-new carton. My stomach no longer feels the anxiety it did before I started, but I'm watching as I eat and saying to myself, "What's wrong with you? Couldn't you wait until dinner?" Of course, the answer is "No."

Even though a part of me can witness my behavior and what I'm doing while I'm doing it, I try to ignore that part. I don't want anything to interfere with my plan to get rid of the feeling. I just want the anxiety to go away.

Stuffing something in my mouth right after I got home from work had become a pattern, and my mini binge eating made me feel guilty and out of control. Thank heavens, it never escalated into a full-blown eating disorder. As a counselor, I worked with students who got caught in that cycle, and I knew too well how all-consuming eating disorders could become. Several years later, I went through an experience that would end my mini binges completely by getting to the root cause—the emotions and actual hunger that were underneath my binging. I described that experience earlier in this chapter in the section on our bodies. It was when my body wrote me a letter. During the time in between, I tried to control my behavior as best I could. I never ate to the point that I felt uncomfortably full, but the timing of my eating was way off.

We all have times when our behavior feels out of control, when we look back and wonder, "What was I thinking?" Many times, we weren't thinking, at least not with rational thoughts. And even if we're able to witness or observe our behavior while we're doing it, the witness part of us gets ignored or shut out. Instead, we go into what I call "space-out" mode, and we often end up regretting our behavior.

Contrast that to the times when we're focused like a laser beam, when every fiber of our being concentrates on a task or project, when we delve into the present moment with such awareness and intention that time becomes distorted, in a good way. We lose ourselves in the now and enter what Mihaly Csikszentmihalyi calls *flow*, a magical place where our behavior reflects complete engagement with whatever we're doing at the time. Most of our lives are spent living some place in between flow and out of control.

Our behavior—what we *do* while we're here on Earth—matters. It matters immensely. Our behavior becomes part of our legacy, a tangible record of the precious time we were given in the school of life. As Gandhi wrote, "My life is my message." The actions Gandhi took during his lifetime became the teaching he offered to the world.

Psychologist Carl Jung once said, "You are what you do, not what you say you'll do." We can all have the best intentions, but if we don't translate those intentions into action, they become lost in our inner world of thoughts. We can profess our values, our desires, our hopes and dreams, but no matter how impressive and noble those might be, they're rendered impotent without action. Talk truly is cheap. We can all speak the words. Putting those words into action with tangible results becomes the real nitty-gritty of making meaning and purpose in our lives.

If some of your behavior is currently problematic, there's good news. You can use the principles of psychology to change it. Psychology tells us that all behavior serves a purpose—it gives us something we want or need. Some aspect of the behavior is reinforcing or rewarding. There's a payoff. In contrast, behavior that isn't reinforced will be extinguished. You'll stop doing it. My mini binge eating gave me an escape from the anxiety that felt so awful, so it definitely served a purpose.

Every problem contains at least one lesson, and all of us are responsible for learning our lessons so we don't get stuck in that particular classroom. One of our jobs as students of life is figuring out what reward or payoff we're getting from problematic behavior and then substituting a healthy reward in its place.

For instance, if you space out while watching television and eat more than you should, maybe the unhealthy reward is that you get to have downtime and total freedom to indulge, because a part of you believes you deserve that. After all, you've worked hard and earned your reward. But if you feel bad after taking your unhealthy reward, in the long run, your behavior doesn't work. Maybe you can tweak the payoffs. Give yourself the downtime by watching TV, but eat something beforehand so you're not hungry when you space out in front of the tube. Keep food away from where you're watching, and then enjoy the reward of feeling good about yourself after the fact. That's just an example. I don't know what lessons will help someone else. I just know people change problematic behavior every day by figuring out what lessons work for them.

In my situation, I eventually learned to acknowledge that I was both anxious and hungry when I got home from work. That's often the case. We're more likely to do things we regret when we're hungry, tired, lonely, bored, or emotionally upset. My body wanted food, just not so much of it. So I started eating a hard-boiled egg instead of the cottage cheese, and that worked. To this day, I sometimes eat one and only one egg when I first get home in the evening. I keep a bowl of already-cooked eggs in my refrigerator, so it's a quick grab-and-eat food. There's something about the protein that satisfies my hunger and gives me plenty of energy to put things away, sort through the mail, and prepare a healthy dinner. Just that one substitution, that one lesson, changed the problematic behavior dramatically.

We can change many of our unwanted behaviors by simply substituting different rewards. Other behaviors are more stubborn and take more time, effort, and sometimes outside help from a professional. However, if we put on our student hats and dig in with determination and intention to switch up the reward system, we can often change problem behaviors rather quickly. Sometimes it's a simple matter of avoiding the problematic behavior to start with. If cookies are your downfall, it might make your life a whole lot easier to just not buy them in the first place. If they're not in the house, you won't be tempted to eat them. You get the reward of feeling good about yourself and your long-term solution instead of feeling semigood only during your short-term indulgence.

I'd like to add an additional emphasis here. If you decide to stop doing something and don't find a substitute behavior, it creates a void. That void often gets filled with anxiety and makes it more likely that you will relapse and go back to what was problematic to start with. For example, switching from cottage cheese to hard-boiled eggs fed my actual hunger, but I wasn't likely to overindulge on eggs. If I just tried to not eat the cottage cheese, it would have created a void, and chances are good I would have found something else to binge on, maybe something even worse. So identify the substitute behavior at the beginning of your efforts to change. Don't leave yourself in a void.

Most of us have behaviors we want to *stop* doing. We also have behaviors we want to *start* doing—new goals to accomplish—which allows us to eventually fulfill our dreams. If we pay attention, our behavior will teach us how to stop unwanted actions and start making new habits, which means we get to pass our classes and move forward in school. Much of chapter 10 focuses on goal-setting techniques.

Frank Outlaw gave us a powerful quote when he said

Watch your thoughts, they become words;
Watch your words, they become actions;
Watch your actions, they become habits;
Watch your habits, they become character;
Watch your character, for it becomes your destiny.

Our behavior distinguishes itself as an efficient, effective teacher because in our school, we can see the consequences of our actions very quickly. We get immediate feedback, which gives us explicit instructions through concrete results on whether we got it right. Either the lesson we chose to change our behavior will work, or it won't. If it doesn't work, we can use our next best guess or hunch on what to try instead. Our task is to keep going until we discover the lesson that our behavior tells us is correct, then practice long enough for it to become a new habit.

You often hear that it takes twenty-one days for behavior to become a habit. In my own life and in working with others, I've found that it sometimes takes longer or shorter than twenty-one days, depending on what it is, so we need to keep practicing a new behavior until it becomes automatic, however long that takes.

We turn our dreams into reality through our routines, our daily habits of doing the work. If we get serious about fulfilling our dreams, we can count on our behavior to teach us how to develop the habits that will help make those dreams come true.

15. *Activities*

Our own behavior will teach us how to make desired changes if we learn to observe the consequences of our actions. Try these activities to get better at breaking unwanted habits.

1. *Identify one behavior you want to stop doing.*

2. *Ask yourself, "What reward am I getting out of doing that behavior?"*

3. *Then ask, "What's a healthy reward I can substitute to help change that behavior?"*

4. *Try using the new reward and see if it works. If it does, keep practicing until it becomes a habit.*

5. *If the new reward doesn't work, use your best guess to pick another healthy reward. Keep trying different rewards until you figure out what works. That's the lesson you need to learn.*

We'll cover behavior change and goal setting in more depth in chapter 10. Please don't do a guilt trip on yourself if you try to change a behavior and it doesn't work. Some of our lessons take longer to learn than others. If you're able to identify what reward you're getting out of problematic behavior, you automatically take a huge step forward in changing it.

Emotions

We can look at our emotions as gifts which add color, texture, and intensity to our lives—the delight in children's laughter, the love we experience for each other, the peace that comes from a life well lived. In the school of life, our feelings are natural forms of physical energy, internal teachers who provide us with crucial information about life, our choices, our likes and dislikes. They serve as emotional guides on our journey, steering us through the ups and downs and helping us make meaning out of our experiences. In an act of sheer generosity, our feelings direct us toward our mission and purpose; by identifying what brings us joy and a sense of fulfillment, we're able to discover what we came here to do.

It's important to understand that we are not our emotions. Even though they can feel so right and true at the time, the energy of our emotions comes and goes rather quickly. We are not our bodies or thoughts, nor are we our emotions, although we may feel like we are.

Our emotions form intricate connections with our other internal teachers, including our bodies, thoughts, and behaviors. It's almost like these teachers gang up on us, in a good way, to make sure we master our lessons.

One of my steps in learning to pass the class on regular exercise involved setting a goal to exercise once a week. If I could get in at least one good workout each week, I could marginally get by, and I actually felt quite a bit better than if I didn't do any exercise at all. If I missed my weekly workout for some reason, I would feel blah, lackluster, and on the edge of irritation. My thinking would tend to become negative and run in the glass-half-empty direction, which is not like me. I didn't get depressed—just negative—so my thoughts and my emotions told me my body definitely needed that workout.

Have you ever found yourself standing in front of the refrigerator with the door wide open, perusing your options for something to eat, when you aren't the least bit hungry? Maybe you're bored, and eating gives you something to do. Maybe you're procrastinating, and getting a bite to eat seems like a legitimate way to avoid what you know you should be doing instead. Perhaps you've got some vague, uncomfortable feeling, you're not sure what, and filling your stomach becomes a way to make sure that feeling never makes it to the surface, because whatever it is, you don't want to deal with it. Our emotions and behaviors form a complex interplay.

We live in a culture that tells us negative emotions are bad, something to avoid at all costs, that we should be positive, happy, and upbeat most, if not all, of the time. And that if we're not, we're doing something wrong. Yet denying any emotion means putting a lid on all the rest. If we don't allow ourselves to feel unpleasant feelings, we limit the extent to which we can experience the pleasant ones. If it's not okay to feel angry, sad, frustrated, or afraid, then we don't get to feel the full extent of our happiness, passion, gratitude, and hope.

By themselves, emotions are neither good nor bad, positive nor negative. The way we experience them is either pleasant or unpleasant, and that's why we label them the way we do. But *all* of our feelings serve a purpose. For example, guilt often tells us that we did something wrong and helps us learn from our mistakes. Fear can protect us from legitimate dangers. Confusion can motivate us to dig deeper to understand what's not apparent. Regret may nudge us to apologize to someone we slighted or to be extra careful not to violate our own standards in the future.

I use what's called **anticipated regret** all the time, because it's such a useful emotion. As author Matthew Hutson states, "this fear of future self-loathing makes us wear condoms, drink less, and eat better." I've found that I can use this feeling for far more than to avoid being mad at myself in the future. In fact, it has become one my best techniques for making decisions.

For example, if I'm trying to make a decision about whether or not to do something, I will project into the future, maybe five years, and ask myself, "In five years, are you going to look back and regret doing this? Yes or no?" I also ask, "Will you regret *not* doing it? Yes or no?" I usually get an immediate response from my gut when I ask those questions, so my anticipated regret gives me the answer I'm looking for. It helps me tap into that invaluable, split-second response from my intuition. It's a quick, easy, and powerful decision-making strategy.

The majority of us were never taught how to deal with negative emotions in positive ways. We haven't learned lessons about healthy emotional expression and how to take the good with the bad. This is particularly true for men in our society. From early childhood, most little boys are taught to deny their fear, sadness, and hurt, to act like a man and always appear strong and in control, never shedding a tear, appearing incompetent, or acting like a coward. Never. Little girls often get more support to express negative emotions like sadness and fear but only to a point. That means most of us grow up with internal censors on which feelings we think are okay to express and which ones aren't. And if we can't express our emotions, we better not experience them in the first place. We end up denying our feelings if we can. If that doesn't work, we suppress or push them down each time they try to pop up. It's a lot harder to use our feelings as guideposts when we're not supposed to have half of them in the first place.

So if our culture frowns on the expression of negative emotions, what incentive do we have to create a space for them in our lives? One big reason—if we don't, our denial and suppression can result in all sorts of serious consequences. Author Steven Covey wrote, "Unexpressed feelings never die. They are buried alive and come forth later in uglier ways." Those uglier ways often include depression, anxiety, physical illness, and the myriad ways we try to numb our feelings through addictions. In the *Big Book,* the basic text for Alcoholics Anonymous, AA cofounder Bill Wilson discussed the buried feelings that often result in alcoholism and stated, "Resentment is the 'number one' offender."

Counseling and therapy often focus on helping people learn how to express negative emotions in healthy ways. Although many people have a hard time getting past their initial resistance to that process, the rewards often prove to be invaluable. I've seen depressed people become alive, spontaneous, and exuberant, with a light in their eyes and a spring in their step that tells me they're going to be not just fine but great. Illnesses suddenly go away, skin conditions clear up on their own, people's stomach problems disappear, and they start living the life they were meant to live.

Very few people can afford counseling because of the time and money it requires. But many people don't need professional help to start allowing feelings to have an appropriate place in their lives. Because positive feelings aren't usually problematic, it can start by simply acknowledging that you have negative feelings you're afraid or ashamed to express, then finding safe ways to express them only to yourself or someone you trust. Here are some suggestions.

1. Name it. Safe ways to express our emotions usually need to start with finding a word that names the feeling you don't want to express. A list of feelings words is included in Appendix A. If you can't identify what you're feeling, use that list to find a word that describes your emotion. When I asked students what they were feeling, they often told me what they were thinking, like "I'm feeling like I don't want that to happen." Our programming runs deep, so this naming needs to be deliberate. Without much encouragement, those same students began to identify negative emotions left and right—like a dam broke—when they were finally free to say what they'd been feeling all along. At that point, they didn't need a list of feelings words. A part of them already knew what they felt.

2. Let them be. After identifying the feelings by giving them names, the next step is finding a safe, healthy way to express them. Sometimes just naming the feelings, acknowledging them, and accepting what you're feeling is enough for the feelings to pass through you and leave on their own. Most of our emotions have a very short life. They come and go quickly if we simply accept them and let them *be*. It's the same process as observing your thoughts. You notice and name the feelings within you. You let it be okay that they came for a visit. Don't argue or defend or try to *make* them go away, and that emotional energy often dissipates and disappears on its own.

3. Notice physical sensations. Another way to work with negative emotions is by simply identifying the physical sensations that go along with them, allowing yourself to observe how the feeling plays out in your body, accepting what's happening with the feeling in your body in the present moment, like you're a detective who's making mental notes of your physical experience. For example, I experience sadness as almost a soreness in my throat, tingling in my face and around my head, and a tightness in my chest. Learning to focus on the feeling as you experience it in your body helps you accept it at a physiological level. It also puts you in the witness position, an arm's distance from your feelings with a healthy degree of detachment.

4. Verbally express your emotions to yourself. If you observe and accept your emotions and they still stick around, you can try expressing them to yourself. When you're alone, you can simply talk out loud by saying things like "I feel sad that my friend and I aren't close any more" or "I feel angry at so-and-so for showing up to lunch twenty minutes late, again."

5. Write in a journal. Many people find that writing about their emotions in a feelings journal gives them ways to express them that become cathartic and therapeutic. When I was going through a divorce, writing in my journal became my saving grace. This may also include writing a letter to anyone involved. You may or may not decide to share the letter.

6. Talk to someone you trust. Some people find it helpful to express their negative feelings to a neutral family member or trusted friend. Just be sure the person you choose to share with understands that all you need them to do is listen. When we hear someone express negative emotions, many of us want to "fix" the situation and give advice about what to do to make the feeling go away, so let the person know in advance that's not what you're asking for.

7. Observe your thoughts. I've learned to work with my negative emotions by observing my thoughts. For example, sometimes I'll start feeling uncomfortable for seemingly no reason. Maybe I suddenly feel anxious, a little scared, or annoyed when nothing I'm doing right then would cause me to feel that way. I can then flip into the observer role and focus on identifying the thoughts I had right before those feelings showed up. Sometimes I have to backtrack in my replay of recent thoughts, but very often, I'll realize that I was thinking about something that resulted in my anxiety, fear, or annoyance. It becomes one of those *aha* moments and allows me to look at the thoughts and maybe do some problem solving around the situations those thoughts represent.

8. Express your feelings through physical activity. Probably my all-time favorite way of dealing with uncomfortable emotions is to channel them into physical activity. The unpleasant emotions dissipate through my actions, and I end up getting lots of things done. I love being productive, so this technique has a built-in reward. Sometimes my physical activity is actually working out at the gym, but more often it's getting things done around my house, like cleaning, organizing, or working on a project. The energy of our emotions wants to be released, and each of us needs to figure out the best ways to do that.

Although many people consistently *underexpress* their emotions, others react impulsively and *overexpress* their feelings. Their emotions get triggered, and they may react without thinking or caring about the consequences, which can cause harm to themselves and others. Maybe they get angry or disgusted, and they lash out at others, either verbally or physically. These people need to learn lessons about how to stall, delay their reactions, and control their impulses. Training in anger management or simple techniques like taking a deep breath and counting backward from one hundred can often change these patterns with enough practice. Those who overexpress can also benefit from learning healthy ways to express the energy of their feelings before they build up and boil over.

Other techniques for dealing with negative emotions are available, but for some people, it's best to work with a trained professional who can gently guide them through the process. If you have any concerns about getting in over your head with your own emotions, find a therapist to work with.

All of our feelings—positive and negative—provide invaluable teachings as we make our way through school, but it's hard to witness our emotions if we're not supposed to have them in the first place. We can miss their instructions if we're busy trying to keep our negative emotions at bay. If you're one of the many who stuff your feelings because you don't know how to deal with them, or if you overreact and cause regrets, now may be the time to learn some new lessons and invite those feelings into your life in healthy ways.

---

16. *Activities*

If you're not currently accepting the gift of experiencing all your emotions, here are some things to try.

1. *Find names for your emotions so you can identify and talk about them. You'll find a list of feelings words in Appendix A.*

2. *Experiment with healthy ways to express your feelings. These can include the following:*

    - *Welcome and acknowledge your feelings; let them be and often they leave very quickly.*

- *Observe and accept the unique physical sensations of each emotion in your body.*
- *Verbally express your feelings to yourself.*
- *Write in a journal.*
- *Talk about your feelings with someone you trust.*
- *Notice the thoughts that accompany or precede your feelings.*
- *Express your emotions through physical activity.*

3. *Find a professional therapist if you need help.*

4. *Ask yourself, "What lesson or lessons are my emotions trying to help me learn?"*

Our feelings can become the fuel that energizes our passion, enthusiasm, and zest for life.

Learning our lessons around healthy emotional expression forms a cornerstone in living a fulfilling life.

Addictions

Many years ago, I flew back to Arkansas to spend Christmas with my parents. During my visit, I got a chance to connect with my longtime friend, Katherine, who recommended that I go to Al-Anon, which is a twelve-step program for friends and family of alcoholics. Katherine knew I had gotten involved with an alcoholic, and although that relationship had ended, she thought I could still learn a lot after the fact. At the close of our conversation, she said, "I suggest that you go to seven meetings in seven days."

I didn't tell Katherine this at the time, but I didn't think I needed to go to Al-Anon at all, much less seven meetings in one week. But I had a break from my job right after Christmas, a small window of time, and almost involuntarily, I decided to take her up on her suggestion. I still can't believe I did that.

I felt a little awkward at my first couple of meetings, but everyone seemed so sincere in their efforts to make their situations better. They focused on improving themselves rather than trying to change the alcoholics in their lives, which made a lot of sense to me. You didn't have to talk if you didn't want to, but because they all agreed on confidentiality, I soon found myself opening up to a group of strangers about my own issues and feeling surprisingly comfortable.

One of the biggest lessons I learned from Al-Anon had to do with **detachment**, which means detaching from the problem behavior of the alcoholic—not reacting to or getting engaged in their problems—but still loving the person. It sounds difficult, but with practice, it becomes that happy medium that can help you keep your relationship and your sanity. To this day, I regularly use detachment with people I know who have all kinds of dysfunctional behavior, not just those with addictions.

However, the monumental *aha* moment came after the fourth meeting. I went home after listening during those four, one-hour meetings as people talked about the alcoholics in their lives, and I realized it sounded like they were talking about *me*. I didn't drink, but I worked like crazy, and I came face-to-face with the startling and overpowering realization that I was a workaholic. That awareness hit me hard, and I felt stunned for days.

I knew I worked long hours, but I always chalked it up to my strong work ethic, which was actually a source of personal pride. I liked the fact that I was a hard worker. Just like with alcoholics, the people closest to me sometimes expressed their frustration that I was so busy working that I didn't have much time to spend with them. But I didn't see my long hours as a problem—or a choice. However, I had never, ever, even remotely thought of it as an addiction. Through the Al-Anon meetings, my unhealthy work pattern became intrusively apparent, and I couldn't deny or rationalize it away.

Being the perpetual student that I am, I immediately set out to learn everything I could about workaholism. A part of me thought that if I learned enough, I could somehow take control of my out-of-control behavior. Of course, I was wrong, but learning about my addiction helped me get at least a cognitive handle on it.

I learned that workaholics often have low self-esteem, and they adopt a mantra that says, "If I work enough, I'll be worth enough." Society plays right into that myth. Don't we collectively admire, respect, and even envy highly productive people, especially those who accrue visible signs of success like money and power? That's a compelling reinforcer.

Workaholism has another cause and built-in reward: it insulates us from intimacy with ourselves and others. We don't have to deal with a lot of complicated and messy emotions within ourselves and our other relationships, because we're always too busy and too distracted by our busyness to have the time. It's a somewhat acceptable excuse not to become too involved and too vulnerable. I've always had a healthy self-esteem, but I already had a divorce behind me, so my own brand of workaholism served to help me avoid intimacy with others.

I eventually decided I didn't want to live a life that put limits on intimacy, and I didn't want to risk getting hooked on the rewards of external accomplishments. I wanted to feel good about me because of who I was, not because of how much I got done or all the things I had.

Addicts are notorious for thinking they can deal with their addictions on their own, that they don't need help. I knew I needed support, but at the time, there were no Workaholics Anonymous meetings I could attend. So I created a recovery program for myself, which included cutting back at work and saying no to extra requests. The results proved quite interesting. Even though I told my coworkers I was working on my recovery, and they said they supported my efforts, they didn't like it when I stopped volunteering to serve on one more committee or help with yet another worthy project. That's when I had to learn how to separate their approval or disapproval from my behavior. By taking a witness or observer position on how our interactions were playing out, I was able to hold my ground and not give in to their requests—most of the time.

During my many years of workaholism, I walked dangerously close to the edge of burnout and actually stepped over that line twice. In each instance, it took almost two years for my mind and body to fully recover. That kind of fatigue can't be undone with a month or two of sleeping in on weekends. I can remember saying to myself, "People shouldn't feel this tired." And I was right.

The work culture in Japan often includes excessive overtime, and those who work twelve- to sixteen-hour days for long periods of time become high-risk for major health issues like strokes and heart attacks. Some die at relatively young ages. The Japanese even have a word for it: **karoshi**, or death by overwork. Like most addictions, workaholism can take a terrible, even fatal, toll on your health.

To make matters worse, workaholics often pick up a second addiction to help them keep going through the long hours. Mine was caffeine. A friend used food, which predictably led to weight problems. Some people use uppers, and also use downers, to help them sleep. It's a destructive, self-perpetuating cycle, one that keeps us hooked on multiple addictions.

Workaholism is rampant in our culture, for understandable reasons. My work addiction resulted in promotions, pay raises, and lots of accolades. It took a while for me to figure out I could cut back to a healthier workload and *still* get those rewards.

Also, for most of us, work isn't an option. We have to work to pay our bills, just like we have to eat to stay alive. Workaholism and eating disorders can become difficult to address because you can't abstain from either one. If I were an alcoholic, I would have the option to stop drinking. If I still smoked cigarettes, I could set a goal to stop smoking altogether. But I can't stop working. That means I have to find a healthy balance that keeps me from overworking to extremes. It's an ongoing process, something I still monitor every day.

Another tricky aspect of workaholism is that it can look identical to someone who works long hours but works out of passion rather than out of avoidance or low self-esteem. Today I see myself as someone who loves what I do and passionately emerges in my work, which actually puts me *more* emotionally in touch with myself and others. We all must go inside our heart of hearts to figure out the underlying cause of our overworking, but please understand that working a lot doesn't automatically mean you're a workaholic. Some jobs require an inordinate number of work hours. And many of us go through periods in our lives when we have to work extra hours out of necessity—for example, we need the money or we're supporting ourselves while we're in school—but we'd prefer not to work so much, and we scale back as soon as we get the chance.

As you can see, my addiction to work became a teacher extraordinaire. It helped me learn crucial lessons that literally changed the course of my life. All of our addictions carry this potential. They offer gifts we can't even fathom until we go through the steps of unraveling their control over us to discover the exquisite jewels they conceal.

The Universe undoubtedly knew it was time for me to learn my lessons around addictions, because for a number of years, I noncoincidentally ended up in jobs that allowed me to work in the area of substance abuse. I was fortunate to work closely with treatment facilitators, a physician who was certified as an addiction specialist, and those who were struggling with the gamut of substance use, abuse, dependency, and addiction. So I got to see the issues from all sides.

Addictions are about relationships, the kinds of relationships we develop with mood-altering substances or activities. At first the relationship may seem to make things better: you feel a sense of well-being or maybe even euphoria similar to falling in love. As the relationship develops, however, you begin to need the substance or activity. You need the fix it provides just to not feel bad. In the latter stages, you become powerless, and the addiction controls you, dictating what you do and when you do it. Generally defined, addictions are obsessive-compulsive relationships with a mood-altering substance or activity that have increasingly negative consequences. Obsessive means we can't stop thinking about it; compulsive refers to behavior we can't stop doing. The purpose of addictions is to keep us numb, out of touch with what we know and feel.

So what kinds of substances do we get addicted to? They include alcohol, drugs—including illegal drugs, prescription medications, and over-the-counter drugs like painkillers—nicotine, caffeine, and food, including sugar. Activity addictions can include addictions to people, sex, work, being busy all the time, money, spending, "keeping up with the Joneses," gambling, electronic devices, exercise, and drama or chaos. Many of the activity addictions create physiological changes in the body similar to the chemical changes that happen when you take drugs. Watch someone who is texting, and you will often see them smiling, with a blissed-out look on their face. In some instances, people become addicted to their own adrenaline, which gets stimulated by engaging in the activity. I've heard addictive gamblers talk about the adrenaline rush they get from their risk taking.

We can also get addicted to internal activities, to processes that go on inside of us. Some people develop obsessive-compulsive relationships with different emotions, like anger, self-righteousness, arrogance, and fear. We can also become addicted to our own thoughts, such as thoughts of being in love, being secure, perfectionism, people pleasing, and thoughts of having money and status. These thoughts become obsessive; we go over and over them in our minds.

Addictions have the ability to stop us in our tracks and severely limit our progress in the school of life. They impair our awareness of what's going on outside and inside of us by numbing our bodies and feelings, distorting our thinking, and controlling our behavior. Plus, they're sneaky. They can grab hold of us under the most innocent of circumstances and operate on subtle levels until one day we wake up and realize we're hooked. My workaholism started when I had to work my way through graduate school. I never suspected it was an addiction until the very day it came crashing into my awareness.

If we're not dealing with our negative emotions in healthy ways, then we're vulnerable to developing addictions, because they help us numb the pain and emotions we don't want to feel and don't know how to handle. Some people become addicted to aversion or avoidance. They get hooked on something as a way to avoid pain.

We can also get trapped in addictive relationships because we crave the initial feelings of well-being, ecstasy, and bliss they provide. In other words, we get addicted to the desire for pleasure. This craving becomes so strong that many people keep going back to the addiction far beyond the time when it stops satisfying the craving, despite increasingly negative results.

Addictions can become increasingly insidious when they serve to help people avoid pain *and* experience pleasure at the same time. Both pain avoidance and desires for pleasure are powerful rewards, which is partly why so many people in recovery end up relapsing.

Even so, people who get serious about their recovery from addictions often make extraordinarily fast progress in the school of life. They sometimes pass through many classes in relatively short periods of time by uncovering what lies hidden beneath their addictions and control issues. In recovery communities around the world, you can see the honesty, courage, and gratitude that result from a commitment to heal. That power becomes motivating and incredibly inspiring.

---

17. *Activities*

1. *As you focus your awareness on your internal teachers and practice being an observer of your inner world, be particularly vigilant for any signs of addiction. Ask yourself:*

    - *Is my body addicted to any substances—maybe alcohol or food?*
    - *Am I compulsively doing things that have negative consequences, like working too much, spending excessively, or ignoring relationships because I'm always on my cell phone?*
    - *Am I hooked on any thoughts or feelings (e.g., thoughts of being secure or wealthy, feelings of anger or fear)?*

2. *If you already know you have one or more addictions or even think you might, thank yourself—not for having an addiction—but for being honest enough to admit it. Opening your awareness to even the possibility of addictions takes an act of courage, which can have tremendous positive rewards.*

3. *If you find that you have an addiction, make a decision about what you want to do about it. Please understand that addictions are progressive and usually get worse over time, so you might want to look for professional help and find a therapist. Many people start by going to a twelve-step meeting. They're free, and most cities have a wide range of meetings and times. You can go and just observe if you want. Like with me, it could be equivalent to enrolling in an exceptionally promising—even life-changing—new classroom.*

Also, if you are addicted to a substance like alcohol, you can look for information on different types of treatments and their effectiveness.

Dreams

Have you ever had a dream that felt significant, even though you couldn't remember all the different parts? Or did you ever have the same dream several times and knew it must have a message, but you weren't entirely sure what it meant? According to sleep specialists, we all dream every night. Some people are better at remembering their dreams than others, and some have no difficulty interpreting their dreams. But all of us can get better at both. It just takes practice to learn how to remember and interpret the wisdom our dreams have to offer.

Years before I knew I would write this book, I dreamed about it. The dream started with me hovering in midair about ten feet in front of this massive waterfall, not quite halfway down. In the dream, my ability to hover above the ground with no effort seemed perfectly normal. I was talking to a small group of people who were going over the waterfall in a canoe, and they, too, had stopped midfall so we could communicate.

I gave the people in the canoe instructions on how to best navigate the journey they were on. They thanked me and then fell the rest of the way down the waterfall, landed upright in the river below, and continued their travels. I went on my way, happy that I had passed along what I had learned about our common journey.

After I got some distance away, I looked back at the waterfall. The people I instructed had returned and were doing the same thing with the next group of travelers going down. Only they were changing the instructions I had given them, improving on what I had communicated based on what they had learned from their own travels.

At first, I felt disappointed that the travelers were changing my hard-earned instructions. Then I realized it was perfect. That was exactly what they needed to do—add their own recommendations for the next group—so the instructions passed down to future travelers perpetually got better.

As I write this book, I'm hoping a similar process will happen. I'm hoping that you as readers will take what I say and modify it or add to it, making it even more helpful and effective both for yourselves and anyone you share it with. That way, we expand and improve our collective wisdom. Who would have known my dream from decades ago would end up becoming so prophetic?

Besides giving us information about the future, like my dream did, how else do our dreams serve as teachers as we navigate through the school of life? Because they come from our subconscious, dreams provide information that we wouldn't ordinarily get from our conscious thoughts and feelings. They can help us understand our inner needs and desires, give us warnings, assist with problem solving and decision making, and comfort us after a loss. For example, many people get reassurance and closure from a dream to help them cope with the death of a loved one.

We can experience all kinds of dreams, from whimsical fantasies to terrifying nightmares. And although some of our dreams contain valuable information and important messages, others may serve as more of an organizing or "housekeeping" function; they help us integrate our day-to-day experiences but aren't particularly significant. Recurring dreams usually do carry deeper meaning and can be a sign that your subconscious is trying to get your attention, so pay special attention to dreams you have more than once.

For years, I had a recurring dream that I was driving my car and the brakes went out. I always woke up just before I slammed into something, but it scared me. The dream seemed to be a warning: don't try to go too fast in life until you're fully prepared because you could lose control and crash. That interpretation felt accurate, especially given my tendency to push myself beyond healthy limits with my workaholism. I needed more recovery time under my belt before I took on a lot more responsibilities.

Information on how to interpret your dreams is readily available, both in books and online. Much of that material gives the meaning of dream themes and symbols based on different cultural or theoretical perspectives, like Native American, Shamanism, and Freudian psychoanalytic theory. Although those interpretations can be a good starting point for understanding our dreams, they don't always fit. Each of us has our own ethnic and cultural background and our own unique set of life experiences, so it's often more helpful to explore the personal significance of your dreams instead of relying on someone else's predetermined interpretation. At least that's what I've found in working with my own dreams and in counseling with others to understand theirs. I believe each of us is the best person to interpret personal dreams.

It's sometimes fun to look at common dreams, those that many of us have. These include the naked-in-public dream, the flying dream, the falling dream, and the dream where someone or something is chasing you. Another common dream is that you are in school, a test is coming up, and you are totally unprepared. This last dream may mean several things, including anxiety about being judged by others or fear of our tests in life. Again, all of us need to interpret our dreams based on what makes sense and feels right for us.

Because our dreams can provide information we can't get to on a conscious level, I sometimes ask my dreams for guidance when I'm having a hard time making a decision. For example, I once had the opportunity to apply for an associate director position within my department, but I wasn't sure that I wanted to go into administration. I started by asking the Universe for help by saying, "Please give me a sign about this job. And please make it obvious, because you know how dense I can be sometimes." Nothing came, at least nothing that registered in my awareness.

With the application deadline the next day, I asked for guidance in a dream the night before. Not only did I not get any messages, but I didn't remember a single dream from that night. So I went to work the day of the deadline in a state of ambivalence, still not knowing what I was supposed to do. Somewhere around nine o'clock that morning, my boss called me into his office and asked, "Are you going to apply for this position?" As it turned out, he wanted me to apply, because he thought I would be a good fit for the job. In the end, I got my sign, and it was definitely obvious.

The point of this story is that even if you don't remember your dreams or don't usually find them helpful, the Universe will still find a way to give you the guidance you need. Just pay attention in your classes, staying open and receptive.

---

18. <u>Activities</u>

1. **Working with our dreams can become fascinating and enjoyable, in addition to giving us another valuable teacher in school. If you have difficulty <u>remembering</u> your dreams, try the following:**

   - *Right before you go to sleep, say to yourself, "I want to remember my dreams tonight."*

   - *Keep a pad and pen next to your bed. If you wake up in the night and remember even a snippet of a dream, write it down. Do not use an electronic device, because those cause deeper interruptions in our sleep.*

   - *When you wake up the next morning, lie still for a few minutes and search your mind for any memories of dreams from the night before. If anything comes to mind, write it down. Most dream memories are extremely fragile and short-lived, and even getting out of bed can make them disappear.*

- *If you don't have time to write it down before beginning your day, go over your dream several times in your head to help strengthen that memory, and then write it down the first chance you get.*

2. *If you want to get better at <u>interpreting</u> your dreams, consider these suggestions:*

   - *Read books or other information on dream interpretation. Even though the universal symbols might not fit, it can help you further explore your personal meaning. Also look for information that helps you come up with your personal interpretations.*

   - *Keep a dream journal. Write down your dreams and what you think they mean.*

   - *Tell your dreams to someone you trust. Sometimes talking about your dreams helps make their meaning more clear.*

   - *Work with a therapist who specializes in dream work or join a dream group.*

3. *Most of us have occasional bad dreams that leave us rattled and unnerved. Try making up a different ending, one that leaves you feeling more in control; write down the new ending or rehearse it in your mind several times to help switch the negative feelings. For example, if someone was chasing you, and your legs wouldn't move, imagine an outcome where you become supercharged with energy and easily run to safety.*

However, if you frequently have disturbing nightmares or wake up terrified, you might want to find a therapist who can help you work with those dreams to get resolution on the underlying issues they represent.

Chapter 6
Intuition, the Ultimate Teacher

Have you ever known who was calling you before you saw their number or answered the phone?

Have you have ever had a gut feeling that something was about to happen without knowing why—and it did?

What about any times in your life when you remember hearing some little voice inside telling you to do something, but you ignored that voice, only to regret it later?

These are common examples of how intuition works in our lives. We may rush right past these experiences or only superficially acknowledge that they happen, but they provide validation for the uncanny wisdom of this natural instinct.

Each of us has an inner guide, an infinitely wise being inside who is just waiting for us to allow it to play a bigger role in our lives. It's the part of us that already knows what we need to know and has already learned all the lessons we came here to learn. Following this guidance means we start moving through our metaphorical classes in life faster and easier.

How is it that certain birds know when and where to migrate? Or that an acorn knows how to grow into an oak tree? Or that mother animals of all types instinctively protect their babies? We all come into this life equipped with that same instinctual wisdom, the same innate intelligence. It's our connection to our souls, which are connected to the divine intelligence of the Universe. And the great news is that we can learn how to sharpen our skills at staying in touch with this invaluable resource. That's because intuition is like a muscle—the more you use it, the stronger it becomes.

When I worked in a university counseling center, I taught a class called "Developing Intuition." The students who participated made remarkably quick progress in learning how to understand their intuitive messages and act on what they were told. And good things happened every time they did. Later in this chapter, I'll step you through the material we covered in that class.

Albert Einstein said, "The really valuable thing is intuition." Different cultures value intuition to varying degrees, but in mainstream U.S. culture, our intuition often isn't respected for the powerhouse of wisdom it provides. Instead, we tend to admire and imitate people who appear logical and unemotional. Gavin de Becker, author of *The Gift of Fear*, goes so far as to say, "Americans worship logic even when it's wrong, and they deny intuition even when it's right."

But the bottom line is that we need both. We need our logical, analytical, critical thinking skills, *and* we need our intuition. Because logic and reasoning skills often come from our experience, that means logic, experience, and intuition all play critical roles in helping us become the best that we can be.

So what exactly is our intuition? It's what we call a hunch, gut feeling, instinct, or sixth sense, that "still small voice inside." It's when we know something but don't know how we know. There's no logical explanation for how we even *could* know. It's when knowledge spontaneously shows up in our awareness without any conscious or deliberate effort on our part. And by definition that knowledge is always correct. Francis Vaughn, the author of *Awakening Intuition,* puts it this way: "If a seemingly intuitive insight turns out to be wrong, it did not spring from intuition but from self-deception or wishful thinking." In other words, it was a bad guess.

How can you tell the difference between intuition versus what you *think* is intuition, like impulsiveness, wishful thinking, self-deception, and bad guesses? Practice. You practice using your intuition, especially in situations that aren't high risk, until you learn to distinguish between the two.

How Is Intuition Helpful?

I read an interesting story about Paul McCartney. This snippet of a song came to him in a dream. It sounded so different from his own songs that he thought he must have heard it someplace else. He went around asking everyone he could think of if they'd ever heard that tune. No one had, so he ended up writing a song around it. And that's how "Yesterday" came to be.

In this example, intuition spoke through a dream as part of the creative process. When you're creative, you come up with something that doesn't exist yet. Think of musicians, painters, dancers, and writers who venture into new territory to create unique outcomes in their artistic expression. Intuition also deserves the credit when successful entrepreneurs find gut-level, creative ways to market and deliver their services. In a more day-to-day example, people struggling with time management may receive intuitive instructions on how to get creative and get everything done.

Sometimes our intuition plays the role of a private detective, working to find answers to our questions, like when research scientists discover new combinations of elements or when people in the business field somehow "get it" about what will become a lucrative financial investment. This private detective role also includes vague feelings about trivial events in our daily lives. For instance, I often get subtle hints from my intuition about where to shop. When I follow those instructions, I always find either whatever I'm looking for or something else I need to buy.

In addition, our intuition serves as a built-in alarm system and protects us from harm. Examples of this type of intuition are examples of divine protection or divine interventions. It's the "uh-oh" or "icky" feeling we teach children to listen to when someone does something inappropriate. Parents feel grateful for a sense that "something isn't right" when they interview a potential new babysitter who wouldn't properly care for their child. On a more obvious level, our intuition is the panic that comes when we're about to step into harm's way.

Mothers often develop a "sixth sense" about their children and know things about them that can't be rationally explained, like when their children need them or are in some kind of trouble. In his book, *Life Code,* Dr. Phil McGraw asks his readers to tap into their "instincts" or "gut" to access vital information about the people in their lives who might be out to do them harm.

People who work in the helping professions, like counselors and those in medical fields, often experience nonverbal, sixth-sense ways of interacting with their clients and patients. Déjà vu experiences tell us we've just stepped into that internal world of wisdom. And many of us develop intuitive connections with our pets, when we know things about them without any rational way of knowing, almost as if we're speaking to each other without words.

So much of life is unpredictable, which means all of us are forced to play the odds and call our shots one way or the other. We have to make decisions about the future without having all the facts. According to Philip Goldberg, author of *The Intuitive Edge,* "We play guessing games with life. Those who guess well are called intuitive; those who are intuitive, however, don't think they're guessing."

Highly successful people in life often have a well-honed ability to tap into their inner guide. For example, Oprah Winfrey credits intuition for all the major decisions around her success. She states, "I take in all the information I can gather. I listen to proposals, ideas, and advice. Then I go with my gut, what my heart feels most strongly."

How Does Your Intuition Communicate?

Everyone is intuitive; we've all been given this gift. Some people find it trustworthy and easily accessible. For others, it remains relatively dormant throughout their lives. A third group of people use their intuition at least occasionally, but they're either not aware that they're using it or don't call it intuition.

Gender differences in the ways that males and females describe intuitive experiences often reinforce a stereotype that women are more intuitive than men, but we all have this innate gift. Women often talk about their intuition as emotions; they frequently have intuitive connections in interpersonal relationships and get an unexplainable feeling when something is or isn't right. Men are more likely to reference "gut hunches." They often use their intuition in some aspect of their work that they can't logically explain, and although it may be chalked up to simple logic, actually it's not.

Many of us, however, were taught at an early age not to listen to our intuition, not to trust the messages it gave us, not to express ourselves truthfully, but to squelch our spontaneity and creativity and to instead be rational. By the time we're in elementary school, many of us have learned that what seemed like inner truth is something to be ignored and maybe even feared.

Why are we so often discouraged from developing our creative and intuitive skills at such an early age? It may be that the adults around us when we're young weren't supported in using *their* natural abilities either, so they do with us what was done with them. And besides that, creativity and intuition can't be controlled; they don't fit into neat categories of right and wrong the way logic and reasoning sometimes do. It's often hard to get a handle on where the intuitive process is headed, so it can become scary or, at the very least, something we're taught to avoid. We live in a culture that worships logic, and many of us try to conform.

But regardless of the reasons, and in spite of where you might be starting from today, the great news is that with practice, you can strengthen the voice of your intuition and begin to follow its advice more often. That's what happened when students took my class, and it didn't take long for them to improve.

Do you know how your intuition talks to you? Do you know how it teaches and communicates, or tries to? That "still small voice" can speak to us in a number of ways.

1. Physical. Intuition sometimes communicates through our bodies on the physical level. This often includes information about ourselves and our environment. For example, we can "sense" danger through physiological changes and sensations, like the sense of apprehension or panic that tells us to leave a situation or place immediately. Maybe we get a flood of adrenaline, a feeling of being trapped, or an irrational urge to bolt and "get out of here." Maybe your intuition speaks through a particular sensation in your stomach or gut, a shiver up your spine, goose bumps, or tears in your eyes.

We can also be given intuitive guidance about needing to take care of our bodies through various bodily sensations, aches, and pains. For example, muscular tension and headaches can be intuitive messages telling us we need to reduce our stress. And intuition can use our bodies to help us learn lessons that are more symbolic than literal. For example, one time I started having problems with my knees, which is rare for me. I finally figured out that I needed to learn a lesson about humility, and my intuition was showing me I needed to be "brought to my knees."

I get chills on my arms and start to cry when I hear something that rings particularly deep and true, as if my intuition is saying, "You just heard something important." Sometimes it speaks through a unique "solid feeling" in the core of my body, like when I understood what the crows were trying to tell me, and I knew that I knew that was correct. If I need to address something in my life that isn't resolved, I sometimes feel this nebulous tension throughout my body, which is different from other kinds of tension I experience. And when I get a burst of energy after making a decision, that's one of the surefire ways my intuition tells me I'm on the right track.

2. Emotional. Many people become aware of their intuition through their feelings. Examples include sensitivity to other people's "vibes," an unexplainable liking or disliking, or a vague sense you're supposed to do something—or *not* do something. Maybe you get an unexpected feeling that you can't trust someone you just met, and that feeling turns out to be correct. Or perhaps you instantly like someone for no reason but only later find out why your first instinct was right.

Our intuition can use any of our emotions to deliver its messages. For instance, positive feelings like happiness and relief after you make a big decision can serve as confirmation that you made the right choice. In contrast, negative feelings like doubt and regret can tell us we might want to reconsider our decision.

3. Mental. The mental forms of intuitive communication can be either ***visual*** or ***auditory***. Visual messages consist of different types of visual images—an inner vision—which may be literal or symbolic. Literal images may take the form of actual numbers or words that we "see" in our heads. Some people see their thoughts as if they're sentences written in their brains. Many musicians report that they literally see musical notes during their creative process, and all they do is write those down. A symbolic vision could be a mother who sees the inner image of a circle, which to her may mean she needs to bring the circle of her conflicted family together. Our intuition often speaks through our dreams, where we may "see" entire stories play out.

Auditory messages are more what we think of as that small quiet voice within. We all have an internal dialogue going on in our heads most of the time. Many people experience this dialogue as just their own random thoughts and aren't aware of any themes. However, sometimes our intuition comes through as a voice inside, providing us with guidance and instructions. Some people hear their thoughts, like a part of them is talking from inside their heads. That internal voice may tell you to get in touch with a family member who needs your help, although you aren't consciously aware that person needs you at the time. It may tell you to finish a project at work before the deadline, and you find out only afterward there was a reason it needed to be completed early. It may tell writers exactly what words to use. Or maybe you've been thinking about a friend for several days, and your friend unexpectedly calls you and says, "You've been on my mind, so I just decided to call."

Sometimes my nagging thoughts, the ones that just won't leave me alone, turn out to be my intuition persistently trying to get my attention. These thoughts may initially look similar to everyday obsessions, but there's often a message that we need to *do* something included in the intuitive thoughts, whereas the obsessions just tend to spin round and round with no clear imperative to take action. Excessive worrying may also be your intuition speaking through your thoughts and telling you to address whatever is going on. And sometimes our mental confusion is a way our intuition gets us to slow down and not act on something right away.

People who have mental health issues sometimes "hear voices" that are frightening and cause them to feel paranoid. Those voices are usually described as outside of themselves, coming from someplace in their environment, like the television, and are not tied to reality. That's not what we're talking about here. Intuitive voices are our own thoughts that come from *inside* of us and provide valuable reality-based messages about real-life events.

To sum this up, when our intuition communicates with us, the messages may come through three different forms: (1) our physical bodies, (2) emotions, and (3) visual or auditory mental images, including thoughts. It may also use a combination of these forms. For instance, your intuition may normally come in the form of visual images, but you may get auditory messages to help you prepare for a speech. Other people may "hear" words of comfort if they're upset. Their intuition may also communicate when they "see" in their minds, images of light, color, pictures, numbers, letters, or words.

Let's do a quick activity to give you some experience in listening to your intuition. It only takes a few minutes.

19. *Activities*

1. *Stop right now and ask yourself the following question. Don't overthink your response. Just go with the first thing that comes into your head. If you're not sure, guess.*

   - *If I were an animal, what animal would I be? Write it down.*

2. *Next ask yourself:*

   - *How did I know what animal I would be?*

Was your answer to the second question something you experienced in your body, like a sensation in your gut? Was it an emotion or some vague feeling? Or was it a mental image—a picture you saw in your mind's eye, or maybe you heard yourself say the name of the animal in your thoughts?

3. *You can also ask yourself these questions:*

   - *If I were a season of the year, which season would I be and why?*
   - *If I were a food, which food would I be and why?*
   - *If I were a car, what kind of car would I be and why?*

Again, ask yourself <u>how</u> you knew the answers to these questions. Was it a physical or emotional response? Or did you get a mental message through something you saw or heard in your head?

This exercise can be fun to do with people of all ages, including children.

Because we don't have any memories of being an animal, season, food, or car, this simple activity pulls for a creative, intuitive response. It is a metaphor, and those help us get past our normal, rational minds and into a more creative part of our thinking. You can use this same activity with all kinds of metaphors.

Another way to start using your intuition more is to look back and identify times in the past when it came through for you. Here's another short exercise to help you connect to your inner wisdom.

---

20. <u>Activities</u>

1. *Think back to a time when you used your intuition. Maybe it was an experience with someone close to you or something that happened at work. Perhaps it was a creative moment when you found a creative solution to a problem or created some piece of art. Maybe it was something as fleeting as a déjà vu experience or a dream with special meaning.*

   - *Identify one intuitive experience—or something that "might" have been an intuitive experience. If you're not sure, guess.*

2. *Now ask yourself, "How did I know my intuition was speaking to me?" Was it something you experienced in your body, like a gut hunch, goose bumps, or tears? Was it an emotion or some feeling? Or was it a mental image—either a visual picture your saw in your head or something you heard coming from inside of you?*

3. *Once you've identified one way your intuition has spoken to you in the past, look for others. Continue to ask yourself, "How else has my intuition tried to get my attention?"*

After you identify one or more ways your intuition has communicated with you, be on the lookout for those same communication methods in the future. Again, the more we use our intuition—and the more we're aware that we're using our intuition—the stronger and more reliable it becomes.

A Lesson on Listening

Writing the first draft of this book was an absolute high. It happened fast and seemed almost effortless. I fell in love with writing. I had found my bliss.

Fast forward several years to when I started exploring possibilities for getting the book published. An agent, an editor, and several writing teachers told me essentially the same thing, "If you want this to be a textbook, you're good to go. But if you want it on the popular market, it needs to be rewritten." One person went so far as to say, "You've done so much academic writing that now you're handicapped." I couldn't believe anyone would say something like that.

But I enjoy being a student, so I decided to dive in and learn everything I could about writing by attending writers' conferences, reading books on writing, and enrolling in writing classes. I did all of that, and although I learned a lot *about* writing, it didn't help me get better when I tried to actually write. I felt blocked and stuck, and in my most frustrated moments, I would admit that I felt intimidated by my own incompetence and the magnitude of the project in front of me.

Even so, I kept going to writing classes. And I kept getting bad feedback. Finally, one of my writing teachers rewrote my work herself to show me how to revise it—and I *still* didn't get it. That's when I said to myself, "I need to drop this for now. Nothing is working. Now isn't the time."

So I waited until I retired and revived my attempts to improve my skills by getting into a writer's critique group. This time, I only wrote personal essays. I was afraid to try to rewrite the book for fear that it would throw me back into the academic writing. But thank heavens, I found my new writer's voice through those short essays. My voice had been there all along. It was actually my teaching voice from all those years of teaching college classes.

After I'd been in the critique group about three months, I decided to try some book rewrites with my newly discovered voice. I promised to bring my work to the group to read, so I had a firm deadline to meet. However, several days before I was supposed to read in the group, I felt stuck, unable to come up with any writing, any drafts, any inspiration, or even any ideas for what I would write. And I knew it wouldn't help to go to a conference, read another book, look online, or consult with my writing teacher. I didn't know how to find a way out of my stuckness.

I started to panic. I needed to write to meet the deadline, but my mind was blank. I've never had problems with writer's block, so this was a totally new experience for me. My heart started to beat faster, and my thoughts began to race, frantically trying to latch onto anything that would help me produce something to read.

That's when I told myself, "Sweetie, this can't be that hard. Just find a bestseller and connect the dots. Don't write the same thing, but make it look the same way." So I grabbed a classic, one of my all-time favorites, *The Road Less Traveled,* by M. Scott Peck. There on the first page, the author began with, "Life is difficult."

I said to myself, "Ah. I could start with something like that. Something simple but profound." But my anxiety got worse. Much worse. In fact, the instant I tried to mimic someone else, my anxiety escalated off the scale. Finally I realized I was having a full-blown, bona fide, clinical panic attack. I started pacing around my house, feeling like I was coming out of my skin. Then, almost miraculously, at the exact moment when I thought I might explode, my intuition spoke up and said in a calm but firm voice, "Your book doesn't want to be written like that."

Oh.

Boy, was that sobering.

It took some time for me to calm down. But I'd learned the lesson: the only way for me to write the book was to write the book. I just had to start writing, even if it was junk, and find my way through to the other side.

Several months after my meltdown, I was telling a friend about it. This friend happens to be a psychologist, and she said, "You should have called me. I would have talked you down."

My reply: "I was too far gone."

Listen, Trust, Act

Experiences like the one I just described make me value and appreciate my intuition even more. I'm so grateful to have an inner compass that points me in the right direction when I start to veer off track. For me, that guidance is priceless.

Although we can't *make* our intuition speak to us, we can open the door and invite it into our lives. In addition to learning how our intuition communicates, learning to listen, trust, and act on our inner voice can help us strengthen our intuitive skills.

1. Listen

Many of us have spent most of our lives trying not to listen, trying to ignore the messages of our inner guide, so our challenge is to develop an attitude of openness and receptivity, a willingness to pay attention to any and all forms of communication. Sometimes the messages may be strong or intense and absolutely clear. Sometimes they may seem muffled, elusive, and doubtful or uncertain. Maybe all you will get is a vague feeling that lasts no more than a couple of seconds. It might be a brief flash in your mind or some image or symbol that appears and then is gone, leaving you wondering if you even saw what you thought you saw. All of these potential forms of communication require heightened awareness. We have to be on the lookout for messages all the time—any place, any time.

A second part of listening means learning to distinguish intuitive messages from all the other jabber we get from our inner world. Is that bodily sensation of hunger an intuitive urge to take care of your body by eating, or is it a symptom of anxiety or boredom that needs to be addressed some other way? Did you immediately dislike that person because of some intuitive wisdom, or did the person unconsciously remind you of someone else you dislike, which is a completely separate issue? These distinctions can be difficult to make, and it takes practice and increased self-awareness to figure out the differences. The better you know yourself, the easier it will be to decipher which inner voices you're hearing. Our conscious and unconscious impulses, desires, and fears may be especially prone to lead us to wishful thinking and bad guesses.

One additional aspect of listening deserves special mention: when we get intuitive messages that are symbolic, part of hearing the message involves the second step of interpreting the symbol correctly. Our intuition often speaks through metaphors, which then need to be interpreted. This same principle applies to dream interpretation. Because of our individuality and uniqueness, metaphors and symbols may have different meanings for each of us. If you get an image of yourself as an animal—let's say an otter—that metaphor may mean something different to you than it would to someone else. A good rule of thumb is to go with your first guess about whatever the symbol means. Just like when you take a multiple-choice test, your first impression about the right answer is usually the one most likely to be correct.

Right now, I encourage you to flip to Appendix B at the back of the book. You'll find a short guided imagery activity, the Inner Guide Imagery Exercise. It will help you communicate with you intuition, or inner guide. The instructions are included. Go ahead and do the exercise now and see how it works for you. You'll need to first start with a question. So identify a question you want or need an answer to, and ask your inner guide for a response.

Just now, when you did the inner guide exercise, did you get an answer to your question? Did you need to take a second step and interpret your answer? And what gift were you given as you left your special place and started back down the path that led you there? All of this information can help you respond to the question you asked your all-knowing, intuitive self.

I did this exercise with a student who was struggling with a decision about which graduate program to enter. She had narrowed it down to counseling and social work, so her question was which of the two choices was right for her. This student already had good insight; she could line up the pros and cons of both options and tell me the predicted consequences of each. She already had all the objective, conscious information she needed, so I decided to see if she could pull in some subjective, subconscious information by doing the imagery exercise.

When we got to the part about "Then wait for your inner guide's response," her whole facial expression changed. Her eyes stayed closed, but her forehead relaxed, and all the tension left her face, replaced by a look of peace. We processed her experience after the exercise, and she told me, "My inner guide held up a sign with only one word on it: trust." When I asked her what that meant for her, she said, "It means I need to trust myself and how I feel about my decision. And I already know I want to go into counseling." In about fifteen minutes, this student had the affirmation she needed to move forward. Her intuition spoke out loud and clear. It had been there all along, just waiting to give her the right answer.

I can't even count the number of times when I've been counseling someone and my intuition guided me to choose the most appropriate technique for that particular moment or helped me say exactly the right thing. Research indicates that in our jobs and professions, in addition to experience, intuition can and does play a major role in helping us work at our best. We may not identify it as a resource we're using, but it's often there.

2. Trust

Another step in becoming more intuitive involves trust—learning to trust your instincts. Sometimes this step becomes difficult because of all the messages we've gotten in the past about how we shouldn't trust our intuition, about how we should only rely on what's rational and fully explainable.

To counter this tendency, start by experimenting in situations that have little or no risk involved. For example, practice making predictions. Ask yourself what color clothes a coworker will wear to work tomorrow. When you're standing in the checkout line at the store—without formulating a mental tally of your purchases, just off the top of your head—ask yourself what your total bill will be. Or try this: guess the chance of precipitation in a city out of your area five days from now. Be sure to pick someplace where you have no idea what the forecast is. Then check the online weather channel and see if your prediction is accurate. This becomes like a simple game of question and answer, back and forth, but it's also a way to start noticing the differences between your accurate intuitive messages and other messages that aren't correct.

Developing trust also includes realizing how your intuition has been there in the past and that it has always been right. Think about the times when your intuition has come through for you before. You might even want to write those down. Acknowledge its previous gifts. Trust will grow as you gain more experience with your intuition and experience firsthand what an incredibly valuable asset it is in your life.

3. Act

The final step in increasing your intuitive abilities is to act on the instructions and guidance it provides. Sometimes we find we are already following many of our intuitive leads, but in this last step, we do that more deliberately and with conscious awareness. Please note that especially when you're first getting used to acting on your intuition, sometimes a "gut check" isn't enough, particularly in high-risk situations. It's always a good idea to pull in all the logical, analytical information you can find and run it past people you trust. Then watch what happens after you follow your intuition—and when you don't.

First, let's look at what frequently happens if we *don't* follow our intuitive instructions. Internally, you may have a feeling of disappointment, separation from yourself, or maybe a distant awareness that you betrayed some inner truth. In terms of external consequences, often we get a sense of somehow being stuck, maybe a need or desire for things to be different, or perhaps an obvious fact makes you regret having done the wrong thing. Sometimes there's a delay in the time it takes to get internal feedback or information back from the environment, so continue to be open to input. One student I worked with put it like this: "I learned to trust my intuition the hard way. I've found out so many times that its right, so now I *wouldn't dare* not do what it says."

Here's an everyday example. When I'm out shopping and find something I really like but am sitting on the fence about whether to buy it, I always do. I can usually take it back if I change my mind, but if I don't buy it then and go back later to try to make that purchase, inevitably I can't. The item is either sold out or no longer available in the size or color I need, or something. It's as if the Universe is giving me immediate feedback that says, "Trust your first impression—and act on it."

So what happens when we *do* allow our intuition to guide our decisions and actions? Very often you will get an increase in your energy level, almost as if your body is telling you, "Yes, you did the right thing." Sometimes there's a feeling of peace, harmony, or contentment. When you get an intuitive insight, some flash of revelation, it's frequently followed by a unique sense of "rightness," along with a certain feeling of being grounded, balanced, and centered. Even when your intuition tells you something you don't necessarily want to hear, there's an emotional "felt knowing" when you know the truth, and you know that you know.

Externally, you may notice that doors open, circumstances fall into place, and you find support for the direction you chose. Things seem to flow naturally, as if you just stepped into a current that was waiting for you all along. As if the Universe is saying, "Yes, you made the right choice." Although not always the case, that's what often happens. And even if your choice involves hard work and long hours, if your intuition guided you onto that path, it will still feel right. If you're familiar with the movie *Field of Dreams,* the line "If you build it, they will come" was a completely illogical but intuitive message to build a baseball diamond out in the middle of a cornfield. Magic happened because those intuitive instructions were followed.

Watch for both internal and external signs of confirmation after you honor your intuitive guide. These provide valuable feedback as you learn to listen, trust, and act according to that inner knowing. It's also a good idea to thank your intuition for sharing its wisdom. We all respond positively to affirmation and gratitude, and this will make it more likely for your intuition to come through for you again.

Our intuition is one of the most valuable of all our *internal* teachers. It uses our other internal teachers—like our bodies, thoughts, emotions, and dreams—to deliver messages and instructions. Developing awareness in all these aspects of your inner world will provide a wealth of information to help you progress through the school of life. This enriches your life and helps you open to the mystery and wonder of the divine play of the Universe as the living, breathing energy we're all a part of.

Intuition is the ultimate teacher when it comes to our *external* teachers as well. No one else can really teach us anything. Whether that teacher in our environment is a person, experience, place, object, nature, animal, or time, it only offers the suggestion; it only provides the stimulus. Our internal response to that stimulus is what causes us to understand. We learn through our own thoughts, perceptions, and intuitive knowing. That's why our gut checks are so important.

If we can learn the lessons about intuition, if we can begin to use that infinite reservoir of knowledge and power, we will always learn lessons from our other teachers that are accurate and correct. Lessons that are in keeping with the divine flow, that are for the highest good of all life. We will intuitively be drawn to the people, places, and experiences that can best help us learn. No one else can tell us or teach us these things.

As Ralph Waldo Emerson said, "We lie in the lap of immense intelligence. We are the receivers of its truth and the organs of its activity." One of our great privileges—and challenges—in the school of life is learning to use the unlimited power and potential we've been given. The Universe always provides the teachers we need to take our next steps. It's our responsibility to recognize, accept, and act on their directions and truth.

---

21. *Activities*

Try these suggestions for strengthening your intuition:

1. *<u>Increase your awareness.</u> Pay attention in school. Your intuition may already be giving you lots of instructions and signs that you're not noticing. For example, some illnesses, injuries, and medical conditions are intuitive messages. If you have neck problems, is there someone or something in your life who's "a pain in the neck"? Have you had a vague but persistent feeling you need to do something but haven't? Explore that. Depending on what it is, it could prevent you from getting a wake-up call—or lead to some unexpected bonanza.*

2. *<u>Identify how your intuition communicates.</u> As you increase your awareness of intuitive experiences, notice how you get messages.*

   - *Is it something physical in your body, like a funny sensation in your stomach?*
   - *Is it more emotional—a feeling that something is right or wrong?*
   - *It may be mental—visual images or auditory information that seems like a thought or sounds like a voice.*

- *Your intuition may also communicate through a combination of these three ways.*

3. <u>Up the odds you'll "get it."</u> *Although we can't make intuition happen, we can increase the chances of it showing up in our lives. We can plant a fertile field for the seeds of intuition to flourish and grow. Frances Vaughn, author of <u>Awakening Intuition</u>, suggests that this takes three conditions.*

   - <u>Relaxation.</u> *If we are tense and uptight, it makes it difficult for our intuition to get through. Be aware of your general level of tension throughout the day. Learn relaxation techniques if you need to.*

   - <u>Concentration.</u> *Learn how to quiet your mind. Meditation is the best way to do this. More on relaxation, concentration, and meditation is included in chapter 9.*

   - <u>Receptivity.</u> *Be open to intuitive messages. Welcome them into your life, even when they give you information you don't want to hear. Thank your intuition after it shares its wisdom.*

4. <u>Practice.</u> *Make predictions, keep a journal of your intuitive experiences, ask your intuition to tell you how to develop your intuitive skills, pray for intuitive guidance if you're the praying type. Also practice interpreting your intuitive messages, keeping in mind that accurate interpretation may be literal or symbolic.*

5. <u>Use guided imagery.</u> *Tape record the imagery exercise in Appendix B and use it to get direct access to your intuition. You can keep using it over and over to answer all sorts of questions. Just get the question in your head before you start, and only ask one question each time.*

6. <u>Research, read, explore.</u> *Do online searches for more information. Read this section of this book again. Read other books or resources on intuition, relaxation, concentration, and meditation. Go to a bookstore when you have some extra time and ask your intuition to guide you to the books you need, and then be open to whatever happens. Let your exploration turn into an intuitive adventure.*

Chapter 7
The How-Tos of Learning

If we're paying attention in school, staying open to the instructions the Universe provides, both from our external and internal teachers, we start to live a life filled with wonder, growth, expansion, transformation, and the advantages that come from a here-and-now, real-life adventure.

As we practice identifying our life lessons and our teachers, following their instructions to the best of our ability, we find that focusing on being a good student in the school of our lives makes it more enjoyable. And more challenging. We're present, alive, and focused—and we're more likely to run into obstacles because of our constant growth. We're covering a lot of ground, so the likelihood of running into roadblocks increases. That's a good thing. It shows that we're immersed in the journey, not watching from the safety and blandness of the bleachers.

However, getting stuck in life can rob us of our confidence and momentum, so we need resources on how to deal with that when it happens. We need to collect a set of tools we can use when we're waylaid so we don't stay stuck on the side of the road for long. Understanding the steps in the learning process becomes one of those tools.

A Model for Learning

One of the most all-encompassing models for learning, a surprisingly simple scheme that many people have found useful, is called the Conscious Competence Learning Model, which was developed by psychologist Noel Burch. Four stages of learning take us from ground zero to the top of the learning curve—from ignorance to mastery, incompetence to competence—in a continuous cycle of growth. It goes like this.

Stage 1: Unconscious Incompetence. In this first stage of learning, we don't know how to do something, but we're not aware of that. We all have blind spots in what we think we're good at; add to that the infinite number of skills we're not even aware we haven't mastered. For example, as young children, none of us knew that we didn't know how to ride a bicycle. In stage 1, **we don't know that we don't know**.

Stage 2: Conscious Incompetence. In this second stage, we become conscious or aware that we don't know how to do something. We realize we are incompetent. Sometimes our mistakes point out our inabilities, or maybe it's something we've never tried to learn. Even though it may feel uncomfortable to acknowledge our incompetence, this awareness often creates the desire to develop a new skill. For example, if we see other people riding bicycles, we almost naturally want to learn as well. Stage 2 means **we know that we don't know**.

Stage 3: Conscious Competence. The third stage of learning comes after we have mastered our newfound awareness of potential, after we have developed a new skill. We can perform the skill, but it takes practice, concentration, and conscious thought; and we may not be able to do it very well or very fast. However, we usually feel a sense of gratification and empowerment after mastering something new. We have stretched, grown, and succeeded. In stage 3, **we know that we know**.

Stage 4: Unconscious Competence. Just like riding a bike, you reach a point where you don't even have to think about it. Bicycle riding becomes an unconscious act, an automatic activity that you do without conscious awareness. In stage 4, you have completely mastered the new skill, you can perform it with efficiency and speed, and you free up your focus and energy to use in learning other things. In other words, you passed the class on how to ride a bike, graduated, and are ready to enroll in other classes. Stage 4 means **we know so well that it's unconscious**.

These four stages of learning repeat throughout our entire lives. We go from ignorance to mastery over and over as we progress through school. Because our school offers an infinite number of subjects to study, we will never run out of classes to enroll in and competencies to develop. More importantly, our potential for learning is limitless. So our job is to use discernment, to selectively pick and choose our classes so they help us learn the skills we need to fulfill the mission that is uniquely ours to complete.

After I retired from my university career, I set a goal to get in good physical shape—and stay that way. I love the way I feel when I'm fit, and I'd already learned the lesson about the importance of physical health. Because of my many past failures in being consistent with my workouts, I knew I needed to find ways to exercise that were convenient, challenging, and fun. I also knew I did great in a classroom setting, so I decided to try a number of fitness classes to see which ones I liked. Most gyms offer free introductory trial periods, so my exploration didn't cost me anything but time.

My excursions included hot yoga, Zumba, circuit training, Pilates, and a class called "Power Sculpt," a traditional barbell class that gives you a full-body workout. I decided to go with the latter two: I liked the way Pilates strengthened my core, and the Power Sculpt wasn't like anything I'd done before—a lot of fast repetitions with lighter weights to upbeat music. Both classes provided not only great workouts but also a healthy dose of humility when I found that despite my athleticism, I wasn't very good at either one.

I had recently discovered the hot yoga; before that I was in stage 1 of Unconscious Incompetence, because I didn't know that I didn't know how to do it. The same proved true with many of the exercises we did in the Power Sculpt class. I was familiar with squats, lunges, and bicep curls, but I'd never heard of kickbacks, upright rows, and reverse planks. My first class moved me into stage 2 of Conscious Incompetence, where I knew that I didn't know. With a little practice, I mastered the exercises and found myself proud to be in the third stage of Conscious Competence, although I still needed to focus to keep the proper form. Now I don't even have to think about doing the exercises. I've made it to stage 4 of Unconscious Competence and feel ready to take on more challenges. I've mastered the goals I set for myself, essentially passing the metaphorical class I enrolled in, so now I'm ready to sign up for new classes in the school of my life.

I went through this same process when I was learning how to dance. At first I didn't know that I didn't know how to dance. Then I became conscious of my incompetence. After taking dancing lessons, I became consciously competent—I could do it when I thought about it. And finally, I became unconsciously competent, where it became automatic. I mentioned this earlier when I went from **I dance to the music**, to **I am the music**, and finally, in Unconscious Competence, where **the music dances me**.

I recently read an article about Lupita Nyong'o, the actress, Oscar winner, and fashion icon. In an interview with *InStyle* magazine, she mentions her enrollment at the Yale School of Drama. In her very first class, Nyong'o was introduced to the Conscious Competence model, and since then, she has used it in learning new skills in lots of other areas of her life. She credits that class with changing her life.

One of the reasons I like this particular learning model is because it shows us a simple sequence of steps we can follow to master whatever skills we might want or need. It breaks down the learning process and takes away any sense of confusion, guilt, or shame when we don't know how to do something. Incompetence isn't a statement of our inadequacy as a person. We don't need to blame ourselves or feel defensive about it. Our incompetence simply means we need to spend more time practicing until we get it right. If we set our intention and devote enough time and energy to the process, almost without exception, we can land in Conscious Competence, knowing that we know, with one more set of skills in our toolkit of expertise.

22. *Activities*

1. *Think of an example of when you moved from stage 2 of Conscious Incompetence—knowing you didn't know how to do something—to stage 3 of Conscious Competence—knowing you knew how to do it. Maybe it was something basic, like learning to cook. (Think of another example besides cooking.) Remember the activities you did to practice enough to finally master that skill.*

   - *One example of when I moved into knowing that I knew how to do something:*

2. *Identify one skill you've learned well enough to move into stage 4 of Unconscious Competence, where you can do the skill automatically, without even thinking about it. Examples include learning to play a sport or musical instrument. Allow yourself to feel a sense of pride and satisfaction for achieving that level of mastery.*

   - *One example of something I've learned so well that my skill is automatic:*

3. *Now identify one area of your life where you're still in stage 2 of Conscious Incompetence—you know that you don't know how to do something—and you want to become competent. Then list one step you can take to master that skill.*

   - *One thing I want to learn how to do:*
   - *One step I can take to become Consciously Competent with that skill:*

Three Steps to Competence

At the age of forty-four, George Sheehan, a successful cardiologist, knew he needed new challenges in his life. He started running and eventually became a successful marathon runner and a writer for *Runner's World* magazine. Dr. Sheehan discovered he had prostate cancer when he was sixty-six and kept running and writing until his death eight years later. In a book about his life, *Did I Win? A Farewell to George Sheehan,* he wrote:

> *I still wonder whether I played this game of life well enough to win. It is so difficult to know what really mattered. It's as if all my life were spent studying for a final examination, and now I'm not sure just what was important and what wasn't. Did I win? Does any one of us know? Is there anything we have done which assures us we have passed the test? Can we be sure we did our best at whatever it was that we were supposed to do?*

Dr. Sheehan understood the metaphor about the exams and tests we're given in life. He courageously questioned the meaning of his own life, whether he used the time he was given to focus on important issues and "whatever it was that we were supposed to do." He wondered whether he did his best and gave his all.

Knowing that someday I could be in the same position as Dr. Sheehan, questioning whether I used my lifetime wisely, makes me even more determined to become a better student of life *now*. The Conscious Competence learning model gives me some of the puzzle pieces, but where I tend to get stuck is going from stage 2 to stage 3 in the learning model, going from knowing that I'm incompetent to knowing that I'm competent.

As the former director of a university learning center, it was my job to understand how students learn, along with the factors that contribute to when they don't. Add to that my own curiosity and resolution to figure out the minute details of the learning process, and I was in an ideal position to observe my own efforts and vicariously learn by observing and working with the thousands of students who were in and out of our office. In fact, those students became some of my best teachers. And what they taught me reinforced my own observations about how the breakdown in learning most often occurs between Conscious Incompetence and Conscious Competence, between knowing you don't know, learning the lesson, and then knowing that you know.

So what actually happens between those two stages? You can divide it into three steps: (1) awareness, (2) skill development, and (3) application.

Step 1: Awareness is where we become aware, first of all, that there is *something* we need to learn. The Universe grabs our attention in whatever way that happens, and somehow we know that we don't know. Next, we become aware of *what* exactly it is that the Universe is trying to teach us. We identify the specific class we need to take, like the one on how to ride a bike. In this first step of awareness, we are dealing strictly with the mind—with thinking, insight, and understanding.

Step 2: Skill development requires us to either access our natural abilities to be competent at something new or take the time to develop a new skill. If the lessons are in an area where we already have some strengths or innate talents, this step may be short and straightforward. Skill development can also take longer and involve more complex and challenging learning, because many of our lessons require us to change our behavior before we can pass the tests. In order to complete this step, we often need to develop behavioral skills we didn't have before. We need to be able to *do* something different.

Step 3: Application is where we apply what we have learned to our everyday life experiences. In step 2, we're developing our skills, and we might be able to ride our bikes well enough to go up and down the driveway. In step 3—application—we would have the skills to ride out on the street, back and forth to the store, and wherever else we wanted to go. We are consciously competent because we know how to ride a bike well, and we know that we know. At times, we may still have to focus and think about it, but we can pass most if not all the tests on bicycle riding. Successfully learning a life lesson means we can pass the tests that life presents with accuracy and consistency. We do it right pretty much every time.

I have such fond memories of Thanksgiving and Christmas when I was growing up, including the twice-a-year meals of turkey and dressing, specialty side dishes, homemade rolls, and, of course, the traditional pumpkin pie. It was good food and good fellowship, marred only by the uncomfortable, bloated feeling that inevitably comes from overeating and makes you want to just lie down and take a nap. It wasn't until I was in graduate school that I finally said, "Enough!" and made a decision not to overindulge in the holiday goodies, thereby saving myself from that sickly feeling of too much food at one time. That awareness and decision started me on a long road of learning about moderation in its myriad variations.

How many of us have learned the lesson on moderation within the context of taking care of our bodies? How many times have we found that when we overeat or don't eat enough, if we sleep too little or too much, when we go overboard with exercise or don't do enough, we end up feeling bad?

Learning the lesson on how not to overeat at holiday meals came relatively easy for me, although I realize it can be extremely difficult for others. Once I had the awareness, I applied a skill I'd already developed and was able to consistently pass the tests that came up every Thanksgiving and Christmas. To do this, I used a counseling technique that is similar to how I use anticipated regret, which I mentioned earlier. With this technique, in your imagination, you project yourself into the future so you can experience the consequences of your decision before the fact. For example, before you overindulge, ask yourself, "What will happen if I overeat? What will that look like? How will I feel? How will I feel after half an hour? How will I feel in the long run—tomorrow, next week, next month? How will I feel physically, and how will I feel about myself emotionally?" All I needed to do was imagine how awful I would feel in thirty minutes if I had one more serving of the green-bean casserole or ate that one last roll, and I could say, "No, thank you," to myself and others.

Learning the lesson on moderation when it comes to sleep and exercise has been a completely different story. If I put myself on a strict, nonnegotiable exercise schedule, I do fine, but I've probably needed to learn the lesson about how there's no substitute for a good, hard workout well over a hundred times. And I still have to stay vigilant in order to get enough sleep at night. All of us are different in terms of where we're likely to get stuck.

When I don't exercise and don't sleep enough, my energy level is low, and my body feels "off." When we get stuck on any lesson, however, we may also end up feeling bad emotionally, feeling that we have somehow failed, knowing on some level we are stuck in the same classroom going over the same material yet one more time. I know a lot of people who struggle with their weight—have for years—and feel bad about themselves because they haven't somehow managed to get past that issue.

In the school of life, there are possible hazardous areas or danger zones in the process of learning our lessons, places where a lot of people hit an impasse. One of the most common hazards is a belief about step 1, about awareness. People think that once they understand what the lesson is, once they know *what* to change in order to move on, then they *should* be able to change their behavior right away, immediately, overnight. If this doesn't happen, then they criticize and berate themselves for not moving directly from insight to applied action.

But many, many times in learning our lessons, **insight is not enough.** Just because you understand something doesn't mean you can immediately *do* it differently. Behavior change may require a totally different set of skills than does developing insight and understanding. With some lessons, behavioral skill development is a difficult, complex, and lengthy process, which requires patience, training, practice, and support over a long period of time. Successful and sustained weight management is often a case in point.

If you currently know of a lesson you need to learn but haven't been able to apply it in your life yet, be kind to yourself. Beyond not being helpful, self-criticism tends to damage your self-esteem and dig you deeper into a rut. The Universe is trying to help us learn and move on. We can facilitate this process by remaining aware and alert to the next set of instructions. We may feel bad, but life isn't punishing us, and we don't need to punish ourselves. Besides, our guilt trips and self-criticism take energy, and we can use that same energy to figure out our lessons and move on.

---

23. *Activities*

1. *Identify one area of your life where you're stuck, even though you understand what you need to do to get unstuck. Common areas include diet, weight, and exercise. Then ask yourself these questions:*

   - *"Do I feel guilty or bad about myself for not getting past this, especially because of the insight I have about my situation?"*
   - *If so, then ask, "In looking back on this situation, has my guilt been helpful? Has it helped me find a solution to this issue and move forward?"*

2. *Whenever you find that you're feeling guilty or bad about yourself, ask:*

   - *What's the lesson or lessons I need to learn?*

Your lesson may involve getting more information so you can figure out a solution. It may mean learning a whole new set of behavioral skills, which could take training, practice, time, and patience. You may need to get support from someone else, like a trusted friend, family member, life coach, or therapist.

Also, be open to the instructions you might receive from external and internal teachers. And remember that continuing to do what you've always done will probably not result in a different outcome, so be willing to try new options. We'll look at this more in chapter 8.

Your Learning Style

After I burned out doing personal counseling, a series of coincidences helped me find a job as an academic advisor in a university athletics program. I still got to work with college students, which I loved, but the one-on-one interaction of advising wasn't nearly as intense or draining. Because of my background in counseling and my work with learning disabilities, coaches and other staff often referred student-athletes to me who were struggling, either with their classes or in some other way. I screened them for learning problems and other personal concerns.

Bryan was referred to me by his head coach, who was frustrated and confused by his behavior. A top recruit out of high school, Bryan was quickly becoming known as "uncoachable" in his freshman year, which was pretty unusual in Division I athletics. By the time they're recruited, high-school athletes have usually been watched and evaluated for several years. They want to do well in their sport, because it means playing time, scholarships, recognition, and possibly a coveted chance to play professionally. Motivation is rarely an issue.

"Bryan won't listen to me," the coach explained. "I tell him to do something, and he just looks at me with this blank stare. I don't know if he's stubborn and doesn't want to do what I tell him, or if he can't do it."

When I talked with Bryan about his coach's concerns, he was also baffled by what was going on. He wasn't able to explain his behavior, except to say, "I did fine in high school. I don't know why it's so hard. I'm trying." Something about the way Bryan said "I'm trying" told me he was truly shaken by his inability to perform. I referred him to a learning specialist for testing that very day.

One of the tests Bryan took evaluated his learning style and how he learned best. It measured three different styles: **auditory**, **visual**, and **kinesthetic**. If you're an auditory learner, you learn best with information you get through your ears—by hearing it. Visual learners do best when they can see what they're learning. And kinesthetic learners need to process new information through some kind of movement or physical activity.

The results of Bryan's testing gave us the answers we needed. The learning styles test showed that Bryan had an extremely weak auditory channel, which meant that information coming through his ears was especially hard for him to process. So no matter how many times his coach *told* him to do something, it didn't sink in. Although his visual channel was stronger than his auditory skills, Bryan was also not a strong visual learner, so watching another player wasn't the best way for him to learn. By far, Bryan's strength lay in his ability to learn by *doing*—kinesthetic learning. His previous coaches used activities when working with their players, so Bryan did great all the way through high school. His learning difficulties only showed up in his sport when he got to college, where there was a different coaching style.

After sharing the results of Bryan's tests with him and his coach, with a slight modification to the coaching techniques, we saw remarkable improvements. The coach would ask another player to demonstrate a new skill, and Bryan would watch and perform the new skill at the same time. This allowed him to use his two strongest learning channels—kinesthetic and visual. Knowing that he needed to *do* something to learn new information, I also gave Bryan tips for how to improve his learning in the classroom, like highlighting important material, taking notes, and using flash cards. No one was happier than Bryan when he also started getting better grades.

One of the most noticeable results was what this newfound learning style did for Bryan's self-confidence. It's tough for many high-school athletes to go from being a big fish in a little pond to being such a small fish in a typical Division I athletics program. They're no longer the star player or the center of attention, and to make matters even worse, they often warm the bench their freshman year. Bryan had actually done fine with that transition, but feeling like he couldn't please his coach was hard on him. With his newly discovered learning style and a different coaching method, Bryan could more than meet his coach's expectations, and he started to really shine. You could tell he felt better about himself; he stood up taller, moved with more self-assurance, and had a brighter light in his eyes.

Do you know your learning style and how you learn best? The questionnaire in Appendix C is the same one Bryan took. I've given it to hundreds and hundreds of college students, and almost without exception, they've told me their results are both accurate and surprisingly helpful.

I've found that most people have a fairly good understanding of their learning strengths and weaknesses. I've taken this particular questionnaire several times over the years, and my scores reflect what I already knew: my greatest strength is visual, followed by kinesthetic, and then auditory. Writing requires both visual and kinesthetic involvement. It's not that I'll never forget, but I'm much more likely to remember something when I write it down. The life lesson—the practical wisdom in knowing this—is that I need to incorporate my strengths into all my learning experiences.

For example, one time I had a supervisor who would try to teach me new computer skills by *telling* me what to do, which was using the auditory channel—my weakest. Once I realized what was going on, I asked if we could restructure our training sessions. So we started hopping onto a computer where I could *see* the screens and actually *do* the different steps as my supervisor talked me through them. That one minor change made a huge difference. After I physically went through the steps on the computer, if they were especially complex, I would also write them down. At that point, I usually felt competent, at least enough so that I could start using the new skills to get my work done. If I got stuck, I just referred back to my notes.

When I taught university orientation classes, I always helped the freshmen identify their learning styles. I wanted them to know how they learned at the beginning of their college careers so they could use that information all the way through school—and life. One time several faculty members attended my class on the day I was giving the questionnaire, so I suggested that they complete the checklist along with the students. After scoring their responses, I asked if they would share their personal styles with the class. One faculty member taught foreign languages, and guess what her style was? Yes, auditory. She had an excellent ability to learn through her ears. Another faculty member was an accomplished athlete and taught in the kinesiology department (which used to be called physical education). She wasn't surprised to find that she was a kinesthetic learner and said the best way for her to memorize new information was by holding the material while walking back and forth, pacing the floor. Sometimes she would rock in a rocking chair. In other words, she intuitively figured out how to use her strongest learning channel by *doing* something while she learned.

Students in my graduate classes often asked if they could have extra copies of the questionnaire so they could give it to a spouse, child, or friend. It can be interesting to compare your learning style with others, and the results can definitely help with communication, like we saw with Bryan. I encourage you to keep your learning strengths in mind and use those to your advantage whenever you are in a learning situation. In general, it's a good idea to use all three channels when learning something new, so you hear the information, see it, and get actively involved. For instance, you can skim or quickly read much of your reading material. However, if you're reading highly detailed material that you need to remember, read it out loud. That uses your eyes and ears, and the movement in your mouth and throat is enough to provide kinesthetic input.

Country singer Carrie Underwood has learned the words to hundreds of songs. During an interview several years ago, Underwood said she figured out while still in high school that she learns best through writing. Now, when she needs to learn a new song, she will write out the lyrics. She stated, "I can't just read it and remember it. I have to be a part of it, like see it, hear it, feel it, write it."

This same strategy holds true for all of us. Although we have individual strengths and weaknesses in the ways that we learn, we enhance our learning by taking in material through all three channels. Doing this can make a big difference in how quickly and how well we learn something, so we're more likely to remember it later.

I hope you will take a few minutes and complete the questionnaire in Appendix C. It's called the Sensory Modality Checklist, and it includes the instructions for scoring. There are no right or wrong answers, just what you prefer. Please note that you give a three to the answer that is *most* typical for you, and give a one to the answer that is *least* typical for you. Additional suggestions on how to use your learning strengths are included in the following activities.

---

24. *Activities*

One of the more helpful lessons in the school of life is knowing your learning style. Even if you think you already know how you learn best, take a few minutes to complete the checklist in Appendix C. Use the instructions provided to add up your responses and determine your strongest learning modality. Then consider the following suggestions.

Suggestions for Learning

<u>Auditory Learners</u>: read out loud; recite material out loud; tape record talks and lectures (with permission) and then listen again; talk with others about what you're learning; use study groups; teach someone else; put new material to songs you already know; take music breaks.

<u>Visual Learners</u>: write things down; outline reading material; examine any charts and diagrams; rewrite your notes; use flash cards; use visual imagery (mentally picture what you're learning);

use color to code material (e.g., highlight similar material in the same color).

<u>Kinesthetic Learners:</u> incorporate physical activities into your learning, like highlighting and taking notes; use flash cards; move your finger under words when reading detailed or difficult material; read out loud; teach or present the material you are studying to a friend; study in a rocking chair or while walking; actually go through the motions when learning physical activities.

After you find out what learning style you prefer, make a mental note to remember to use it when you're learning something new. Using your strong suit makes it easier for you to learn; using all three channels—auditory, visual, and kinesthetic—works best. That's why when I teach classes, I always find ways to have students use their ears, eyes, and some kind of physical movement to learn the material. You can do the same when you're helping another person learn.

Now, let's move on to the next chapter to find out how to deal with those inevitable obstacles in the school of life that, paradoxically, can become some of our best teachers.

Chapter 8
Turning Obstacles into Teachers

I'm a recovering procrastinator. I used to drag my feet with the best of them, pulling off unbelievable feats in the final hour. For example, I would piddle around the house before I needed to leave for an appointment, fly into a frenzy to finally get dressed and out the door, and show up at my meeting with *maybe* three minutes to spare. I'd wait until the last second to pay my bills and marvel at how I always made it on time. One of my more over-the-top experiences was when I was a dirt-poor graduate student. I had to use my laundry quarters to put just enough gas in my car to drive to the bank, make a deposit, and beat a check I'd already written before it hit my account.

Nothing caused me any serious negative consequences, except for the crazy amounts of unnecessary stress. But my behavior was definitely a pattern. During that time, a good friend said to me, "LG, you run your life like you're going to a house afire." That's what my procrastination looked like to her.

The Universe has interesting ways of trying to help us learn our lessons. After completing my graduate coursework, I did a predoctoral internship that included—would you believe—teaching a class on procrastination. That's when I learned that some procrastinators just need to be taught time management techniques, and then they are fine. I refer to another group as "hard core," because they will continue to delay despite knowing how to manage their time and regardless of severe negative results. These include people who create conflict in their personal relationships by stalling on their promises to others, those who get demoted or even fired from jobs for missing their deadlines, and the many people who put off personal health issues until something major comes along.

I discovered my own hard-core procrastination streak when I started my first full-time job after graduate school. I continued with my pattern of barely making it to meetings on time. Knowing that the meetings wouldn't actually start until five minutes after they were scheduled, I systematically made it a habit of showing up five minutes late, just as the meetings began. I always felt guilty, and I knew my behavior was not only unprofessional but downright rude. Still, I couldn't seem to change. No one on our staff said anything to me, but I could feel their silent awareness and nonverbal questioning each time I walked in late.

One day, after making my usual tardy entrance, my guilt finally forced me to seriously ask myself, "Why are you always late?" My response surprised me and made me feel embarrassed and exposed. The answer came from deep within: "Because it feels powerful."

So that was it. My chronic lateness gave me a sense of power in an environment where I didn't always feel that way. I was working harder than I ever had. I was giving my coworkers my all and then some, and showing up late was my immature way of asserting my power and independence. I might have to go to the meetings, but I would do it on my own time.

Figuring out the benefits of being tardy opened a door for me to examine the other ways I procrastinated and look for the built-in rewards. For example, my last-minute efforts to pay my bills gave me an exciting rush, wondering if I would make it by the due date. That rush was caused by adrenaline, and it finally dawned on me that I was addicted to my own adrenaline, which is the fight-or-flight stress hormone. No wonder I felt energized and even high when I pulled off some feat in the eleventh hour. I could also end up feeling like a hero when I succeeded. Because my timing was almost always right, that wonder-woman feeling of success became my normal way of life, along with the habits and behaviors that caused it.

In looking back at my experiences with procrastination, I sometimes still feel astounded at what an amazing teacher it became. It taught me that procrastinating created excitement in my life. We all want a certain amount of excitement now and then. It taught me I wanted to feel powerful. We all want and need a sense of power. I felt a sense of personal power when I met my deadlines. I was also trying to create that feeling by having power and control over other people. That didn't work. I needed to learn how to feel powerful within me because of my competencies, successes, and the ways I could help others. That's *empowerment*, which is distinctively different from power or control over others.

So now I make sure I keep excitement and a sense of empowerment built into my lifestyle. But they come from healthy, constructive activities—not my stress-producing inner drama. I no longer need procrastination for the rewards it provided, and it's very rarely a problem anymore. In fact, I try hard to avoid the kinds of situations I used to create with my procrastination, because

I don't like those stressed-out, anxious feelings. Instead, I've found that hitting my deadlines early feels empowering and provides a new and exhilarating kind of healthy high.

So what kinds of obstacles are you dealing with? These could be i*nternal obstacles*, like my procrastination, ***external obstacles***, or both. Do you have inner conflicts that create unnecessary stress in your life, like my procrastination did? Maybe you're in a constant battle with your weight or struggle with physical fitness and regular exercise. Do you face external roadblocks, like not enough time or money? Maybe you dream about a different life altogether, a life where you feel happy and fulfilled, but it remains a distant dream. Whatever is getting in the way of you living that dream can become your teacher to help you get there.

As a personal counselor, I spent decades listening to people's personal stories. These were the kinds of stories we usually don't talk about in everyday conversations. They shared their pain, sadness, and frustration caused by the problems in their lives. They talked about their unhappiness, because their lives weren't the way they wanted them to be. Maybe they had goals they wanted to attain, but something always got in the way. Sometimes their frustration came from feeling lost and uncertain about which goals to choose or which direction to take. Some of them appeared to be successful by anyone's account, but they didn't feel any real joy in their lives. Most of us have gone through similar periods in our lives. Those times can become our teachers, prompting us to learn our lessons, pass the tests, and get on with the next adventure.

Hazardous Zones

After hearing thousands of stories about problems from clients, and after observing my own life and the lives of others, I began to see common obstacles where people got stuck. Those obstacles showed up so regularly in people's lives that I could frequently predict that people would run into specific issues at certain times. Not always, but often. That meant I could warn them about what to watch out for so they didn't stumble or fall. It meant they didn't always have to repeat a class in the school of life in order to pass the exams and move on.

I started calling those obstacles **hazardous zones.** Just like when you're driving in your car, and you see road signs warning you of construction or danger up ahead, certain events in life carry metaphorical signs to pay attention so you don't have a wreck or end up stranded on the side of the road. The following obstacles often say "Caution" or "Hazard Ahead":

1. Time management. You set a goal and then find out you don't have enough time to accomplish it. This hazardous zone is so common that I will address it in depth later in this chapter.

2. Procrastination. This is a variation on time management, but the reasons we procrastinate can be different. More discussion follows in the section on procrastination.

3. Limiting beliefs. Our unconscious beliefs probably stop more of us from achieving success and greatness than any other single cause. This internal obstacle deserves special attention, which I include at the end of this chapter.

4. Fear. It's a well-known fact that as humans, we're afraid of the unknown. We tend to cling to what we know, even if it makes us unhappy, because jumping into uncertainty often feels like a much worse fate. That means a part of us is afraid of change, because who knows where it will lead? Yet life is about change, so we often end up on this teeter-totter, going back and forth between seeking change and avoiding it.

But there's another aspect to our fear, one that's often more subtle. Our fear frequently keeps us trapped in small dreams and limited visions. Who are we to think too big? And if we so dare, will fear stop us from acting on the magnitude of those dreams? Our fear can become one of our most powerful teachers if we learn how to break it down into small pieces and extract the wisdom it provides. That's what I did with my procrastination. The same process can be used with any obstacle on your path.

5. Stress. With change comes stress. Even when change seems positive, like marriage or a job promotion, it puts demands on us to adapt, and those demands can cause stress. Then there are those of us who create all kinds of unnecessary stress by our inner conflicts and poor choices. Techniques on how to manage stress are included in chapter 9.

6. Unhealthy boundaries. In an earlier part of this book, we looked at the life lesson on moderation: finding a balance between overeating and not eating enough, sleeping too much or too little, overexercising or not doing enough. All of these extremes make us feel bad. They represent ***internal boundaries***, limits we need to set for ourselves. We can identify myriad other examples where we need to set healthy internal boundaries, like with drinking, working, or the amount of time spent on our tech devices. Any activity can be done to excess with negative results, and our extremes may turn into addictions. We can also get lost in our desires, allowing our unbridled thoughts to place too much value on money, status, power, or other goals. These excessive, out-of-balance thoughts can cause us to forsake our authenticity and purpose in life.

Unhealthy boundaries can also wreak havoc in our interpersonal relationships. These represent issues with **external boundaries**. Many of us have gotten involved with someone whose dysfunction jeopardized our equilibrium, even if just for a short time. It's the friend who becomes too needy or demanding. Couples sometimes get caught in the destructive dynamics of their interaction, and neither one is able to set the kinds of boundaries that would make their relationship better. We see it with bullying on the Internet, in schools, and in the workplace. Financial scams victimize people where they sometimes feel the most vulnerable. We watch as people try to set boundaries and protect themselves from someone else's intrusions. It goes on every day, and it can keep us stuck in the school of life until we learn the lessons that healthy boundaries have to offer. Unfortunately, sometimes those intrusions are unavoidable.

7. Sacrificing our authenticity. It happens so often. We want to please others, so we become who we think they want us to be. We do the things others want us to do. We let others dictate who we are and how we act, trying desperately to be someone we're not.

Sometimes others come right out and tell us how to live our lives. A less obvious version of this comes from social psychology and is called *impression management*. That's where you try to control how others see you by doing the things you *assume* will impress them. Our efforts leave us living in a fantasy world of assumptions. Instead of striving to live from our authentic core, we jump onto a path of trying to figure out who others want us to be. Then we spend inordinate amounts of time and energy attempting to become that person. In the process, we lose ourselves and what makes us special and unique.

Another way we sacrifice our authenticity is in comparing ourselves to others. When we compare, we end up feeling like we're better than or worse than someone else. Either way, our judgments create distance in our relationships. Instead of applauding others and cheering them on, we become competitive. This process of judging ourselves in comparison to others impedes our own progress because it takes our focus away from doing our best and running our own race. A healthy competitive spirit certainly has its place, but not when our goal becomes beating the other person instead of doing what's ours to do.

8. Learned helplessness. Psychologist Martin Seligman did a number of laboratory experiments with dogs. Some were given electrical shocks but were allowed to escape. Others were shocked but could not escape. The second group of dogs became passive and gave up. In subsequent experiments, the passive dogs were allowed to easily escape the shocks, but they did nothing. They had learned not to even try.

Seligman called this concept *learned helplessness*. He realized how people also learn to be helpless based on their previous experiences and how that often creates problems later in their lives.

Seligman struggled with the ethics of his experiments and felt determined to use the results of his work for good. He now offers a message of hope: based on his research, he published a book called *Learned Optimism: How to Change Your Mind and Your Life*. Just as we can learn to be helpless, we can also learn to be optimistic.

One example of this comes from chapter 5 on internal teachers, the part about emotions. We looked at how many children are discouraged from expressing their emotions, especially what we consider negative emotions like anger, fear, jealousy, and hurt. Those around them often respond to their feelings with things like "Don't be scared" or "Big boys don't cry." As a result, many of us grow up not knowing how to deal with our feelings. We've learned to ignore them or pretend they aren't there, only to have them spill over into our lives in unhealthy ways, like through stress, illnesses, or addictions. In other words, we learn to be helpless when it comes to expressing our feelings, and our helplessness often becomes a debilitating hazardous zone. That same chapter also includes suggestions for healthy emotional expression.

We can learn helplessness simply by observing others around us. For instance, if no one in our family or close circle of friends shows us how to get motivated, take on realistically challenging goals, and succeed at those goals, we may vicariously learn that same helpless pattern. By observing others, we may adopt unhealthy attitudes like pessimism, or perhaps we blame others for our failures rather than take responsibility for our own actions. We may learn to see our obstacles as adversaries, enemies to struggle and fight with, rather than perceiving them as a normal part of life and something to work through.

Learned helplessness is different from the fear we covered under the fourth hazardous zone. We're not afraid to think big and move forward. Instead, based on our past experiences, we honestly believe we can't or won't succeed, so why bother to try? Like the dogs in Seligman's experiments, we become resigned to our lot in life and passively accept the perceived limitations that come with it.

9. Ignoring intuition. In chapter 6, we explored the phenomenal gift of intuition and the many advantages it offers us as students in the school of life. It takes practice to learn how to use this natural instinct, and it's common to ignore or miss some of the wisdom it provides. We need to experiment with listening to our inner voice and trusting that gut feeling when we "just know." Developing the courage to act on our internal guidance often becomes a lifelong pursuit, because you can always fine-tune your skills. But when we do, we open the door to a powerhouse of opportunities.

10. Inadequate goal-setting skills. I've taught goal setting to hundreds of people, and it always surprises me how many of them start out with goals that are unrealistic. Maybe they set a goal to exercise more. When I ask them to get specific, they say, "I want to work out six days a week." When I ask them how many days they're currently working out, they'll reply with something like "One" or "None."

That's just one example of how people can unknowingly set themselves up for failure. We don't typically change overnight. It sometimes happens, but we don't normally go from zero to sixty just because we set a goal to dramatically change our behavior. Learning new habits usually takes time and practice. We need to nurture ourselves along the way, setting small baby steps until we can successfully pull off something like a goal to exercise six days a week, especially if we want to sustain it over time. A more realistic goal would be to exercise two days a week, then modify and fine-tune your approach to your goal based on any interferences that come up when you try to achieve it.

Goal setting can also become difficult until we figure out that *insight is not always enough*. This hazard was mentioned earlier. We think our insight will automatically result in behavior change. If it doesn't, we may feel frustrated and incompetent.

For example, let's say you want to go to bed earlier so you can get more sleep. You have good insight about what will result in more sleep, which is an earlier bedtime. It's easy, right? Maybe not. You may need to figure out a host of other issues in order to make that happen, like adjusting schedules with others in your household, restricting your caffeine intake later in the day, figuring out the best time to exercise, and shutting off your tech devices shortly after dinner. Sometimes behavior change requires a whole lot more than insight.

Another way I often see people get off track with setting goals relates to fear. Yes, they want to change, but no, they don't want to change. Often, people are afraid of the consequences of what will happen if they change, so instead, they sit tight and stay stuck.

I used to teach assertiveness training through weekly group sessions. Each week, participants were asked to set a goal on how they planned to be assertive outside the group. Part of our training involved identifying what are called "stoppers"—the beliefs and fears people had about becoming more assertive. Maybe they thought others wouldn't like them or would see them as aggressive instead of assertive. Or perhaps they were afraid of upsetting the balance of power that kept a relationship intact. Sometimes the stoppers they mentioned seemed highly unlikely to ever happen, but nonetheless, they were very real in the minds of the participants.

Once the group members identified their stoppers, we looked at whether they were willing to risk those negative consequences in order to move forward. Almost every single time, they felt it was worth the risk. And many more times than not, their fears never materialized. However, if you don't identify your fears or stoppers, you may end up caught in the ambivalence of wanting change but avoiding it.

Solid goal setting skills are a must if you want to make significant changes in your life. There are so many ways we can run amuck when we set out to change specific aspects of our thoughts, behaviors, and habits. Yet that kind of change is required of us if we want to make our dreams come true.

Chapter 10 contains an entire section on goal setting. It includes structured activities so you can start practicing with your own personal goals.

---

25. *Activities*

The ten hazardous zones we just reviewed often create obstacles as we try to move forward in the school of life. But there's good news. Obstacles can be friends or foes, depending on how we deal with them.

Based on your life as it stands today, respond to the following:

1. *Identify one of the ten hazardous zones that is currently holding you back. It could be an obstacle like fear (e.g., fear of change) or unhealthy boundaries (e.g., too little sleep, too much time on social media). Write down at least one obstacle.*

   - *One obstacle I'm currently dealing with is*
   - *Then ask, what rewards could my obstacle be providing?*

It's important to be honest here. For example, I didn't want to admit my procrastination made me feel powerful, but it was an essential piece in figuring out how to stop it.

- *Look at the built-in rewards and identify a healthy way you can include that reward in your life. I needed to find constructive ways to feel a sense of empowerment in order to stop dragging my feet.*

One healthy reward I could start to include in my life in place of the unhealthy reward is

- *Especially if you have difficulty identifying the reward(s) your obstacle provides, also ask, What lesson or lessons is my obstacle trying to help me learn?"*

   2. *If you're dealing with additional obstacles, go through these same steps for each one. Figure out the reward(s) and find healthy ways to incorporate them into your life. Also answer this question:*

      - *What lesson or lessons are my obstacles trying to help me learn?*

Time Management

Imagine that someone tells you that you will be given $10,000 if you read a short book and write a report on it within the next two weeks. All in all, the reading and writing will take you about ten hours to complete. The assignment isn't hard; it will just take time. You can't miss any work (or school if you're a student), you can't cut back on your sleep, and you have to keep up with all your other priorities. Would you be able to find the time?

When I asked this question to students in my university classes, almost every hand went up. Of course, they would find the time. If the rewards were high enough, most of us would figure it out.

We would suddenly get creative. We would rearrange our schedules. We would quit fiddling around with things that weren't important. And we would get faster at doing our daily chores, finding ways to shave time off our routine tasks.

So what's the point of this example? As untenable as it may sound, I contend that *a part of us already knows how to manage our time more effectively.* We've probably already learned about time management techniques that would help us become more productive, but we often don't act on those. I also believe we intuitively know how to better use our time, but many of us don't listen to or act on that internal advice. So you may be able to manage your time better right this minute. You may already have the techniques or the intuitive creativity to pull that off. What may be missing is the right reward, a more compelling incentive to get you motivated. So in this section, let's talk about techniques *and* motivation.

Left- versus Right-Brain Techniques

Technically, we don't manage time. Instead, we manage ourselves in relationship to time and call it time management. That being said, advice for how to better manage your time is readily available in books, online, and through seminars and various types of training, especially in the business world. I've found that most of the material is written by those we think of as left-brain dominant, people who thrive in a world that is organized, logical, and structured. It comes from their linear, sequential thinking—*A* leads to *B*, which then leads to *C*. Living much of their lives according to a well-planned schedule feels perfectly normal to them. Those kinds of techniques work well for a lot of folks, but they're not effective for everyone.

People we think of as right-brain dominant often live in a world that is more creative, intuitive, spontaneous, and go-with-the-flow. Sometimes these more "artsy" free spirits rebel against structure and need to find more organic ways to get things done, ways that feel more natural for them.

Recent research on brain dominance has debunked our long-standing beliefs about how the two hemispheres of our brains work. As it turns out, all of us use both the left and the right sides of our brains for most tasks. However, the distinction can still be helpful when we look at our own characteristics and how we typically get things done.

Do you identify more with left-brain dominance? Do you work well within a structured schedule, find comfort in rituals and habits, and love the feeling of control in knowing exactly when you will get something accomplished?

Or are you more of a right-brain, go-with-the-flow person who doesn't like to be pinned down by lots of scheduled activities? You may get as much or more done as the left-brain folks, but your world unfolds in a looser structure rather than fitting into time segments on a calendar.

Most of us use a combination of left- and right-brain strategies to accomplish our goals and get the results we want. But it's helpful to know your preferred style when experimenting with new techniques.

Intuition and Intention

Intuition is an incredibly powerful right-brain technique for managing your time. Yet very little of the time management material I've seen looks at the role that intuition can play in helping us use our time more wisely. In fact, it can be one of our greatest tools if we can learn to tap into the advice it has to offer. If you've ever been faced with a short, unexpected deadline, you may have unknowingly benefited from the creative, intuitive guidance that's always there—and not realized you were using it.

Another right-brain technique you rarely see in the time management literature has to do with intention. We previously discussed the astounding potential of this readily available resource, which is free for the taking. In many cases, it works in tandem with our intuition when we get inspired to complete a project that's important to us. Not only do we benefit from our own creativity, but "all of Providence moves" to assist with the pieces we can't control, helping us to achieve extraordinary results in almost unbelievably short amounts of time.

I've watched couples juggle multiple jobs, child care, and sometimes also care for their own parents, and I've marveled at how they manage to cram so much into twenty-four hours. I usually assume that their intention is to do their absolute best for the sake of their families, and that whatever-it-takes commitment, combined with their creative inner guidance, allows them to achieve close to superhuman feats.

The Role of Motivation

Remember the $10,000 question at the beginning of this section? If you have a powerful motivator, the how-tos of time management often fall into place. You'll do whatever it takes to get something done, which often calls intuition and intention into play.

One of my good friends tended to be a workaholic like me, working well past the forty hours a week required for her job. She tried to cut back but found it difficult.

Then she had her first child. Presto. The workaholism went away, and she left the office on time, every time. Her child became her motivation, and it forced her to become more efficient at work, creating a much healthier work/life balance. She probably had the knowledge of how to cut back all along. It just took the right motivation for her to act on that.

So what motivates you to get more done? What lights your fire? What gives you energy just thinking about it and makes you want to do whatever it takes to accomplish it? That passion, that aliveness, that deep-seated, heartfelt commitment will help motivate you to find the time management techniques to make it happen.

Because here's the deal. In all my years of teaching time management to all kinds of people, I've found that no one can tell you *exactly* how to better manage your time. People can give you strategies that work great for them and other people, but you still need to try out those strategies to see if they work for you. Having a compelling incentive, a reward you're willing to work hard for, makes the process a whole lot easier. It gives you the energy and motivation to keep going until you discover the specific techniques that help you to get more done.

What Works for Me

I'm motivated to learn how to make good use of my time, because I don't want to get to the end of my life and regret the fact that I didn't complete my purpose for being here in the first place. Above all, time becomes my teacher, offering me instructions every day as I try to get better at managing myself. On occasion, time seems unrelenting. The ticking of the clock never ends. When my self-management is going well, time feels like a comfortable and predictable friend, assuring me that I'm on track, making progress, certain to reach my goals, and enjoying the ride. In addition to seeing time as my teacher, here are my favorite, tried-and-true techniques. They may also work for you.

1. Use intuition. We explored ways to access your intuitive potential in chapter 6. It might be helpful to use the guided-imagery activity in Appendix B and start by asking your intuition, "How can I make better use of my time?" Modify the question if you need to.

2. Tap into intention. Once you set your sights on what you want, make a 100 percent, no-holds-barred commitment to achieve it. Let your emotional enthusiasm, cognitive clarity, and physical efforts work together to create an end result. In doing so, you will invite the Universe to join you to provide the necessary resources and take care of the details that are out of your control.

3. Keep to-do lists. I don't like a lot of unnecessary clutter in my head, and I don't like having to remember things that could just as easily go on a to-do list. So I keep several lists: one for shopping, one for things I need to get done that are out of the ordinary (like finding a new pet sitter), and other lists for goals and miscellaneous tasks that I want to make sure I complete. For me, they work. I rarely miss deadlines or fail to follow through on commitments. Plus, it's really rewarding when I get to cross the completed items off my lists. I love it! One of the tricks is to keep your lists where you will see them so they will remind you of what needs to get done next. Some people keep everything in their phone, some use a tablet or computer, others use hard-copy lists. Find what works for you.

4. Prioritize. At times, our to-do lists get long and somewhat overwhelming. We obviously can't do everything all at once, so we need to prioritize. Different strategies for prioritizing are readily available in books. For example, you can use numbers, letters, or Roman numerals. I like to use letters, where you identify your most important tasks as *A* goals, the items with medium value as *B* goals, and the least valuable tasks as *C* goals. Sometimes the *C* goals naturally drop off your lists over time without having to complete them. The point is to finish your most valuable *A* goals first. In other words, "Work your *A*'s off."

Once you prioritize your lists, then you can use what's called the "80/20 rule." This principle says that 80 percent of the value comes from doing 20 percent of the work. So for example, if you have a to-do list with ten items, you can get 80 percent of the value of all the items by doing the two that are the most important. If you can complete your top priority items first, then you get to ride the wave of good feelings that come from making substantial progress. Be sure to review your priorities regularly; they often change over time.

5. Set long- and short-term goals. So how do you identify your *A* items? Sometimes life dictates what's important when. If you only have so many days to get a birthday gift in the mail, that may become your priority. However, if we want to go someplace in our lives other than where the wind blows, we need long- and short-term goals that reflect our values and how we want to invest our time. Chapter 10 includes an entire section on goal setting.

6. Set deadlines. Our goals can float out in the future like wishful thinking and never materialize, unless we have deadlines for their completion. Sometimes the goal carries its own deadline, like holidays and income taxes. Sometimes we need to set our own deadlines. For instance, it's easy to add "due dates" to your to-do lists. That also helps with prioritizing. There's more on this in chapter 10.

7. Use prime time. Once we identify our goals, we need to figure out exactly *when* we are going to accomplish them. This relates to the time-on-task technique we discussed earlier, where we devote enough time to accomplishing our goals to turn them into realities. I'm a morning person. It's a lot easier for me to focus and concentrate when I first get up in the morning. So that's my *prime time*. Some people focus better during the day, and others are night owls and work better at night. The point is to figure out your prime time and use that window of time to your advantage. If you can, schedule an appointment with your goal on your calendar. Focus your attention and effort on your goal during your prime time, and work on your most important and most difficult goals. You'll save time by doing that.

8. Use a month-at-a-glance calendar. I keep a large calendar in my kitchen, tacked up inside the cabinet where I keep my water glasses, so I see it several times a day. That's where I keep my personal appointments and reminders like doctor visits, anniversaries, and travel dates. It shows the whole month and easily lets me see what's coming up in advance, so I get lead time to make plans and prepare.

I find it's easier to keep my business appointments in my phone, synchronized with my computer calendar. I usually add in personal appointments or travel so I won't double schedule. My electronic calendars include monthly, weekly, and daily views. Some people prefer physical calendars. Some like reminders on their phones. It just depends on what works best for you.

Also, when you schedule your daily activities, be sure to leave time for unexpected delays and interruptions, which are bound to happen. That way you have some flexibility and don't set yourself up to get stressed when things don't go exactly according to your plan.

9. Visualize success. I often use visualization exercises with people when I'm helping them with goal setting. When I worked with college athletes, it usually focused on enhancing their sports performance, but you can use it with any kinds of goals. We did a visualization activity on intuition in chapter 6. I'm including another one in chapter 10 on goal setting. The research is clear: when we add visualization to goal setting, we tend to get better results.

When I feel like I need some extra help to achieve a particular item on my to-do list, I will visualize myself successfully completing that item. Usually I do this right before I fall asleep, the night before I plan to complete the goal. I pay close attention to see in my mind exactly *when* during my day I will get the item done. Almost without exception, I complete the task quickly and easily. It's as if I've already succeeded by visualizing it first, and all I have to do is follow through with action.

I like to combine this technique with the one on prioritizing. Often I will ask myself in the evening, "What's the main thing I need to get done tomorrow that will make me feel good tomorrow night?" I'll pick something, decide on the best time to get it done, then I'll visualize actually doing it. Almost without exception, I succeed at following through—and at feeling good because of it.

10. Create a compulsion to closure. Another one of my favorite time management techniques is what I call my **compulsion to closure**. I have a high need to finish projects, to get them done, tied up with a bow, and crossed off my to-do lists. It's *almost* like a compulsion; it doesn't drive me nuts when I can't get closure, but the lack of closure becomes a compelling incentive to complete the items on my lists, kind of like an itch you really want to scratch.

This compulsion is what's called the **Zeigarnik effect**. A psychologist named B. Zeigarnik postulated that some people have an inherent compulsion to finish a task or attain a certain result. Apparently not all of us have this strong need, but if you're one of them, you can use that to help with time management. It means that once you start a task, you'll get some extra energy to finish it. So if you complete just one step, one small part of your to-do item, that will trigger your need to keep going. It's like a little gift of motivation. So write the item on your to-do list or calendar. That's a start. If your item is to see a doctor, schedule an appointment. Any small, preliminary step toward getting your item done will make it easier to complete.

As you can see from my Top 10 list, I use a combination of left- and right-brain time management techniques, some that help me structure my priorities and some that allow me to go with the flow (like intuition, intention, and visualization). I also use other strategies like delegating, depending on what I need to get done, but these are my everyday strategies.

You can also do left-brain activities in right-brain ways. For example, I buy large kitchen calendars with bright, bold colors, ones that appeal to my artistic side. Then I use different colored felt pens to schedule events (e.g., green for birthdays and anniversaries, blue for appointments, and purple for travel), which is another right-brain add-on. A day or two before or after New Year's, I have a left-brain ritual of creating my calendar for the coming year, writing in all the predictable, fixed events, but I usually do it while listening to music, so both sides of my brain get to be happily involved in what might otherwise be a boring, repetitive task.

With all these time management techniques, I need be clear that I'm not encouraging workaholism. I don't want you to come away from this section with the idea that I'm suggesting that you try to be productive every minute of every day. We need downtime, fun time, social time, definitely sleep time, and time to just *be*. Often, those unstructured times spontaneously open up in natural, right-brain ways. If you tend to be a workaholic or a highly structured left-brain person, you may need to deliberately schedule them into your calendar.

Unstructured time provides some surprising benefits. Our left brains are detail oriented, good at grasping individual parts of the whole, whereas our right brains see the big picture. When we give our left brain a chance to disengage, time when it doesn't have to keep up with the minutiae of our lives, we create space for our right brain to kick in. That's when we may get some of our most creative epiphanies and revelations. For instance, when we meditate, walk or run outside, play with our pets, listen to music, sit with nature, or swing on a porch, we may open the door for our intuition to offer us a stroke of genius. One such lightning bolt of intuitive insight can make half the items on our to-do lists irrelevant, because it may point us in a grander, more expansive direction.

You never know when that gift might come. Opening a space for holistic, right-brain messages to appear in your life on a regular basis through unstructured time can lead to an entirely new world of possibilities. As I described in chapter 1, that's how I got the inspiration for this book—while sitting in a park, simply observing the trees. That one magical moment in unstructured time showed me my calling and changed the entire course of my life.

I've practiced with different time management techniques for years, so now I have a good idea of what will work when. I want you to also have a toolbox of strategies to pull from, so you can build a brighter future for yourself and others, accomplishing what's important with the least amount of stress. It takes experimenting with different techniques to find out exactly what works for you, but it's so worth the effort.

---

26. *Activities*

Some of the more important lessons in the school of life have to do with effectively managing our time. If you want to get better at it, try these activities.

1. **Identify at least one goal in your life that's motivating enough for you to learn new time management techniques. What would serve as a big enough reward to make you want to explore and change?**

2. **Write down the time management techniques you're already good at. If you know they work for you, sometimes you can find new ways to apply them, especially in problem areas or with more challenging goals.**

    - *Time management techniques I'm already good at include the following:*

3. *As you read through the ten techniques described above, did any of them stand out as something you might want to try? Pick one of the ten techniques and experiment with it in your own life. Practice using it in different situations so you really give it a fair chance to see if it will work for you. Or pick another time management strategy you want to explore and try it out. You may want to start by selecting a technique that matches your left- or right-brain preference. The point is to develop more skills.*

4. *Make an ongoing commitment to let time be your teacher. Let it instruct you on which techniques to use and how to get the most benefit out of the time you have available. Your life can become dramatically richer and more fulfilling because of it.*

Procrastination

Let's say that you already know a number of time management techniques. You've found some strategies that work for you, but you're still having problems with procrastination. What now?

First of all, know that you're not alone. Almost everyone procrastinates to some extent. Maybe you're good at keeping up with things at work, but you tend to drag your feet when it comes to your social life. Or perhaps you stay on top of your responsibilities with household tasks like paying your bills, but you neglect certain aspects of your health. Most of us have areas of our lives where we sometimes (or regularly) drop the ball.

So what exactly do we mean by procrastination? It's when we *needlessly* delay on getting something done. We have the time or could make the time to do it, but we keep putting it off to the future. It's the *mañana syndrome*. We act like it can wait until tomorrow when maybe it really needs to get done today.

Procrastination takes two different forms: **comfortable procrastination**, which has no negative consequences, and **problem procrastination**, which causes minor or major negative consequences. For example, I may need to clean my garage, but waiting until later is fine, because a delay won't cause any negative results. But if you don't pay your bills on time, you'll get a penalty fee. If you drag your feet when dealing with health issues, they can turn into something serious.

If you know time management techniques and don't use them, despite repeated negative consequences from your delays, you may be considered a "hard-core" procrastinator, like I was. As I mentioned earlier, I developed a pattern of showing up late to meetings at work in spite of knowing my behavior was unprofessional and disrespectful to other people. My late arrivals also stressed me out, so I experienced both external and internal negative consequences. I knew all of this at the time, but I couldn't seem to change my behavior. It was almost like something inside of me wouldn't *let* me change. The whole pattern seemed irrational and strangely baffling—*until* I identified the rewards I was getting out of it.

Procrastination or Overcommitment?

Before you label yourself as a procrastinator, you need to ask one important question: "Am I procrastinating, or am I **overcommitted**?" The two may look the same, but each requires a different solution. With overcommitment, you may simply need to cut back on your obligations. Procrastination can be a bit trickier to resolve.

I used to work with students who had been disqualified from the university because of poor grades. They had to meet with me and develop a plan for success, an outline of the things they would do differently if they were allowed to return to school. Many of the students I met with were business majors, going to school full time and working twenty to thirty hours a week. Some also had family responsibilities.

Most courses in the business major required class attendance and a lot of time-consuming homework assignments outside of class. The students I saw were highly capable and could easily complete the work in their classes, but only if they devoted enough time. They weren't procrastinators, needlessly delaying on their studies. No, they were overcommitted. They didn't have enough time to get their schoolwork done. They either needed to go to school part time, reduce their work hours, or some combination of both. They couldn't keep up with all their responsibilities *and* get the grades required for a business degree.

Strategic Delays

I've gone through periods in my life when I wanted to plow through my to-do lists and get everything done, leaving no time for procrastination to sabotage my agenda. However, there may be times when putting off a task is a smart thing to do. It makes sense and becomes part of an overall strategic plan. One strategy consists of simply rearranging your priorities to take advantage of better timing. Other strategies may be more complicated.

Here's an example. Sometimes when I'm faced with a particularly daunting task, it can make me feel overwhelmed, frustrated, or inadequate, especially if I don't know how to do it. Those emotions generate anxiety, which can make it even more difficult to focus on the task at hand. So I will intentionally delay through what's called **contingency procrastination.** Getting my priority task done becomes *contingent* upon doing something else first. Sometimes I'll clean my house or maybe respond to e-mail instead of buckling down and doing what I need to do. Or maybe I'll do several smaller tasks that need to get done before jumping into my top priority. But those contingent behaviors help me dissipate anxiety, which usually allows me to focus better in the long run. After a short stint of draining off anxious energy, I'm almost always ready to get down to business, so the strategy normally works. I end up getting my task completed by any deadlines, and I crank out quality work. No negative consequences.

However, if I decide to use contingency procrastination as a deliberate strategy, I have to be extremely careful, because my procrastination can fool me into thinking I'm in charge and moving in the right direction. That's because procrastination often takes control by being sneaky, clever (in a bad way), and full of tricks that bamboozle us over and over. You turn on the television, only intending to catch the news, and then find yourself surprised when you look up and see that two hours have gone by. You think you have plenty of time to do whatever, but then you realize time is slipping away, and you haven't even started.

Sometimes the damage done by procrastination is more subtle. We may not notice when it lulls us into thinking we're getting a lot done and making progress, and all the while we're focused on busywork or less important tasks, losing critical windows of time. We may be unaware of the extent to which it erodes away our opportunities, keeps us from developing our potential, and snatches our dreams. Procrastination may also hide in the shadows as it undermines our self-esteem. We need to feel good about ourselves, to have a healthy sense of self-confidence in the ways we manage ourselves and our time in order to move forward and truly shine in the school of our lives. If we're not paying attention, procrastination can take all of that away.

When I bring up the topic of procrastination in casual conversations, people will often halfway smile, roll their eyes, and make a joke about their own issues. And I have funny stories to tell about my own antics as well. But problem procrastination is a serious issue, which sometimes results in dire consequences. For example, during one of my procrastination classes, a young woman said she no longer had a car. She had procrastinated on paying her parking tickets, the fines went up, and she couldn't afford to pay the tickets and the impound fee to get her car back. I know of a couple where the husband procrastinated to gain a power position over his wife, rarely following through on his promises. That couple is now divorced. She finally had enough. And I just heard about two women who knew they had lumps in their breasts but never got around to seeing a doctor until it was too late. They lost their lives because of their delays.

Stop Procrastinating: Things to Try

Sometimes I see procrastination like a necklace that's gotten tangled up. It has lots of knots that need to be untangled. It sometimes takes focused efforts to understand the knotted-up wad of positive and negative consequences of procrastinating and then patiently work to get out all the twists and loops. But once you do that, your procrastination in that particular area is not likely to come back. And the really good news is that you can use these same steps to change any bad habit.

In order to break a pattern of procrastination, we need to begin with our eyes wide open. Awareness and self-observation are crucial if we want to catch our thief in midaction and regain control of our time. Here are some suggestions.

1. Identify where you procrastinate. Most of us have a couple of areas of our lives where we procrastinate. We may do fine on most things, but those few areas consistently trip us up. For example, maybe you're good at keeping up with family obligations but sometimes struggle to stay connected with personal friends. Or perhaps you take care of your finances on time but tend to put off personal health issues.

I suggest that you stop reading right now and make a list of the areas where you procrastinate. It may be helpful to first think about broad categories where you might have problems. Jane Burka and Lenora Yuen, coauthors of *Procrastination: Why You Do It, What to Do about It NOW*, identify six areas where people tend to procrastinate: household, work, school, personal care (including health), social relationships, and finances. So take a few minutes and write down specific tasks where you procrastinate in these broad categories. It's a great way to start dealing with your issues.

2. List the consequences of your procrastination. Usually we find that good and bad things happen when we procrastinate. This can make it more difficult for us to break our bad habits. So again, right now, I suggest that you get a piece of paper and draw a line down the center of the page, making two columns. At the top of the left-hand column, write "Positive Consequences." At the top of the right-hand column, write "Negative Consequences."

Next, pick an area where you procrastinate—let's say paying bills. Then take a few minutes to brainstorm and jot down all the positive and negative consequences you can think of. For example, a positive consequence may be that your procrastination helps you avoid feeling anxious, especially if money is tight. A negative consequence is that late payments eventually hurt your credit. Notice that our positive and negative consequences can be both internal (anxiety avoidance) and external (damaged credit history).

3. Decide if your procrastination is comfortable or problematic. Look at your lists of positive and negative consequences. If your lists include a lot of consequences that have a significant negative impact on you and your life, consider that your procrastination is problematic. But if your consequences are mostly positive with just a few insignificant negative consequences, you may instead be dealing with comfortable procrastination. For instance, I have a landscaping project planned for my backyard, but it's no big deal if I keep putting it off. If I decide that something is comfortable procrastination, I may decide to do nothing.

4. Determine whether you're procrastinating or overcommitted. Ask yourself if it's humanly possible for you to get everything done that you're trying to do. Are your to-do lists even realistic? It's important to be honest with yourself here. If you're overcommitted, you need to somehow cut back on your commitments. You might delegate some of your tasks, decide to do some later, or find other ways to reduce your load. Overcommitment calls for a different solution than problem procrastination.

5. For problem procrastination, identify the underlying cause. As we've discussed earlier, behavior that's not reinforced will fizzle and go away. You'll quit doing it. So you need to find the reward that's reinforcing your problem behavior. In other words, what are you getting out of it? You may have several rewards. Try to be honest with yourself, even if you don't like what you discover. You rewards will include the positive consequences you identified in item number two above. They may also run deeper. Here are some possibilities:

- Ask yourself, "Am I afraid of failure?" We may intentionally or unintentionally avoid our goals to protect ourselves from the possibility of failing. If you never try, you never have to find out that you might not measure up. A variation of this fear involves perfectionism. You don't try because anything less than perfection would feel like failure. If this could be a cause of your procrastination, ask yourself, "What am I afraid of?" or "What am I trying to avoid?"

- Also ask, "Am I afraid of success?" Although it may not make logical sense to fear success, many people fear they will be held to higher standards after succeeding and that they won't be able to meet those standards. They may also fear the kinds of changes that might occur following success. For example, people will only like them for their success, not for who they are as individuals. Or they will be thrown into a world of scary uncertainties, which seem very real in their imaginations.

- Maybe you're like me and enjoy the excitement and intensity procrastination created in my life. That thrilling feeling eventually resulted in getting hooked on my own adrenaline.

- Procrastination can be a great antidote to boredom. You create, direct, and star in your own drama. Unfortunately, our personal dramas become an unnecessary waste of our time and energy.

- One of my biggest rewards became the sense of personal power I experienced after I procrastinated up until the last minute, then miraculously managed to pull the rabbit out of the hat and met my deadlines just in the nick of time. I felt like superwoman.

- When I procrastinated by being chronically late to meetings, I experienced a sense of power and control over others. Withholding or delaying on our promises to other people may feel like you're getting the upper hand, but it's disrespectful and can cause major conflicts in our relationships.

- You may feel unmotivated to complete a task, so you stall on getting it done. Or you believe you should wait until you feel inspired, which may never happen.

- I worked with many students who put off doing term papers until the last minute and told me, "I work best under pressure." It's true that deadlines can cause us to find sudden energy and motivation to complete a task, but it's a stressful way to get our work done, and we often don't leave enough time to check our work and make final revisions, so we sacrifice quality.

- You don't know how to complete a task, or the task is unusually difficult or complex. This situation can cause us to feel intimidated, helpless, and incompetent, so we avoid the task and the emotions that go along with it. We can actually get addicted to avoidance of our negative feelings.

- Sometimes we don't feel like we have the energy to get something done, so we put it off until later. Fatigue and burnout can be real issues, which need to be separately addressed.

- Some people are lazy and don't want to exert the energy required to do something. Others are easily distracted and can't find ways to either eliminate or distance themselves from their distractions. And sometimes we get caught in our own rebellion and think, "I resent having to do this, so I'll wait until I damn well feel like it."

- Remember the first time you procrastinated. Maybe it was when you were a child, or perhaps it was an experience from later in your life. Sometimes you can identify the rewards of your delays by looking at the first time it happened. A short exercise on this is included in the activities that follow this section.

The causes of procrastination can vary, depending on the individual, the task, and the situation. Each of us has a personal history of experiences with putting things off. What we learn from those experiences often creates irrational beliefs, and those beliefs underlie our pattern of repeatedly creating negative results.

6. Find healthy ways to build the unhealthy rewards of procrastination into your life. Although we may feel in control when we're the ones calling the shots, waiting to do things when *we* want to do them, the bottom line is that we are not in control. In those situations, we don't have all of our choices available. We're reacting to people or events in our typical knee-jerk fashion rather than putting all our options on the table and choosing how to best respond.

One of the fastest ways to stop procrastinating is to find healthy ways to build the rewards it provides into our lives. For example, if you are protecting yourself from possible failure or success, learn how to take strategic, calculated risks in the direction of your goals with small incremental steps that you feel you can handle. Watch what happens, and then decide on your next strategic steps. If you need more intensity, power, or motivation in your life, find new challenges that will cause you to stretch and grow, goals you feel excited about, believe in wholeheartedly, and will enjoy doing. If you don't know how to do something, put on your student hat and figure it out. Mastering a new skill is highly rewarding. Plus, many rewards end after we experience them, like the pleasure of eating delicious food. But we carry new skills with us for the rest of our lives, so the rewards never end. Learning how to stop procrastinating is itself a new skill and provides its own built-in rewards. It's empowering in positive ways, boosts our self-esteem, and makes us a lot more likely to succeed at almost any future goals.

7. Identify *why* you want to stop procrastinating. What is your motivation? Remind yourself of what made you want to complete a task to start with. If you procrastinate on keeping in touch with friends, remember how nurturing it feels to maintain those close relationships and how they help you grow and enjoy life.

8. Ask yourself what will happen if you stop procrastinating. When we change our behavior, we usually find there are positive and negative consequences. A part of us knows this in advance, so unconsciously, we may drag our feet to avoid what we anticipate or imagine will be negative consequences if we change and stop procrastinating. For example, maybe you're afraid that if you succeed, people will be jealous or ask too much from you. We may need to identify those fears in advance. And sometimes those fears aren't real. We just thought they were.

The answer to this question may be identical or similar to your underlying cause of procrastination. And it may be included in your list of positive consequences. It may also turn out to be something different.

9. Slide into an easy start. Begin by just doing one thing toward your task or goal. It could be something as simple as making a phone call or writing one e-mail. This can help you break the pattern of resistance. Or set a five-minute contract with yourself. Agree to do just five minutes of activities toward completing your task, promising yourself that you can stop after five minutes if you want to. But often, those five minutes are the hardest we face to get going. So if you can, do your five minutes and then do another five minutes, and another, until the energy of the task kicks in and starts to carry you forward.

This technique of simply getting started can trigger the ***Zeigarnik effect*** that we discussed earlier, which refers to the need to finish what we started. So if you just do five minutes toward completing your task or goal, it may make it more likely that you will want to complete it. Use that to your advantage.

10. Find outside support. Ask friends or family to help you stay accountable with regard to completing your goals. Promise to report to someone on your progress. Read books or online articles about procrastination. Work with a professional life coach, counselor, or therapist. Do whatever you think might help. I could begin to untangle the knots in my own bad habits when I started teaching a class on procrastination because it forced me to learn more about it.

11. Understand that procrastination may be a message that you're not *supposed* to do something. Your delays might be your intuition trying to create a roadblock to keep you from heading off in the wrong direction. Always allow for the possibility that your procrastination is trying to tell you to wait, for a perfectly legitimate reason. If a task seems particularly difficult to complete, stop and examine whether you need to do it at all. You might need to either wait or let it go completely.

12. Use time management and goal-setting techniques. Sometimes you can self-correct and overcome your procrastination by completing the previous steps. And sometimes you need to deliberately start to use time management techniques to make sure you stop your needless delays. However, if you're dealing with an area of problematic procrastination that's especially resistant to change, use both the time management techniques previously addressed and the goal-setting techniques covered in the next chapter until you discover what works for you.

---

27. Activities

1. *Take a little time to write down your areas of procrastination. Think in terms of broad categories like work, household, and personal care. You might be surprised by your results.*

2. *Ask yourself, "Am I procrastinating or overcommitted?" Sometimes the answer is both. If you're overcommitted, look for ways to cut back.*

3. *Remember the first time you procrastinated.*
   - *What were the circumstances?*
   - *What were the consequences?*
   - *How did it make you feel?*

- *What were the rewards for your procrastination?*
- *What did you learn as a result of that first experience with putting something off?*

4. *Pick one of the techniques we just covered for stopping procrastination. Try it. Give it a fair chance, and see if it's effective. For example, I started with suggestion ten by reading about procrastination.*

5. *Then select another technique. Experiment to see if it works.*

6. *Keep trying different techniques until you get a handle on your behavior, until any remaining procrastination becomes comfortable, without negative consequences. If you start with suggestion five and identify the underlying cause and the built-in rewards, this often provides a shortcut to gaining control and self-confidence around how you use your time. Sometimes people need to follow all the suggestions to break up long-term habits.*

7. *If you have difficulty cutting problem procrastination out of your life, you might want to get support from a life coach, counselor, or professional therapist. Don't let procrastination keep you from honoring your values or achieving your goals.*

Limiting Beliefs

While writing this book, I discovered a limiting belief I didn't know I had. I stumbled across it at exactly the same time I started writing this specific section, of course, on limiting beliefs. It's hard to believe the timing of that was sheer coincidence.

Here's what happened. I felt like I was getting stuck with my writing, like I couldn't sit down and crank it out like I normally do. That's when I started wondering if I was procrastinating, being lazy, or maybe I was just a slowpoke in my ability to get things done. Those kinds of negative labels aren't in my normal internal banter. I don't think about myself like that. I've learned that's usually a sign I need to stop, take a break, and figure out what's going on.

So I went to my computer and started writing. Just stream of consciousness. Whatever came to mind. Unplanned, undirected thoughts that seemed to want to be written. I wrote four single-spaced pages before my limiting belief showed up, as if it had been buried inside of me for years, hiding in the deep dark recesses of my subconscious mind.

But there it was, written on the computer screen in black and white, like an imposter or culprit who involuntarily got exposed to the light of my awareness. It came out as a cluster of thoughts packaged together:

> *I'm afraid if the book is a success, it will make me arrogant and egotistical and send me off on a power trip. Undo my progress in connecting with my authentic self. I'm happier now because my focus is on helping other people. I'm scared I'll go backward. Become self-serving. Get more self-absorbed.*

Whoa. Where did that come from? I thought I'd worked through most of my limiting beliefs, at least the major ones. But I would certainly count a fear of success as something major.

Uncovering that belief felt surprising, even shocking. Plus, it made me feel embarrassed on two counts. First of all, how presumptuous and probably naïve of me to think the book would meet with that kind of success. After all, hundreds of thousands of books get published in the United States each year, so you're looking at astronomical odds.

And second, I'm a recovering procrastinator. I've worked on my issues for years. Besides that, I teach procrastination to others and always go over how the fear of success can result in unnecessary delays. How could I have missed it? But I can honestly say I never saw a fear of becoming more egocentric as a version of fear of success.

Yet it makes sense. I've seen it often in others. Some of the nicest people you'd ever meet become successful in their fields and change because of it, and not in good ways. So I've been unknowingly afraid success might make me a little snooty, a bit smug, draw me off my focus to use this book to help others and instead get caught up in self-promotion. My belief about success has probably been laying low as I've written the book, but now that I'm almost done, it stepped things up a notch by getting in the way of my writing.

Maybe that's also why for the past several weeks, with my writing, I felt like I was driving with one foot on the gas and the other on the brakes. Our limiting beliefs can create conflicts around our goals. Those conflicts may result in ambivalence and tension from our push-pull dilemma, and we may take one step forward and one or two back. Or we might stop working on a goal altogether. Worse yet, we may never set goals in the first place.

What Are Core Beliefs?

Our core beliefs are the thoughts we believe to be true about ourselves, whether or not they are true, and whether or not other people perceive us that way. They are the essence of how we see ourselves. Core beliefs can be either positive or negative. For example, you may see yourself as worthy, lovable, and competent, or you may believe you are unworthy, unlovable, and incompetent.

We usually form our core beliefs early in life, often as the result of what we learn about ourselves in childhood. Sometimes we develop our beliefs later on, when they're influenced by life circumstances, traumas, and individual experiences.

Once we decide on our core beliefs, we often continue to think they're true, regardless of contradictory evidence from our environment. For instance, I used to counsel students who had low self-esteem. No matter how much success they achieved, and regardless of how many people expressed their affection, respect, or admiration, the students still saw themselves as failures, less than, or unworthy. They clung to their beliefs despite tons of feedback to the contrary.

In other words, the students continued to perceive themselves as inferior, and their perceptions created what they experienced as reality. That's the danger with limiting core beliefs. We believe with absolute certainty that something is true. And that certainty often becomes a self-fulfilling prophecy. You think it will happen, you feel like it will happen, you act *as if* it will happen, and then, lo and behold, it does happen. It proves you were right all along, and that proof can strengthen your other core beliefs without your knowing it.

In our minds, our core beliefs are not just possibilities. They're facts—bound to happen. Unknowingly, we may use intention in a bad way to create a reality that matches our negative beliefs. We may also ignore contradictory evidence or distort our perception of reality so our reality matches our core beliefs. Regardless of how it happens, if our core beliefs are negative, we usually end up with negative results.

Here are some common core beliefs that limit our experiences in the school of life:

- I'm not as good as other people. I don't measure up.

- No matter how hard I try, I can't be successful.

- I'm stupid, unattractive, fat, lazy, too young, too old, weak, unable to change, and so on (this list can be endless).

- People won't love me if they know who I really am. I must impress them by trying to be someone I'm not.

- I always get rejected in relationships. I can't maintain long-term relationships.

I've found that many people have five or six limiting beliefs they carry around for years. Usually one or two of those focus on body image—things about their bodies they don't like or feel ashamed about. Several more beliefs usually relate to their lack of ability—beliefs that put a cap on what they're willing to try or even consider. They never think about setting a particular goal, because they're already certain they couldn't attain it. They're not "that kind" of person.

We need to bring those negative core beliefs out into the light of day by shining our awareness into the nooks and crannies of our subconscious mind where they live. But first, let's look at other kinds of limitations.

Other Limiting Beliefs

Besides our core beliefs, those we hold to be true about who we are, most of us have additional beliefs that get in the way of doing and being our best. Some of these beliefs come from childhood experiences of growing up in our families and are called "family rules." Every family has its rules or expectations, which can be positive or negative, healthy or unhealthy. Although these rules are rarely spoken or talked about, they usually don't need to be. Even as a little kid, you *just knew* what they were. Our unhealthy family rules can cause problems, both at the time and later on. For example:

- Do as I say, not as I do.

- You're just like so-and-so (another family member). You'll never amount to anything.

- Follow the rules. Don't rock the boat.

- You're the big brother/sister; your needs aren't as important as your younger siblings' needs.

- I need to do that for you. I don't think you're capable of doing it for yourself.

Dysfunctional families, including those with alcohol or drug addiction, often have common family rules. Claudia Black, author of *It Will Never Happen to Me*, identified three rules that are usually present in dysfunctional families:

- **Don't talk.** It's not safe to talk about real issues. Don't mention that Mom seems depressed or that Dad drinks too much.

- **Don't trust.** It's not safe to trust other people in the family to be there for you. You can't count on others to take care of you or keep their promises.

- **Don't feel.** It's also not safe to feel what you're feeling. It's better to ignore your emotions. Besides, no one will listen, no one will nurture you if you're upset, and no one will understand.

Do any of those sound familiar? Many of us get at least parts of those rules in our families.

We can also learn limiting beliefs from culture and society, like "Boys don't cry" and "Girls aren't good at math." I grew up in the South, where there's a strong work ethic. One of the things I heard repeatedly as a child was, "Idle hands are the devil's workshop." Now I look back and think that kind of cultural message probably contributed to my workaholism. Then there are all the "shoulds" and "musts" that we hear from lots of different places like:

- You should be perfect.

- You shouldn't fail. If you fail, don't admit it. You should feel ashamed of any failures.

- You must be rational and logical all the time. Don't get too emotional.

- You must be liked by others, and if you're not, there's something wrong with you.

Notice that these limiting beliefs are often stated in absolutes like "always" and "never."

Additional beliefs come from our individual experiences and can include ones like:

- I'm the peacemaker in the family, or the quiet kid, the clown, or the black sheep.

- It's not okay to be too powerful.

- Don't outshine the people around you.

When you look at all the ways we can pick up unhealthy beliefs, it's a wonder most of us function as well as we do. That's a testimony to our resiliency. But now may be the time to clear out any lingering problem beliefs and open the door to new possibilities.

How to Identify Your Limiting Beliefs

When we identify our negative thoughts, we take a huge step forward in the process of changing them. At least then we know what we're dealing with. If our beliefs continue to lurk in the shadows of our subconscious mind, we're often stuck in a reactive mode, wondering why we keep acting in certain ways or why things keep turning out the way they do.

And identifying them isn't that hard. That's the good news in this process of unlearning. Sometimes they just pop out when you give them a chance, when you create a space for that to happen. I experienced that after I got stuck while writing this book and started writing undirected stream-of-consciousness thoughts. My limiting belief showed up, reluctantly, but also like it almost wanted to get exposed and transformed. Besides stream-of-consciousness writing, here are more ways to identify your limiting beliefs.

1. Identify problems. Look at the problem areas in your life and ask yourself, "Do I have any thoughts or beliefs that might be contributing to these problems?" You can also try asking, "What's the lesson I need to learn?"

2. Brainstorm. Write down all the negative beliefs you can think of, even if they seem outlandish or don't make sense. Don't judge your beliefs or question them at the time. Just jot them down. You can go back and evaluate them later on. You can brainstorm in two ways:

- Set aside at least thirty minutes, go someplace where you can remain uninterrupted, and write down as many negative beliefs as you can in that time frame. Don't overthink. Just write. If you're still writing after thirty minutes, keep going.
- Get together with a trusted friend or a small group of people and brainstorm together. Same thing: write down all the negative beliefs that you're carrying around or even might be carrying around. Usually the beliefs mentioned by others will cause you to remember more of your own.

3. Use intuition. Ask your intuition to help you identify beliefs that are problematic.

4. Try imagery. Do the imagery exercise in Appendix B and ask your inner guide to tell you your limiting beliefs.

5. Write in a journal. Keep a thoughts journal on your thoughts and write in it regularly. Look for themes in your thinking. Those themes might point toward underlying problem beliefs.

6. Get more information. Do more reading on limiting beliefs, in books or through online research.

7. Observe. Take a witness or observer position and watch your thoughts in action. Notice any that stand out as troublesome or cause you to feel uncomfortable.

---

28. Activities

Review the methods for identifying your limiting beliefs. Select the one that seems like it would work the best for you, and try it. If it turns out not to be effective, then select another method and try that out. Or think of a method that's not listed, and try that. Keep exploring methods until you find one that helps you get your negative beliefs on paper.

Look for limiting beliefs from the various sources. See if you can come up with at least several limiting beliefs from each of the following:

1. *Core beliefs around not being worthy, lovable, or competent.*

2. *"Family rules" that focus on what was normal and expected in your family growing up, like don't talk, don't trust, don't feel.*

3. *"Shoulds" we all get from society, like "You should be logical all the time" and "You must be liked by everyone."*

4. *Limiting beliefs that come from our individual experiences, for example, "People only like me when I'm funny" or "My role in friendships is to take care of the other person."*

It's important to dig through and unearth the beliefs that limit us. Just writing them down starts to diminish their power over us. Then at least we know what we're dealing with.

How to Change Limiting Beliefs

One time during a budget crunch at work, I was asked to take on three jobs. There was absolutely no way I could get everything done, so I tried to cover the most critical aspects and hoped nothing major fell through the cracks. I felt overwhelmed about 90 percent of the time. Because two of the jobs were new, it was hard to prioritize my responsibilities. Sometimes my mind would start racing so fast with all the items on my to-do lists that I would become paralyzed and couldn't do anything at all.

Thank heavens for my meditation. I could observe my racing thoughts and watch myself as I became overwhelmed. That's when I came up with one question that saved me. Every time I noticed I'd gotten worked into a tizzy, I'd ask myself, "Is this helpful?" And of course, the answer was, "No."

Asking and answering that question broke the negative cycle. It brought me back to the present moment and allowed me to figure out the next thing I needed to do. I realized my paralysis was due to a limiting belief that said, "This is too much for me." Yes, it was a lot. But as long as I stayed focused in the now, I could manage to get it done.

This example illustrates the power of awareness in changing negative thinking. If you're paying attention in school, you will at least have a chance of catching your unproductive thinking in the here and now, as it happens. Maybe you won't be aware of the thoughts as you're thinking them. But you can sometimes backtrack and figure out the thoughts by noticing your uncomfortable emotions or maladaptive behavior. My temporary paralysis, in addition to my distressing emotions, told me my thoughts were getting me stuck.

Besides becoming more aware of when your limiting beliefs are getting in your way, try these suggestions for changing them.

1. Use logic to question whether your belief is realistic. Does it even make sense? Once it's out on the table and you have a chance to examine it, you may find that you don't even think it's accurate. Seeing that a belief doesn't ring true can quickly take away its power. If the belief keeps returning, remind yourself each time that it's not realistic and train yourself to let it go.

That's what happened to me with my belief that the success of this book would make me egotistical. I've never been like that with other successes in my life. But now I'll be especially on the lookout for any signs I'm getting cocky. Plus, I have a great group of people around me. I know I can trust them to tell me if it looks like I'm sliding into self-importance.

2. Do the thought-stopping activity. As was previously mentioned, many of us have five or six limiting beliefs that we carry throughout life. Thought stopping is a simple technique for changing those. First, it helps you identify the negative thoughts that are limiting your options and keeping you stuck. Writing those down helps you start to take your power back. Then you come up with counterthoughts—ones that are positive and realistic. When you catch yourself falling into your negative thinking, you substitute your positive thoughts instead, either mentally saying them to yourself or actually saying them out loud.

The point is that you don't want your negative thoughts to have the last word. They need to be challenged and uprooted. You'll need to practice substituting positive thoughts for the negative ones, but over time, it becomes automatic. The negative thoughts lose their foothold, and you're left with positive, empowering thoughts that help you move forward.

Turn now to the Thought-Stopping Form in Appendix D and follow the simple instructions. It only takes a few minutes, and I think you'll be surprised at how good you feel after you complete it.

3. Keep a journal. Keep a running log of your limiting thoughts and learn to counter them by replacing them with thoughts that are more positive and realistic, like in the thought-stopping exercise. Continue to use your journal as a tool until the negative thoughts lose their ability to control you.

4. Identify your strengths. Make a list of your strengths, the things you do well. Remind yourself of your strengths when your limiting beliefs start to get in your way. Use affirmations and practice saying positive things about yourself.

5. Use visualization. Ask yourself, "What would it look like if I were no longer controlled by that belief, if I were free to be my completely healthy, confident, and competent authentic self?" Also ask, "What would that feel like?" Practice visualizing your optimal outcome.

6. Pretend. Act *as if* you already were free to live your authenticity. As the saying goes, "Fake it till you make it." There's surprising power in that approach. Because each time you act *as if*, you're neurologically setting the stage to repeat your behavior. You're creating neurological connections in your brain that make it easier to do that same behavior again. So if your limiting belief is that you're too old to do something, act like you're not, and do it anyway.

7. Work with a professional. Some of our beliefs can be especially well concealed, stubborn, and resistant to change. Often we learned them as a way to protect ourselves. They might have kept us safe at the time, and maybe we believe they still do. Sometimes you need to find a trained professional who can help you get to the root of the belief and make the changes you need.

I used to do assertiveness training with university students, where we did a lot of role-playing. For example, I would tell the students to think of something they wanted to ask for, and then we would act out how they would make that request. If students wanted to ask a professor for a grade change, I would play the part of the professor, and they would play themselves.

Sometimes students would start out timid, with poor body posture, a weak voice, and hesitancy in their speech. Even if students felt they deserved a higher grade, this usually happened if they anticipated rejection or had a core belief about being unworthy. Then I would ask the students to imagine they had all the confidence in the world. They knew they deserved that higher grade, and they had every right to ask for it. The differences were amazing. The students would stand up straight, look me square in the eyes, and, with strong voices, assertively ask me to change their grades.

Limiting beliefs are one of the most dangerous of the hazardous zones as we try to find our way through the school of life. They affect our conscious and subconscious thoughts, our behavior, our emotions, and our self-esteem—all the ways we think and feel about ourselves. Those beliefs become our "script" in the story we tell about ourselves.

All of us have stories about our lives. Sometimes our stories serve us well. But most of us have a few parts of our stories that don't serve us and reflect either erroneous or outdated beliefs that need to be uprooted, examined, and changed to fit with our authentic selves, who we're meant to be, and the life we're meant to live. You can always rewrite your script. It's never too late to change your story.

29. *Activities*

Correcting our limiting beliefs can take courage and work, but the results are almost always more than worth the effort. Try these steps.

1. <u>Identify one problem belief.</u> Look back at the limiting beliefs you identified in the previous activity. Maybe it's around money. Or perhaps relationships. Maybe it's in your career, and you can't seem to find or keep a fulfilling job. Whatever it is, shine your light of awareness and bring it out into the open where you can work with it. Write it down.

   - *One limiting belief that is a problem in my life is*

2. <u>Decide on a plan to unlearn your problem thinking.</u> Do you want to work on it by yourself? Or will you ask someone else to help you, like a trusted friend or trained professional? Read through the section "How to Change Limiting Beliefs," and develop a plan of action. For instance, I often start by writing stream-of-consciousness thoughts about how I can get past my limiting belief. That often leads me to some specific action steps I can take.

   - *One action step I can take to change my limiting belief is*
   - *Another action step I can take to address this limiting belief is*

3. <u>Follow through with your plan.</u> Undo the limits set by your problematic beliefs by learning new ways of thinking and acting. It may take some time to unravel the different layers of how that faulty thinking has messed you up. It may take additional time to change your related behaviors. Keep practicing.

4. <u>Continuously monitor whether your plan is working.</u> Are you seeing positive changes in your problem area? For example, once I identified my limiting belief about the potential success of this book, I started writing again—that very day. And I enjoyed it,

which was another sign I'd had a breakthrough. However, it often takes longer than a day to see a turnaround, so stick with it.

5. <u>*Keep repeating the above four steps until you work through the other problem areas in your life.*</u> *Most of us have at least a handful of negative beliefs that keep tripping us up. Set your intention to unlearn those, and replace them with healthier alternatives.*

6. <u>*Be gentle with yourself.*</u> *You've probably lived with your negative beliefs for years, and it takes time to change them. That's okay. Just keep going. Don't let limiting beliefs keep you from having the life of joy and abundance that you deserve.*

Chapter 9
Continuing to Grow

I was fortunate to work with university students for more than twenty-five years, and they became some of my greatest teachers. The students covered a large age span, from not quite eighteen-year-old freshmen to those returning for degrees much later in life. They also came from a wide range of racial, ethnic, religious, and economic backgrounds. And every day they reminded me of our common humanity and how much our journeys through the school of life are alike.

Through personal counseling, hundreds and hundreds of students shared their innermost private lives, the places most of us hide from the world. The places where our deepest doubts and fears and pain reside. Where we struggle to break free from our past, accomplish our goals, and find some semblance of happiness and peace.

Because of my students' honesty, vulnerability, and willingness to be seen, I learned so many lessons. Like how all of us have been wounded, and therefore all of us have issues. Even the people who look perfect on the outside, the ones we perceive as having it all together. Even *those* people have wounds and issues that remain a part of their daily, inner lives. Many of us find coping mechanisms, ways to block the pain and fear so that even *we* may not know it's there, but that doesn't mean it isn't still buried inside, alive and well.

Although our inner pain and fear may go unnoticed, it will often become blatantly obvious when we try to make changes in our lives. It's like this baggage we carry through life. We're used to the weight; it's normal for us, and we don't even think about it. But when we try to make changes that trigger those inner issues, they can rise to the forefront and interfere with our plans. For example, how many people buy gym memberships with the intention to start working out but then end up wasting their money when they never go? And there are those who decide to quit saying "Yes" to so many requests from other people, but somehow they always end up back in the same boat, unable to say "No." Our invisible inner issues often cause us to dishonor ourselves and sabotage our goals over and over again.

Because our emotional baggage can make significant change difficult at best, I've found that it's sometimes important to first make other kinds of changes in our lives, ones that are easier to accomplish. These easier changes can minimize the interferences with our efforts to take on more difficult challenges. They form some of the essential elements that can help us increase our learning curve. Successfully putting these other pieces in place can also help to build momentum and self-confidence to help us take on more challenging changes. It can make our goals easier to achieve because we drop part of the baggage we have to carry in trying to reach them.

By dealing with these issues, resolving them, and letting them go, we're free to learn our lessons faster and to more readily make progress in the school of our lives. In other words, we can develop a lifestyle that facilitates our learning and growth. We can create a fertile field where our goals and dreams can sprout, take root, and grow.

This chapter covers four of the most common interferences: (1) stress; (2) our personal energy level; (3) clutter, which includes our material "stuff" as well as mental and emotional clutter; and (4) a mindset for change and growth.

Managing Stress

Stress is inevitable. Life is about change, which means life is about stress. The definition of stress is anything that makes demands on us. That means every change, even a change for the better, causes stress because of the demands we must meet to accommodate it. But some stress can be positive. Taking on a new challenge, like earning a college degree or mastering new job responsibilities, even though demanding, can add adventure, intensity, pleasure, and meaning to our lives. It can require us to stretch and grow beyond who we once were.

I think stress in general sometimes gets a bad rap. We're so used to thinking of stress as something negative that it makes it difficult for us to take advantage of positive stress, the kind that can motivate us to move forward in life. Positive stress provides energy and incentive to take on new challenges and accomplish our goals.

Optimal Stress Level

Each of us has what is called an optimal level of stress, the level where we function best in a particular area. For example, some people may need a high level of stress in how they spend their recreation time and do dangerous sports like rock climbing. Others may like to relax and unwind when they have free time by maybe hiking, gardening, or knitting. I know people who thrive on a fast, high-powered work environment and others who prefer a job that's more relaxed and slower paced. The key is knowing how much stress is right for you and learning to balance the different aspects and changes in your life.

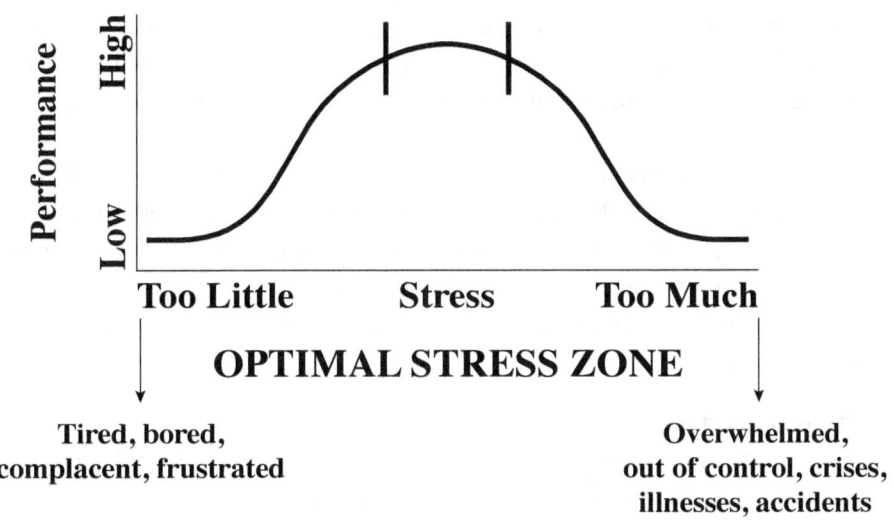

An optimal level of stress allows us to perform at our peak. The diagram above shows the level we need to attain in order to reach our peak performance. The horizontal axis measures stress, and the vertical axis measures performance; both show levels from low to high. For instance, if we have too little stress in our lives, we often feel tired, bored, or frustrated. If we have too much stress, we can feel overwhelmed and out of control. We may also get sick, be more accident prone, or experience other kinds of crises as a result of stress overload. The curved line represents levels of stress in relationship to performance. We perform at our best when we stay at the top of the curve, between the two markers.

---

30. *Activities*

Think about your life today, right now. Where do you see yourself on the curve? Put an "X" on the curve to indicate if you are:

- *At the top of the curve in your optimal zone.*
- *Over to the left, with too little stress in your life.*
- *Over to the right, in stress overload.*

This simple self-assessment gives you a starting point for developing a plan to manage your stress.

The goal is to try to stay in the peak performance zone, where you maintain your optimal stress level over time. However, the tricky part is that your optimal level can change every day, depending on a whole host of factors. These include being sick, how much sleep you got the night before, whether you have pressing deadlines, and whether you're having conflicts in a relationship.

On top of that, stress is cumulative. That means we can't separate our different sources of stress. It's our concerns about money, worries about a family member, fears about where the world is headed, and those extra five pounds we've been trying to lose for months. On any given day, the combination of all those factors will influence our stress level and can dramatically impact our peak performance.

Sources of Stress

To simplify potential sources of stress, let's start with three basic areas. Stress can come from: (1) your environment, (2) your body, and (3) your thoughts. Examples of environmental stressors include the death of a loved one, a change in residence, interpersonal demands, and time pressures. Physiological stressors from our bodies include chronic tension, illness, poor nutrition, and sleep disturbances. Thoughts can also be sources of stress, depending on how you interpret your experiences and what you predict for the future. Thoughts that become stressors include excessive worrying, perfectionism, and low self-esteem. For example, putting yourself down for not doing as well as you would have liked may be more stressful than accepting how you did and learning what you need to do different the next time.

---

31. <u>Activities</u>

Just off the top of your head, think of your top three stressors, the things that are causing the most stress in your life right now. They could come from your environment, body, or thoughts. Write them down.

    1.

    2.

    3.

The way we manage our time is often closely related to stress, so also ask yourself, "What is my number one time waster?" and jot it down.

My number one time waster is:

___

Our finances often fall into the category of environmental stressors. Sometimes money creates stress for me, and sometimes it doesn't. During my graduate school days, my parents paid for my books and tuition, and I paid for my living expenses. I was fortunate to get university internships that gave me valuable experiences in my field, even though they never paid much. At all. In fact, for a number of years, I literally lived below the poverty level.

But my lack of money at that time rarely stressed me out. Almost all my fellow students were poor, just like me, so we found ways to live, entertain ourselves, and have fun that didn't require money. However, I remember going home one time to visit my parents, and my mom noticed that I never went shopping. When she asked me about it, I replied, "I don't have money to buy anything, so why look?" I know she felt bad for me, but she also understood the circumstances, and both she and my dad helped me as much as they could.

What's interesting, though, is that in looking back, I can see that period of poverty was one of the happiest times in my life. As soon as I realized that, I learned another significant life lesson: ***I don't need money to be happy***. Wow. That was a big one. Yes, it's important to have enough money to cover basic *needs* and necessities. But I can be happy without getting my *wants* and desires fulfilled.

I also realized that part of the reason my poverty didn't bother me was because of how I *interpreted* my lack of money. I knew it was temporary, just until I could complete my degree and start to work. Plus, my poverty was voluntary. I willingly put myself in that situation, knowing finances would be tight. So the fact that I chose that path also made a difference in how I interpreted it.

Contrast my graduate school poverty with a later time in my life when I went into stress overload because of money. I worked through a year-to-year contract with a university and never knew until the last minute whether or not I would get hired for the next year. My stress led me to think about the worst possible outcomes, and at one point, I even worried about becoming homeless. I knew that employers in the private sector were reluctant to hire people out of education, so my worry had some merit. However, I anticipated poverty as almost an inevitable fate. I was afraid of something that hadn't even happened. In other words, I interpreted my uncertain situation in a way that created even more stress.

Here's the big *aha*, the major life lesson, in comparing these two situations. *It's not the event but the way we **interpret** the event that causes us to feel stress.* In graduate school, I interpreted my poverty as a necessary means to an end. No big deal. Later on, I interpreted my *possible* poverty as a catastrophic event, something that could lead to homelessness. And that interpretation sent my stress level soaring.

Here's another example: some people who get divorced feel devastated and over-the-top stressed out. Others may feel some stress but mostly relief. It all depends on how you interpret the situation. The good news is that even when we can't change or control situations in our lives, we always have the option to change the way we interpret those situations.

In looking back, I could have interpreted my yearly contract in ways that didn't stress me out, at least not as much. If nothing else, we can always interpret stressful circumstances as an opportunity to practice effective stress management techniques. See if we can get really good at it, like shooting for an A in the classroom on stress in our metaphorical school. As you identify your sources of stress, know that the way you think about those sources can make a huge difference in how much stress they create. Also, look for the silver lining in whatever is happening, and try to find a reason to be grateful, even if it's for other things in your life.

Another way we get stressed out? We interpret *all* stress as negative and something to be avoided. But remember, some stress is positive. It provides motivation and a healthy amount of anxiety or excitement, which are forms of emotional energy. We can channel that energy into getting things done, overcoming our challenges, and accomplishing our goals. It all starts with how we interpret our stress.

Right now, let's take a quick stress break by doing the following exercise.

---

32. *Activities*

Breathing is one of the easiest and fastest ways to lower your stress level. Try this simple activity.

1. *Sit in a comfortable position.*

2. *Focus on your breathing. Don't try to change anything. Just breathe normally.*

3. *Count your breaths. With each inhalation, silently say the word "One."*

4. Continue saying "One" each time you breathe in.

5. Do this for several minutes.

Keep this breathing exercise in mind when you need a quick stress break. It can help clear your mind and calm you down.

You can also try different variations of this activity. For example, count your inhalations by silently saying, "One. Two. Three. Four." Then start over again and count up to four. Experiment and see what works best for you.

Symptoms of Stress

How do you know if you're experiencing stress? One of the first things that happens to me is that I get annoyed. Little things start to irritate me, things I usually don't even notice, like time constraints and certain noises (for example, gum chewing, dripping water, and ticking clocks). Another one of my symptoms? I forget things. I can't remember simple things that I normally don't even have to think about.

If you want to manage your stress, it's essential that you learn how to recognize your symptoms. All of us need to know when we're stressed out so we can do something about it. The following symptoms are common stress responses. They may last a short time or for longer periods. Although they may make you uncomfortable, acknowledging your stress signals is part of a healthy approach to reducing your stress and starting to develop a stress management plan.

1. Physical symptoms: fatigue or exhaustion; insomnia or sleeping more; underactivity or procrastination; hyperactivity, overworking, or an inability to slow down; health problems (e.g., overeating/undereating, headaches, digestive problems); spending excessive time on technology devices; using or abusing alcohol or other drugs

2. Emotional symptoms: emotional numbing or denial; oversensitivity; guilt; an excessive sense of vulnerability; feeling inadequate, overwhelmed, or out of control; depression; helplessness; hopelessness; emotional withdrawal; anxiety; fear; uncertainty; apprehension; impatience/irritability/agitation; cynicism; anger

3. Cognitive symptoms: confusion; poor concentration; impaired memory; difficulty making decisions or solving problems; nightmares; obsession (inability to stop thinking about something); scapegoating; blaming; suspiciousness

4. Spiritual symptoms: loss of meaning in job and/or life; sense of grief; hopelessness about life in general

---

33. <u>Activities</u>

Think about how you experience stress. Write down your three main stress symptoms, whether they're physical, emotional, cognitive, or spiritual.

    1.

    2.

    3.

Become an observer, and learn to notice when you first begin to have symptoms of stress.

Most of the time we can handle short-term stress. In fact, it's healthy to periodically take on challenges that put demands on us and give us short, bite-size pieces of stress. That's positive. But long-term stress can wreak all kinds of havoc with our minds and bodies. Some estimates indicate that 75 to 90 percent of all doctor visits are for stress-related issues. By tuning into your symptoms of stress, you take one step in learning to prevent at least some of the long-term negative stress we all need to avoid.

Also, please note that what you might think is a symptom of stress may instead be the sign of a more serious medical condition. Be sure to see your doctor if you have any concerns.

Taking Care of Yourself

Stress becomes problematic when you have too little stress and become bored or when you have too much and it exceeds your optimal level. If you have too little stress and feel stagnant or complacent, you can always add more stressors to your life by taking on new challenges. In other words, there's usually a quick fix for too little stress. So for the rest of this section, let's mainly focus on when you're overly stressed.

Many times the source of our stress is environmental, like money, problems at work, or relationship conflicts. Basic psychology suggests that if your stressors come from your environment, you have three options:

1. Leave
2. Change the situation
3. Change your reaction to the situation

For example, let's say your stress comes from your job. Some people choose the first option—to leave. They quit or retire. However, most people can't leave their jobs, because they don't have another source of income. You may also try the second strategy, changing the situation, to make your job less stressful. Maybe you can suggest changes in company policies or ask to modify the way you do your job, but sometimes these possibilities are limited. However, we *always* have the option to choose the third strategy. We can always change our reaction to the situation. For instance, you might find ways to minimize your interaction with irritating people or learn how to interpret events at work so they don't create stress, at least not as much.

What if you're feeling stressed and overwhelmed, but you can't pinpoint any one source of stress? This kind of general stress can easily creep into our lives, because stress is cumulative. It's not one thing in particular but rather the combination of all the things we're dealing with. We might be able to choose the second option and change the situation by rearranging our lives, maybe cut back somewhere, so that all of our responsibilities combined don't take us beyond our optimal stress zone. But regardless of which option we choose, it's important to have a handful of stress management techniques we can use when we need them.

The people who tend to have the most difficulty with stress are those who either *underreact* or *overreact*. If we underreact, it's important to find ways to express our stress and the feelings it creates. As we discussed earlier, these can include anxiety, fear, impatience, frustration, anger, guilt, helplessness, and feeling overwhelmed and inadequate. Unexpressed, these feelings can get buried in our bodies and come out as an illness or injury. We may also hold feelings in for so long that we eventually explode and inappropriately express our pent-up emotions all at once. In contrast, those of us who overreact to stress need to find ways to relax, kick back, and give ourselves periodic breaks from our stress and the emotions that go along with it. We covered this in chapter 5, the section on emotions.

Things to Try

Depending on where you are at any given time, you may need to express your feelings of stress more. If you're already overwhelmed, you may need to distract yourself and get away from your stressful emotions. Whichever situation you're in, consider the following suggestions.

1. Breathe. When you notice your symptoms of stress, take a few minutes to focus on your breath and breathe more deeply and slowly than you normally do. It's one of the quickest ways to relax.

2. Reinterpret whatever is causing you stress. Whenever you find yourself in what you think is a "bad" situation, find a way to reframe it and see it in a more positive light. For example, instead of seeing a new work assignment at your job as a source of stress, think about it as an opportunity to learn new skills and life lessons. And then set your intention to let that situation bring out the best in you. Aim for an A in that metaphorical stress management class. Dig in, and let your attitude and effort help you not only rise to the occasion, but really shine.

3. Use affirmations. When you get stressed out, there's a good chance that your thoughts are making things worse, so pay extra attention to your self-talk. In addition to reinterpreting the stressful event, deliberately change to self-talk that calms you down. For example, "I can handle this," or "I'll get through this just fine. It's okay to relax and enjoy the ride." I often use what's called *paradoxical intention* by saying something like "The more stress I experience, the more calm, focused, and productive I become." Experiment and find out what works for you. You can say these affirmations out loud or silently to yourself.

4. Practice gratitude. When we focus on the things in our lives that we're grateful for, it helps to put our problems in perspective. Especially when you feel stressed out, take time to focus on the blessings in your life. Writing down the things you're grateful for on a regular basis helps to develop a more positive, can-do attitude about life in general. When the curveballs of life inevitably come along, you're more able to keep it all in perspective.

Here's an example of how to combine gratitude with reinterpreting the source of stress. There's a dog in my neighborhood that sometimes barks for hours, which can stress me out and drive me nuts. People have tried talking to the owners, and it's helped some, but when they're not home, the dog can go on and on. This is a situation where I can't leave, and I can't change the situation. But I can change my reaction to what's happening. I can reframe the situation. So instead of getting mad at the dog and its owners, I tell myself that I'm so glad the dog has a home and isn't in some shelter in a cramped cage. My gratitude that the dog is being taken care of helps knock the edge off the annoyance factor and is surprisingly helpful. And if it really gets bad, I can always put in ear plugs.

5. Talk about your stress with those who are supportive. Find family members or friends who can be good listeners.

6. Pay attention to your physical health. Get enough sleep, eat a healthy diet, and exercise regularly.

7. Find healthy escape activities. Read, watch television, go to a movie, enjoy music or sports. Be careful about alcohol and other drug use, and avoid abusing substances as a way of dealing with your stress. Also observe the amount of time you spend on tech devices; they can become an unhealthy way of avoiding situations that need your attention.

8. Be happy. Every day include at least one activity that makes you feel happy, something you look forward to. This can help you hold on to a positive attitude, which is essential for us to interpret the events in our lives in ways that prevent or minimize our stress.

9. Keep busy. Stay active, but alternate that with taking time to relax. Stress-reducing physical activities include walking, bicycling, running, and yoga.

10. Do more. Sometimes when your to-do lists get overwhelming, it can help to do more. I know this may sound counterintuitive, but if I have a long list of things that need to get done, and I can't put any of them off for a later time, it reduces my stress when I dig in and complete some of the smaller items—the ones that don't take much time. If I can cross those off my list, it frees up my focus and energy for other items on my list. Plus, crossing items off my list shows me I can be successful at getting things done quickly and helps to boost my confidence and mood.

11. Find ways to express your emotions. Laugh, have a good cry, keep a journal, play, vent through physical or artistic activities (e.g., gardening, cleaning, dancing, drawing, singing). See the section on emotions in chapter 5 for more suggestions.

12. Figure out what you can change in your life and what you can't. Change what you can, but learn to tell the difference. Many of us spend inordinate amounts of time and energy trying to change things that are completely outside of our ability to influence. For example, we usually can't change other people, but we often try.

13. Use your time wisely. People who feel more in control of their time usually feel less stress. Use your time wisely and in ways that increase your self-esteem.

14. Learn new skills. If you need to learn stress management techniques, consider classes, books, or online resources. We all need to know how to slow down. Activities such as relaxation, breathing exercises, and meditation can help. In addition to time management, learning other skills may be needed. For example, learn how to become more assertive so you can say "No" to other people's requests and to your own tendency to take on too much.

15. Find some type of creative expression in your life. Examples include art, music, hobbies, volunteer or community work, and exploring different approaches to your job—whatever you do with passion that feels rejuvenating.

Remember: a healthy stress management plan includes seeking out positive stress in your life while at the same time incorporating some type of stress-reducing activities. So take on healthy challenges, and then for short periods every day, find ways to stop the "stress juices," primarily adrenaline. Don't wait for your annual two-week vacation to finally relax. It's best to build that relaxing downtime into every day.

Developing a Stress Management Plan

Stress management needs to be individualized. What may be emotionally expressive for one person may be an avoidance technique for another. Plus, various techniques may work differently for you at different times. Experiment and find out what's effective for you. Also, listen to your gut—that intuitive inner voice—for what technique would be helpful when.

It's important to be aware of how you typically respond to stress. Do you usually react, underreact, or overreact? An effective stress management plan includes several healthy escape activities (sleeping, watching movies, surfing the Internet) and a couple of ways you can express emotions (talking to others, venting through physical activities, writing in a journal). That way you don't become too dependent on any one technique. If your stress management plan gives you ways to both avoid feelings and express them, it can help you take your emotions a little at a time and put them into small, manageable pieces that you can handle without getting overwhelmed.

What Works for Me

Over years of experimenting with a variety of stress management techniques, I've developed a personal plan that works, at least most of the time. It starts with my "foundation"—four cornerstones that help keep me centered and positive: (1) a healthy diet, (2) adequate sleep, (3) regular exercise, and (4) meditation. If I get off base with any of these four, my body lets me know right away, and that feedback helps me get back on track.

Although I usually react appropriately to stress, sometimes I overreact, depending on the stressor. The symptoms of my overreactions usually include irritability, forgetfulness, anxiety, obsessive thinking, and hyperactivity. Especially when I overreact, I need to make sure I find ways to escape my stressful feelings and nonstop thoughts by incorporating enjoyable "time-out" activities.

At different times, I use all fifteen of the strategies listed under "Things to Try." But my main, go-to, de-stressing technique is music. It serves as both my great escape from stressful feelings *and* my near-perfect activity for emotional expression. Sometimes music gives me a temporary time out from my angst and, at the same time, helps me feel the emotions of my stress. It's amazing how that works.

I often listen to music at home, and I almost always play music in my car. I usually pick artists whose songs have upbeat words, something like "Happy" by Pharrell Williams. I sing along with the songs and frequently dance around my house. Sometimes I find songs that express what I'm feeling at the time (like anger) or what I need (like courage), and I sing them over and over.

I also sing in my car, sometimes so loudly and for so long that I'm actually hoarse. It feels great to exhaust myself that way, like when you finish a hard physical workout. Afterward, I'm relaxed, my problems seem smaller, and the world seems like a better place.

My plan usually keeps heavy duty stress at bay, and it definitely helps me through the rough spots in life that all of us periodically encounter. It's important to turn your stress management plan into daily habits, things you do automatically without having to think about them. That way you'll be in better shape to handle major bouts of stress when they come your way.

Now it's your turn to create a stress management plan you think will work for you. You can write it out like I just did. Or you can make a list or an outline—whatever makes the most sense.

34. Activities

Taking into account what you know about how you react to stress, write a stress management plan to help you deal with negative stress. You can choose from the activities under "Things to Try," or maybe you already know what you need to do. Include ways you can relax and take a break as well as activities that will help you express your stressful feelings.

Also, identify ways to minimize or prevent negative stress. For example, if I simply get a good night's sleep, things don't stress me out as much the next day.

<u>*My Stress management Plan*</u> *(include at least three ways to better manage your stress)*

1.

2.

3.

After you incorporate these three changes into your day-to-day life, add a few new techniques for managing your stress. Make your plan a growing, evolving process that helps you continually get better at staying in your optimal stress zone.

Now ask yourself, "What's the main thing I need to remember about managing my stress?" Write down your answer.

After you draft a personal stress management plan, you'll need to find ways to implement it. That usually means setting goals and achieving them. We'll cover goal setting in the next chapter titled "Doing What You Came Here to Do."

Increasing Your Energy

"Meet you at the pool today?" I asked my friend Melissa as we passed each other in the hallway at work.

"Yes, see you there," she replied as she hurried off to her next meeting.

Melissa and I had worked in the same department for several years. We had a lot in common, including our love for athletic activities. We decided to swim together once a week after work, so we met at the pool of a local junior high school every Wednesday afternoon at five thirty for an hour-long workout.

I love to swim, even though I'm not that good at it. Melissa and I joined a Masters Swim Club for adults, which meant we could swim as many days as we wanted during the designated times. We swam with a group of people who were training for triathlons, and I was definitely slow in comparison. But it didn't matter. Swimming makes me feel better than any other type of exercise I've found. I would feel energized for two days after a workout in the water.

But then I learned that at least 80 percent of kids pee in the pool, so I stopped swimming and switched to other workouts. Plus, I knew the chlorine was horrible for my health. One of my goals is to someday build my own heated lap pool and use something besides chlorine to keep it clean.

Mostly through trial and error, I've found what exercises my body thrives on. Swimming tops the list. Running comes in second, although it doesn't work my whole body, and it's hard on my knees. Now I do a combination of cardio, weights, and stretching, which is okay, but I still want to get back to the swimming.

I've gone for periods of time without working out, usually when I've gotten extra busy, traveled, or when the weather turned bad and I was exercising outdoors. Here's what I learned: nothing takes the place of exercise. Nothing. You can't fake the benefits it gives you by doing other things. No matter what else I do to beef up my physical health, I won't feel as good, have as much energy, think as clearly, or function as well without exercise. It's an absolute must if I want to do and be my best.

That doesn't mean I haven't looked for shortcuts. I can trick my body for short periods of time by doing caffeine. It definitely gives me an energy boost, but then it wears off, and I come down to a level lower than where I started. I know lots of people who use sugar the same way. It takes their energy level up but then drops them off, leaving them craving more sugar just to keep going. This becomes a never-ending cycle and doesn't address the underlying cause of low energy in the first place.

If we want to become better students of life, it's essential that we find ways to naturally increase our energy in healthy ways. When we increase our physical energy, it simultaneously boosts our mental abilities and helps balance out our emotions. My whole attitude about life improves when I exercise regularly. If I miss a couple of workouts, I tend to become somewhat negative. It's not depression, but I'll start to see the glass as half empty, which isn't like me. As soon as I notice this negativity, the first thing I ask myself is, "When was the last time you exercised?"

So what else can we do to increase our energy? I've found a formula that works for me, but what works best for any given person is highly individualized. No one size fits all, which means each of us needs to figure out what to do in order to feel great and truly thrive.

However, you can look at several areas that need to get addressed, and use those as a starting place for discovering exactly what will work best for you. Besides regular exercise, the cornerstones of my foundation include diet, sleep, and meditation.

1. Exercise. This one is absolutely essential for me. I feel a lot better when I exercise every day, for a total of four hours each week.

2. Diet. I pay a lot of attention to nutrition, because I've seen a direct correlation between what I eat, my overall health, how I feel, and how much energy I have. With so much information available about what constitutes a healthy diet, much of it contradictory, it's sometimes hard to know what to eat. That's why I've learned to listen to my body about what it likes and doesn't like. Does a particular food make me feel better or worse? Does it increase my stamina or only provide a short-term energy spike?

To see if my diet is working, I periodically get blood tests to make sure everything stays in the healthy range. I also work with a nutritionist and try to keep up with at least some of the latest in health research when making decisions about what foods are right for me.

But here's the kicker. Finding an optimal diet falls into that category of life lessons that are **changing**. The lessons change over time. What worked beautifully for me five years ago, two years ago, or even six months ago may not be what works best today.

I would love to think I could find the perfect diet, and it would be perfect forever, and I wouldn't have to keep tweaking what I eat to meet the needs of my body as it changes over time. I used to get mad about that. Now I know with absolute certainty that my lessons about a healthy diet will continue to shift, and I accept that. I've developed a habit of constantly being on the lookout for the next way I can improve the nutrition my body needs.

Am I happy about this constant change? Not always, especially when it means reading about the next direction, substituting foods on my grocery list, and learning to cook new recipes. But I make small modifications over time and only take on what I think I can succeed at. Also, I've tried ignoring my body's transitioning needs, and I don't like where that goes. So my alternatives aren't very attractive. We'll cover this more in the next chapter on goal setting.

3. Sleep. We live in a nation of sleep-deprived people. Recent research from the Centers for Disease Control shows that 35 percent of adults get less than the recommended seven hours a night. And I've been right there with them, thinking I could cut my sleep short and get away with it. Yes, I usually can get by with less sleep for short periods of time, even though I notice, and studies show, that even one night of too little sleep can affect our mood, memory, motivation, concentration, and decision making.

But it's the long-term sleep deprivation that really takes its toll. I used to go through crunch periods at work when I missed getting enough sleep for several weeks at a time. My whole body ached, and I felt like I had the flu. I knew if I kept going like that I would eventually get sick. I also knew my mind wasn't functioning at 100 percent. But sometimes you just need to struggle through.

I've found that my body's needs for sleep are pretty consistent over time. I feel my best on seven hours a night. If I get less than that, I can sometimes take a twenty-minute power nap the next day and wake up feeling great.

I've been taking midday naps for years. After I completed some training in hypnosis, I started exploring self-hypnosis suggestions. During my lunch hour at work, I would often close my door and either put my head back on my chair or stretch out on the floor. I gave myself the suggestion that I would wake up at a certain time, and over years and years of doing this, I never once overslept. Now it's easy for people to set the alarm on their cell phones and wake up when they need to.

If you haven't already discovered power naps, I encourage you to experiment. Health experts now tout the benefits of a quick daytime siesta to help you feel more alert, increase productivity, and decrease stress. Naps have also been found to help prevent heart disease. I became a fan when I noticed how those few minutes gave me so much more energy, concentration, and enthusiasm for the rest of my day and into the evening. Try it and watch what happens.

4. Meditation. While I was in graduate school, I took a class on yoga and immediately got hooked. I noticed that when I focused on what my body was doing, it took my thoughts away from their normal nonstop chatter and gave me a much-needed break from my own thinking. After the class, I felt more relaxed and at peace. Poof. My worries were gone, at least for a while.

That experience made me more open to learning meditation. After exploring several different types, I found what works for me. The goal of meditation is to find something to focus on—a word (like peace), a visual image (maybe a candle flame), or a motion (like your breathing). You start by focusing on whatever you've chosen and then watch how your thoughts start darting out in all directions, pulling your attention with them. When you notice you've lost your focus, simply bring your attention back to the object you've chosen. That's it.

Because my thoughts are so hyperactive, I use all three ways of focusing. I might concentrate on my breathing and silently say one word when I inhale and another word when I exhale. I may also use visual imagery, sometimes imagining that I'm encircled in a bubble of golden-white light or seeing a small radiant white light in my mind's eye. The point is to find what works for you, whether it's an auditory word or sound, a visual image, or a kinesthetic movement. Your most natural technique—auditory, visual, or kinesthetic—may be the same as your predominant learning style that we covered in chapter 7. If you want to learn specific meditation techniques, look for instructions in books, classes, or online materials.

Some people aren't the type to sit still for meditation, even for twenty minutes. They may do better with what's called **movement meditation**. Any repetitive movement can work. For instance, take walking. I can pick a word (maybe joy, light, or love) and say it silently to myself with each step I take while I go about my day.

I've also noticed how sports and athletic activities can give people some of the same benefits of meditation. Many of the college athletes I worked with went into a "zone" while participating in their sport. Playing gave them a one-pointed focus that kept them in the present moment and prevented extraneous thoughts. They were usually physically exhausted after a workout, but their minds had gotten a break. This can happen with all kinds of physical activities, whether it's a sport like basketball or golf or something like knitting, gardening, or playing a musical instrument. If I'm concentrating on my singing, it naturally prevents other thoughts, because my voice becomes my single point of focus.

Once considered esoteric, meditation is quickly becoming mainstream in American culture, especially as more research shows its benefits. Studies have documented improvements in physical and mental health, reductions in stress, better mental clarity, heightened creativity, and more emotional resiliency, among others. The results I notice most in my own life include greater awareness, improved concentration, a pervasive sense of peace and optimism, and the ability to stay mentally and emotionally grounded in situations that used to upset me. It can sometimes take several months of meditating to notice the results, but most people find that good things happen if they're willing to stick with it.

Staying Ready

When I keep my four cornerstones in place—exercise, diet, sleep, and meditation—I'm more ready for whatever comes along, whether that's an unexpected curve ball or a beyond-belief opportunity. It means I'm more prepared for the next lesson and that I get to pass my classes faster, with less effort and stress, and then graduate and move into the next class in the school of my life. It means I increase my overall learning curve.

I used to play some tennis when I was an undergraduate. The cornerstones of my foundation are analogous to being in the "ready" position in tennis—feet apart, knees bent, bending forward slightly with my racket centered in front of me. I can easily move forward, backward, use my forehand to the right, and return with my backhand. I'm set.

Most of the time, I find it fun to experiment with different health practices. Plus, it helps me stay in my optimal stress zone. Sometimes it feels like work, but it's always been worth it.

Even so, I didn't used to be *this* focused on increasing my energy or improving my health. When I was younger, I had loads of energy and never *needed* to give it much thought, although I always dabbled in different ways to stay healthy. I also know a lot of older folks who sail through life with energy to spare and don't appear to do much to keep it that way.

But aging has changed me. I've become keenly aware of how much I need an abundant supply of energy in order to finish doing what I'm here to do. I see so many opportunities in the future, and I know I'll need to keep my body and mind in prime shape in order to take advantage of them. I'm acutely aware that our time on this planet is finite, and I don't want to get to the end of my journey, look back, and regret the fact that I didn't do more. Much of that "doing more" depends on how much energy you have to work with.

Meditation Techniques That Don't Take Extra Time

One of the main reasons people don't meditate is because they don't have the time. Our time is precious and often scarce, especially when we live such jam-packed lives. To reap the greatest rewards from meditation, we need to do it twenty minutes a day. Taking that time actually increases your productivity throughout the day and is practiced by extraordinarily busy people like Oprah Winfrey, Jerry Seinfeld, Arianna Huffington, and Paul McCartney. And the late Steve Jobs swore by it. However, if you just don't have twenty minutes, there's good news. You can practice meditation without setting aside any extra time.

Make no mistake: you don't get full benefits if you don't put in full effort. But you can still get some of the benefits, and a little bit of meditation is better than none. So if this sounds doable, try experimenting with the following:

1. Breathing techniques. Using our breath as a focal point easily lends itself to inclusion in our hectic lives, because our steady in-and-out movement remains a constant throughout the day. In many traditional meditation practices, you sit still and focus on your breath. You can just observe your breath or count each one. So for example, silently say to yourself the word "One" every time you inhale. Or say "One" as you inhale and "Two" as you exhale. You might count each inhale up to four, and just observe your exhale. Another variation is to pick a word like "peace," "calm," or "relax," and say it in time with your breath. This technique is simple and highly portable. It can be done anytime, anywhere.

I use this technique often. For example, if I feel pressured to get a lot done in a hurry, I'll start focusing on my breath, saying one of my favorite phases with each in-out cycle. I find this works best when I'm doing habitual tasks like cooking, dressing, and household chores—activities that don't require much thought. To get started, you can pick a routine task like taking a shower and practice saying a word or phrase in time with your breath, at least while the water is running.

You can also do this while waiting to be seen in a doctor's office or standing in line at a store. It works great whenever you have a forced time out in your day.

Another time I use this is when I'm particularly worried about something. Focusing on my breath while saying a word or phrase keeps me from getting into my obsessive cycle, where my thoughts begin to race out of control and I go over and over the same things. Obsessing often leads to negativity and feeling powerless and stuck, so I try to head it off at the start.

I've also found it helpful to focus on my breathing when I get surprised or unexpectedly stressed out. For example, if I'm sitting in a meeting where there is a lot of confusion or animosity, and especially if I feel myself getting caught up in that chaotic energy, I'll focus on my breath and silently say a word or words with each inhalation and exhalation. You can say "calm" or "kindness" or whatever feels right for you and for the circumstance. I can quickly ground myself with this technique, while still participating in the discussion off and on, and no one knows what I'm doing. When I take this momentary step back from the interaction, it also allows me to listen for what's *not* being said that needs to be said. I can offer that information to the group and sometimes help us get back on track or move toward a resolution.

I also like to use this technique while I'm working out. If I'm on an elliptical machine, it's easy to say a word or words with each breath. When I used to swim, I would repeat one word with my inhale and another word with my exhale. It made my swimming even more fun and relaxing.

Research shows that meditation increases our neurotransmitters, including endorphins, which are feel-good chemicals in the body. Add that to the neurotransmitters that naturally flow when you exercise, and it's no wonder I feel high after a workout. If you try this and start to feel spacey or disoriented, stick with meditation techniques done in a safe, controlled environment, at least until you get used to keeping your focus on the activity *and* your breath.

2. Movement meditation. Meditating while moving can be similar to breathing techniques, except you focus on the movement and silently say a word, phrase, or sound with each repetition. Walking is an easy one. Instead of saying something to yourself with each breath, you say it with each step. The same goes for jogging or running. Say a word or phrase to yourself each time your foot hits the ground. You can add this meditative component to lots of different physical activities, especially if they involve repetitive motions.

3. Visual imagery. Movement meditation can also be combined with visual imagery to provide both kinesthetic and visual focal points. This brings your thoughts into the here and now and gives your mind a chance to rest. I used to have good posture, but I've noticed I'm starting to slump. Every time I become aware of my bad posture, I focus my attention on my spine, straighten up, and imagine golden-white light flowing from the top of my head all along and down to the bottom of my spine. This technique takes maybe two seconds, and it's surprising how that quick physical adjustment, combined with the visual imagery, can boost my energy and give me a can-do attitude.

Another technique I benefit from is this: imagine that with each inhalation, you're breathing in everything you need, like relaxation, peace, courage, love, and joy. With each exhalation, imagine you're breathing out and letting go of everything you don't need, like pessimism, stress, and fatigue. Breathe normally for a few minutes while doing this imagery and see if you feel better.

4. Music. Music lends itself to meditation because of the repetition of the underlying beat. For example, pick a phrase—maybe something like "I'm grateful for my life" or "Love and light surround me" or "Today I choose joy"—and sing along with the melody, using your phrase instead of the words to the song. Most songs have a four-count beat, so you can sing your phrase within those four counts.

Sometimes it takes real concentration to stay on task, which gives your mind a challenge in the present moment. There's no worrying about tomorrow when your mind is trying to repeat your phrase, especially if it's a fast song! If it's too difficult to impose your phrase over the song's lyrics, start by singing your phrase to instrumental music. It's like a game, but one where even a little effort means you're definitely going to win because of the positive outcomes from meditation. You can do this anywhere. Again, just be sure to also pay attention to what's going on around you so you stay safe. I often do this in my house where my environment stays predictable.

You can modify all these suggestions in order to find take-no-time meditation techniques that work in your own life. For instance, visualize light surrounding your spine, helping to give you perfect posture, while you're walking. You might not notice big differences right away, but over time you may find that you're more aware, peaceful, and creative, and you have an increased energy that's calm and centered.

---

35. *Activities*

As you read through the examples of meditation techniques that don't take extra time, did any of them stand out as something you might want to try? Here are some suggestions:

1. *Pick one of the techniques mentioned and experiment with it. For instance, you could start with a breathing technique and practice using it when you're in the shower or brushing your teeth.*

2. *Select another technique and try using it at a specific time in your day. Maybe you could visualize golden-white light surrounding your spine every time you walk to and from your mailbox.*

3. *Keep exploring different techniques until you've experimented with all four types. You may find that some are easier and feel more natural than others. But you won't know that unless you try them out. Once you find what works for you, start practicing*

until it becomes more automatic. If you're like me, you may find yourself looking forward to practicing because of the good feelings that follow.

Plugging Your Energy Leaks

I've learned and relearned that improving even one of my cornerstones of exercise, diet, sleep, and meditation gives me more energy. For example, it happens every time I get a solid night's sleep and wake up eager to greet the day. It happens when I tweak my diet one more time and find the next right combination of foods to give my body the nutrition it needs. The longer I meditate, the more I notice a peaceful optimism permeating my life, which helps to prevent stress before it begins.

But there's a second half to this equation. We can also increase our energy by eliminating what I call **energy leaks**. Most of us constantly lose energy as it drains out of us due to a variety of reasons, most of which are fixable.

Imagine that your body is a vessel carrying life-giving vitality, but you've sprung a leak. In fact, you may have sprung lots of leaks. It's impossible to keep your body fueled to its capacity, and you go through life running on less than full. That automatically means you operate below your potential.

So what kinds of leaks do we spring? Leaks come in a variety of shapes and colors and are highly individualized. So each of us needs to do the work of discovering ours and then find ways to repair them. Think of yourself as a plumber who's been called out on a job to help someone (you) stop the constant loss of energy out of their body. Ready to get started?

Let's begin with the obvious leaks in the physical or material world. I don't know about you, but every project I haven't completed, every messy corner of my house, and every item I own that's broken and needs to be fixed—they all drain me. I can't forget them. They're like one of those pesky gnats that won't leave me alone. How do I know this? Because as soon as I finish the project, clean the corner, or fix the item, I get a somewhat subtle but clearly noticeable rush of energy. It's like my body says, "It drains me when you don't keep your house in order." That disorder also takes up a little bit of space in my head and my psyche, preventing me from doing and being my best.

Let's start with the assumption that everything in life that is uncompleted takes your attention and mental energy. We may use mental energy to figure out how we're going to complete a task, or we may spend energy trying *not* to think about it. Either way, it drains us.

As the plumber, your job is to examine all areas where there might be energy leaks and then fix them—plug them up so they don't waste such a valuable resource. The more you do this, the more you move into present time and become "current" in your life. You let go of the things from your past that are draining your vitality and catch up with the here and now.

---

36. *Activities*

Write down your responses to the following areas that many of us need to complete in our material worlds. Identifying incomplete tasks is the first step in plugging your energy leaks.

  1. *Places I need to clean:*

  2. *Things I need to fix:*

  3. *Projects I need to complete:*

  4. *Personal health issues I need to address:*

  5. *Other areas where I need to stop procrastinating:*

When you consider personal health issues, keep in mind that sometimes these can be addressed by improving your exercise, diet, sleep, and mediation. At other times, you may need medical help, so be sure to see your physician if you have questions or concerns.

Problems in our relationships can also drain our energy. This includes our relationships with other people and our relationship with ourselves. To regain the energy you may be losing, start by responding to the following.

---

37. *Activities*

Consider all the people who are now in your life as well as those you've known in the past. Write down your responses to the following areas.

  1. *People I need to apologize to:*

  2. *People I need to thank:*

  3. *People I need to forgive (including myself):*

4. *Other people I have unfinished business with:*

5. *Relationships I need to improve:*

Before trying to repair a relationship, consider whether your efforts might make things worse for the other person. Don't let your attempts at closure cause you to possibly hurt or upset someone else. Also, know that sometimes other people won't be receptive to your efforts. Learn to let it be okay if relationships can't be fixed, and realize that benefits can come from making your best effort.

When I taught classes on this book to college students, we went over these lists, and many of the students felt overwhelmed just thinking about all the unfinished projects and unresolved relationship issues they needed to fix. I felt that way, too.

It's important to remember that the lists represent *possible* areas to put in order. After I realized I needed to deal with some of my own unfinished business, I started by identifying a couple of things that would be quick fixes, like replacing a broken lamp and sending a thank you note. Completing those didn't take much time, felt great, and got me motivated to take on more. At some point, I developed an intention around resolving my past issues, and circumstances started naturally occurring that helped me make things right. Now I work hard not to create any additional unfinished business as I go about my life. In other words, I avoid all the new leaks that I can.

Clearing the Clutter

After I retired, I looked at my house with a fresh set of eyes. I knew my house would be my office and that I'd be spending a lot more time at home. I wanted to enjoy my time there, and it gradually dawned on me that in order to do that, I'd need to get rid of at least some of the clutter.

Not that my house was completely out of control to start with. But I enjoy decorating and tended to fill most spaces with an arrangement or sit-around. I love my "stuff," most of which has some special meaning or reminds me of something important in my life—like family mementos, the two-foot statue of a woman meditating that sits on my coffee table, and the picture of a young child drawing, which symbolizes spontaneity and creativity.

But then there were those old clothes I would probably never wear again. The shoes that were out of style or hurt my feet. The kitchen gadgets I'd had for years and used maybe twice. The boxes of folders I'd saved from previous jobs that I knew I'd never need. My stuff suddenly seemed heavy, and I realized I needed to lighten my load in order to fully embrace a new chapter in my life.

My stuff wasn't so much disorderly, but there was definitely too much of it. I felt like I needed empty space in my house and my life, space that could get filled with the newness of the now and the opportunities of the future. So I gradually started paring down—donating, giving away, throwing away, recycling, or selling the things that needed to go. I developed several criteria for my decisions:

1. Do I like the item? Some things I'd kept for years, and I didn't even like them.

2. Do I want the item? I might like something, but do I really want to keep it? If the item made me feel good when I looked at it because of the memories it evoked or because of its aesthetics or because I just thought it was cool, I kept it. I like having feel-good items around me.

3. Do I need the item? I had kept a lot of stuff I knew I would never need.

4. Can the item be replaced? If I didn't need the item right then but might in the future, could I go out and buy a replacement without major expense? If so, I let it go.

5. Does the item have sentimental value? The items that reminded me of a special relationship or time in my life were some of the hardest to even consider parting with. I learned that if I took a picture of the item, it was easier to let go. Knowing the memory could be preserved in a photo helped me realize I didn't need to hold on to the item itself. If I started to feel guilty for letting go of something that had been given to me by someone as an expression of their love, I reminded myself it was the love—not the item—that was important. And that love would always be in my heart.

6. Does the item support my life purpose? Would the item help me move forward with my goals, dreams, and mission? This question remains one of my most important bottom-line criteria. Each time I ask myself that question, it reaffirms who I am right now in my life and the direction that I'm headed.

7. Does it feel especially difficult to let go of a particular item? Even when I knew I needed to get rid an item, sometimes I started feeling anxiety, apprehension, and doubt when it actually came down to parting with it. So I made a deal with myself. I placed the item in my garage and left it sitting there for several weeks. If I still had misgivings in two to three weeks, I knew I could always keep it. But in every single case, I eventually decided to let it go. And my final decision always felt right in the long run.

These questions worked for me in clearing out the physical clutter in my life. You may find that other questions provide better guidance in making your own decisions. If you're already living a clutter-free life, congratulations. But if you're among the majority of us, I encourage you to experiment with letting go of some of your things. Like me, you may find that you feel happier, lighter, more energized, more powerful, and have a sense of liberation that you never would have known until you went through this process. Try it and watch what happens.

If you want more information on how to declutter, you're in luck. In the recent past, the material available online and in books has mushroomed. You can even hire a professional to help you clean your closets and downsize your house. Ask a friend or family member to help, or support each other as you both clean out your stuff. I've found that the ecstatic "Yes!" feelings I get from decluttering are pretty immediate, so once you start, those positive feelings help keep you going.

After I made some progress getting rid of the extra weight of my physical belongings, it felt so good that I wanted to continue. So I cleaned out my files, updated my finances, and finally got serious about putting my paperwork in order, including everything required for when you die—like a will, trust, medical power of attorney, and advanced medical directive. Again, lots of information is available in books and online. If you're resourceful, it doesn't have to cost much, although if you do it yourself, I recommend a final review by an attorney in your state.

I thought I was putting my affairs in order for those who would be left behind, but when I finished, I felt this heavy weight lift off my shoulders. I realized my procrastination had created a dark spot in my psyche. I'd been dragging around this undone task for years, and when it finally got completed, the sense of closure felt incredibly freeing. Yes, my paperwork was a gift to others. It also turned out to be a surprisingly valuable gift to myself.

Several years ago, my next-door neighbor died suddenly from a stroke, leaving her remaining relatives without a stitch of paperwork about her affairs, not even a list of assets. I watched as these relatives struggled through the maze of trying to figure out what to do, all while they were trying to deal with their grief. Believe me, the life lessons about putting your affairs in order are best learned on the front end of your departure. If you think you even might need legal documents, and especially if you have children or sizable assets, move that task up to the top of your priorities. None of us knows when we'll get that inevitable call to go home.

38. *Activities*

Most of us have "stuff" that we don't like, want, or need. It fills up space in our lives and weighs us down, sometimes without us knowing it until we let it go. Think about what you might need to let go of and write it down—not the actual items—just the categories:

1. *Physical belongings I need to let go of like knickknacks and clothes:*

2. *Paperwork I need to recycle, shred, organize better, or scan and file on my computer (like magazines, bank statements, or tax records):*

3. *Procrastination I need to address by completing the following tasks (e.g., updating a budget, reviewing insurance coverage, or writing a will):*

If cutting through your clutter seems too daunting, remember: you can always start small and go slow. Clean out one drawer or clear away just one pile of papers. You can get great ideas for downsizing from books and online information, and you can always ask someone else to help you.

Cognitive Clutter

We often have physical clutter in our lives that zaps our energy and keeps us from having full access to our potential. But there's another, more subtle kind of clutter that most of us carry through life. It's an invisible yet frequently debilitating energy leak, something that can keep us from even thinking about fulfilling our dreams. I call that kind of energy drain **cognitive clutter**.

What do we mean by cognitive clutter? It's the thoughts and memories we carry in our minds, the ones that constrict and often undermine our choices and options. These thoughts include the lessons we need to unlearn and replace with lessons that are more current. It's the limiting beliefs that we discussed in chapter 8, the ones that need to be examined, questioned, and either modified or unlearned altogether. It's the pockets of pain that remain in our minds after we go through hurtful or traumatic experiences. Cognitive clutter also includes our negativity, worrying, and obsessive thought patterns—unproductive thinking that takes up space in our heads. The fact of the matter is that most of us could use a good "head cleaning."

So how do you clean and declutter your mind? Let's take a look.

1. Limiting beliefs. I believe limiting beliefs do more to restrict how we live and who we become than any other factor. That's because all of us learn cognitive structures early in life that tell us who we are and how the world works, and those thought patterns often define a very narrow role that we can play in the world. So no matter what else you do to try to get ahead or live out your dreams, those beliefs can stop you in your tracks. You'll often self-sabotage and end up feeling frustrated and defeated, despite thinking that you gave it your best effort.

Why is that? All of us want to be true to who we think we are. We crave that consistency. It's an innate need. Otherwise it creates what's called ***cognitive dissonance***, where there's a discrepancy between our self-image and our thoughts and behavior. When we step outside our self-perceived identity, even when we're not fully aware of what that is, it makes us feel like we're betraying ourselves. If you think of yourself as a good person, and you have evil thoughts toward someone else, it will probably make you feel guilty. If you consider yourself a responsible person, and you do something irresponsible, it will likely cause internal dissonance and discomfort.

One of my limiting beliefs is this: "It's not okay to be too powerful," which is another version of "Don't outshine others." A lot of us hold that belief. I work hard to not buy into that faulty thinking. But remnants still remain in my head, and I have to stay vigilant so it doesn't dictate my choices.

If you're not sure about the beliefs that may be holding you back, go back to the exercise in chapter 8 where you brainstormed for limiting beliefs and dysfunctional family rules. You may also want to review the techniques that are included for changing them. It's essential that we don't let those beliefs create ceilings on who we become and how far we go.

2. Wounds. We've all been wounded in the course of living our lives. Unless our wounds sufficiently heal, we continue to carry these pockets of pain in our minds, bodies, and emotions.

Our wounds are often inflicted by others, either intentionally or unintentionally. The severity of the wound depends on the nature of the infliction, which can range from abandonment, severe abuse, neglect, and trauma to situations where someone barely hurts our feelings. We can also be wounded by life circumstances, like going through a natural disaster, witnessing some horrific event, or losing a loved one and not grieving. Most of us go through experiences that weren't anyone's fault but that still leave us feeling victimized.

Sometimes our wounds heal over time, and sometimes they don't. If they don't heal properly, they can change the entire course of our lives, usually for the worse. For example, people who have been bullied are likely to struggle with self-esteem issues. Those who have been sexually abused often have difficulty with sexual intimacy later in life.

We also inflict wounds on ourselves. We don't take care of our relationships, our health, or our finances, and we eventually have consequences to pay. We ignore problems in our lives, thinking they will go away on their own, then one day they show up uninvited and bite us. We try to squelch our burning desire to strike off on a completely different path in life and pursue a heartfelt dream. When we ignore or deny our dreams and goals, we may crush our passion and spirit in the process.

Sometimes our self-inflicted wounds are intentional, and sometimes we never meant for them to happen. For instance, if we act in ways that violate our ethics or values, if we make decisions that are inconsistent with who we believe we are as a person, we're often left with guilt, shame, remorse, and regret. In a way, that's a good thing. Those feelings tell us we have a healthy conscience and need to get back on track. In these situations, our emotions serve as teachers who are trying to help us live up to our own standards.

Some of our wounds are easily visible, and some are barely perceptible, if at all. If your life is going well, you may not need to dig up painful experiences from your past. But it you've been stuck for a considerable time, you may want to look into your past for long enough to figure out what's holding you back. You can start by simply asking yourself, "Could I be stuck because of a past wound?" Also ask, "How have I been wounded that might cause me to get stuck like this?"

For example, maybe as a child, you were told you weren't good enough. As the result, you may find yourself going through life trying to compensate by either overachieving or not even trying to achieve, because, after all, it would never be enough. Or maybe you wound yourself by being a perfectionist or setting your expectations for achievement too high, and then you feel like a failure when you don't meet what's unrealistic to start with.

A full discussion of how to heal wounds is beyond the scope of this book. Just know there's a range of what might be required, from letting time heal to extensive therapy. In between, I've seen people heal through insight into a situation or just by a shift in perception, like realizing that everyone in a traumatizing situation was doing the best they could at the time. This new perception allowed them to forgive each person involved, including themselves.

But here's the deal. It's important that we not stay stuck in a wounded victim position for long. Simply acknowledging our wounds is often a critical first step. Healing usually involves developing insight into what happened, emotional expression, learning new behavioral skills to get back to normal (if needed), and finally, forgiving whoever hurt you. Forgiveness becomes a gift to yourself. It means you no longer have to bear the mental and emotional weight of the wound. Self-forgiveness sometimes starts the process as the first step, or it may end up coming last.

If you have old wounds that are affecting your life today, it might be time to put on your student hat and learn what to do to help yourself heal. The life lesson here involves *moving from victim to student.*

You may be able to heal through journaling, talking with others, reading about how others have healed, getting into a support group, or working with a therapist one-on-one. Regardless of how you go about it, remember that each one of our experiences of wounding has at least one life lesson embedded in it. The amount of effort required to learn that lesson is usually well worth the time it takes.

3. Unproductive mindsets. Mark Twain wrote: "I've had a lot of worries in my life, most of which never happened." Sometimes I'm like Twain in worrying about things that aren't likely to occur. Or I'll worry about things I can't control. If I'm not careful, my worrisome thoughts can take off into a flat-out run and turn into obsessing, and I can't stop thinking about something. And every once in a while, I'll slip into a glass-half-empty attitude, where I see and expect the worst. When any of those things happen, it means my mindset is unproductive. My thoughts are inefficient and ineffective. They're draining my mental energy and creating obstacles to getting where I want to go.

Take worrying, for example. Worry can give us ulcers, increase our anxiety and fear, contribute to depression, and suck the joy out of life. Most of us worry at least a little, which is normal. It may not take up a lot of time and mental energy, and it might not stress us out. But worrying covers a range of intensity, so it's important to monitor your thoughts and make sure it doesn't become excessive.

Our worrying can escalate and turn into obsessive thinking, which often has its roots in fears, limiting beliefs, or wounds that haven't healed. Sometimes when we go over and over the same things in our heads, it's annoying but doesn't get in the way of our day-to-day lives. Obsessive thoughts can also take over the airwaves of our minds, drowning out healthy thoughts and preventing us from staying focused in the here and now.

Some people obsessively think about their weight, their health, or their relationships. According to a recent survey conducted by the American Psychological Association (APA), the number one source of stress in this country is money, so it stands to reason that many people worry, and maybe even obsess, about their finances.

Have you ever found yourself putting a negative spin on something that might turn out to be a positive experience? Sometimes I'll start to dread an event in the future, like a mandatory meeting, a chore around the house, or writing a touchy e-mail. My feelings of dread tell me I'm probably anticipating a glass-half-empty experience, so I'll try to change my attitude.

Sometimes I can only shift my attitude to a neutral position, where at least the dread goes away. I can tell myself something like "It might not be that bad" or ask "Can you do something to make this a more positive experience?" And many times I'm pleasantly surprised when I find that I actually enjoy whatever I'd been dreading.

I may put on some music while doing the chore or focus on how I can help improve the situation that requires a difficult e-mail. Just like with stressful situations, *we can always change the way we react to our own negative attitudes.* It's sometimes amazing to watch how that mental shift on our part helps intention kick in. We can actually create a more positive experience for ourselves and others by looking on the bright side and bringing optimism into the situation.

To recap, we can change a negative attitude through: (1) self-awareness and (2) a conscious, deliberate decision to shift our perception and let some light shine in. If you're a worrier or tend to get into obsessive thinking, you can try a variety of different approaches, like meditation, thought stopping (see Appendix D), and becoming curious about the underlying cause by asking yourself, "Why am I so focused on this particular issue?" Or set aside a specific amount of time, maybe thirty minutes, and focus only on your worries. Write down everything you're worried about. Putting it on paper helps to get it out of your head. Then take your list and start doing problem solving—looking at ways to resolve what's bothering you—or deciding on a technique to address your needless worrying if it's about something that's not likely to happen.

Once I identify a problem, my mind sometimes grabs hold of it and goes over and over the situation. I get stuck in my thinking by what's referred to as ***paralysis by analysis***. Motivational consultant Tony Robbins offers a great suggestion for this. When considering a problem or challenge, spend no more than 20 percent of your mental time analyzing the problem, and put 80 percent of your time and energy into working on a solution. This rule of thumb can do wonders to help you keep from getting bogged down at the front end of a challenge.

Other ways to address worrying include focusing on your blessings instead of your problems and being grateful for future opportunities to create positive experiences for yourself and others. If worry is a serious issue, you can also ask a counselor for help or just read more about it on your own.

It's important to discriminate between unrealistic worries and those that are grounded in reality. Be sure to ask yourself if your nonstop thoughts are attempting to give you a message. They may be trying to alert you to something you need to take care of.

I need to mention that sometimes our unproductive mindsets involve an actual mental illness. Most of us get anxious at certain times, but if your anxiety is pervasive or stops you from doing ordinary things in your life, it may be an anxiety disorder. Many of us get negative and down on occasion, but if your blue mood is accompanied by bleak thoughts and lasts for more than two weeks, it might be depression. Lots of people get obsessive and compulsive, but if their thoughts and behaviors interfere with their day-to-day activities, it could be the sign of a clinical concern.

If you think you might have a mental health issue, if your faulty thinking and unproductive mindset are making you miserable and causing you to change the way you live your life, please see a mental health professional. Effective treatments exist today that can help you get back on track and start enjoying life again.

Whether it's limiting beliefs, unhealed wounds, worrisome thoughts, or other forms of cognitive clutter, every piece of mind clutter has important lessons to teach us. If nothing else, it gives us a chance to learn how to stay in the present moment with our thinking, to witness what's happening in our heads. Each of us holds the power to add at least a sliver of optimism to our mindsets. Acting on this power opens the curtain for intention to enter the stage. The Universe responds to our hopeful attitude with assistance from seen and unseen sources. Practice observing how this happens.

39. <u>Activities</u>

Even though they may be invisible, our limiting beliefs, wounds, and unproductive mindsets drain our energy and restrict who we become and how much we accomplish. In considering where you are in your life right now, write down your answers to the following:

1. *One limiting belief that's restricting my life is*

2. *One unhealed wound that may be keeping me from moving forward is*

3. *Ask yourself, "Do I worry too much?" and "Could I improve my attitude?"*

After you answer these questions, ask, "Which one piece of cognitive clutter could I deal with right away?"

Next, write down one step you could take to address that clutter. You might want to first review the suggestions included in the previous discussion. For example, if you find yourself with a gloomy outlook, start to ask, "How can I learn to see the bright side?" or "What can I do to make this better?"

One step I could take to deal with my cognitive clutter is

Remember: a positive, can-do attitude goes a long way in propelling us along our journey of self-healing. Setting your intention to clear out restrictive clutter invites all Providence to move to help you out.

Becoming a Growth Seeker

On Tuesday mornings I go to the gym for a forty-five-minute workout. It consists of time on an elliptical machine, pedaling forward and backward, and about twenty-five minutes on a treadmill. If you're not familiar with an elliptical, you stand on pedals as your feet go around in a motion similar to riding a bicycle; hand holds cause your arms to go back and forth each time you pedal.

I've been doing this routine for quite a while, so you'd think I'd get bored. But actually, this workout is anything but boring. That's because in addition to doing other workouts, I find ways to switch things up and make it enjoyable and challenging.

For starters, I take my own music, which gives me energy and puts me in a great mood. It also drowns out other noises in the gym and helps me concentrate. I feel like I'm in my own little world.

During my workout, I alternately focus on my breathing, shift my awareness to different parts of my body, and work on improving my balance. I also include what's call high-intensity interval training, where you do short bursts of intense exercise for around thirty seconds and then rest for a couple of minutes. Research shows this cycle gives your body the benefits of longer workouts.

I love this routine and feel amazingly energized when it's over. I realize it's a form of movement meditation, because there's no way I can challenge myself like this and have my mind wandering away from the task. I have to stay focused in the present moment, so it gives my body a great workout and my mind a break from its normal chatter.

I know I'll eventually get tired of this workout and move on to new routines, but for right now, it works. It's something I look forward to. When combined with the music, it takes about ten to twelve minutes for my feel-good neurotransmitters to kick in. That's when I notice I have a big grin on my face. And the energy from the forty-five minutes I spend usually lasts all day.

So what's the point of describing all of this? The point is that I'm continuing to ask my body to meet new challenges. Safe, calculated challenges where I'm almost certain I can succeed. This workout gives me a physical, concrete activity that has become a metaphor for how I want to live my life—constantly stretching and growing.

Sports naturally cause us to want to get better. If you play golf, you're always trying to get a lower score. Competitive sports like tennis automatically put you in a mindset of improving your skills and winning matches. And even if they know they'll never win a race, runners usually try to beat their own times and do their personal best. It gives them a goal. Something to aim for.

Most people already have at least one area of their lives where they are always reaching for the next level, where they voluntarily and consciously seek growth and improvement. People into cooking are usually looking for new recipes. Parents often search for the next best childrearing practice. Business owners stay constantly on the lookout for ways to improve their profit margin. Homeowners often have an ongoing urge to complete the next improvement project. And I know lots of people who are *way* into their tech devices. They're always looking for the latest and greatest smartphone, app, or gizmo in a constant quest for something better. It's almost like a game for them.

So here's the good news. Given that most of us already have experience with this kind of enthusiastic learning, it's possible to transfer that same enthusiasm over into learning our life lessons. And when we do, it leads to personal growth. The practical wisdom from our lessons eventually guides us toward developing more of our potential, and we become more of who we're capable of being. Our individual lives get better. They expand into new territory. We pass our classes in the school of life and graduate into more advanced classes, where more choices, potential, and opportunities await. Our worlds get bigger, richer, fuller.

But there is a hazardous zone in this process that I often see in myself and others. That hazard has to do with **changing lessons** in life, those that change over time. Most of the lessons we learn about the world change. And *we* change. Our bodies, thoughts, emotions, and relationships are in a constant state of flux. How we relate to the world changes as we grow and mature from childhood to old age. So it makes sense that the lessons we learn along the way will also change.

Many of us get stuck when we try to hold on to lessons that no longer serve us. We found what was valid and true at one time, used it to grow, but then often didn't realize that it was no longer effective. For instance, many of the lessons I'm learning now about what makes for an ideal exercise routine will change as my body's needs change over time. And today's tech gadgets will be obsolete by next year.

The nature of changing lessons means we need to **unlearn** what once worked and then learn new life lessons. We may need to make midcourse adjustments in our planning as the landscape shifts. Our agility, speed, and accuracy at learning life lessons depend, in part, on how well we're able to unlearn what used to work and then learn something new.

But once we have the idea of changing lessons in our heads, we can be on the lookout for when we need to update. The key is to keep from getting stuck trying to apply a previous lesson, one that was perfectly good at the time but no longer works.

It is human nature to resist change. We almost instinctively fight against it, even when we know the world is rushing ahead, and we'll get left behind if we try to stand still. The world changes daily, and as human beings, we constantly grow, transform, and evolve.

Change necessarily means moving out of our comfort zones and into the sometimes scary darkness of the unknown. So change often makes us uncomfortable and afraid. But discomfort and fear are only emotions that come and go. The key is learning to become friends with all of our emotions, including those that are uncomfortable and frightening, and preventing those emotions from getting in the way of our growth and forward progress. We covered this in chapter 5. It's also important to note that sometimes our fear is a teacher, telling us there's a legitimate danger in the change ahead. In those cases, our job is to address that threat and make sure we stay safe.

It's also important to recognize how much change we can handle at any given time. All changes—good and bad—make demands on us and cause stress. If you are already stressed from circumstances or changes in your life, it may not be the right time to voluntarily take on more.

The bottom line is that we live in a sea of change which permeates our external and internal worlds. Knowing how it's normal to resist change, we can decide to become more deliberate in welcoming change into our lives—when the specific change and the timing are right. We can also add in the use intention to purposefully move forward in positive, growth-producing ways.

Seeking growth, combined with the use of intention, becomes a powerful force, helping us make progress at beyond average speed, because there's nothing inside of us putting on the brakes. Here are some of the areas where I'm currently using intention to stretch and grow.

Becoming a better student of life:

- Pay attention in class, identify life lessons the first time they come around, and learn from the astounding variety of teachers that the Universe puts on my path.

- Continue to hone my intuitive skills, which serve to guide my every move, even when I don't know I need guidance.

Becoming a better me:

- Continue to reflect on what I learn about myself, my relationships, the coincidences that appear in my life, and how they all tie together.

- Look for ways to practice being more enthusiastic, resilient, loyal, purposeful; stay focused on character and integrity issues within myself; keep doing the next right thing.

Nurturing my relationships:

- Give more and love deeper in my relationships with others, including family, friends, those whose paths cross mine only briefly, and those I never meet but share a connection with nonetheless.

- Practice becoming more vulnerable with those I can trust, say "I'm sorry" sooner if I need to, and say "Thank you" more often.

Improving my job skills:

- Keep getting better at writing self-help material.
- Find more ways to make my motivational talks fun and inspiring.

Supporting my purpose:

- Continue to honor my authenticity, the one-of-a-kind me that I am.
- Share my talents and gifts with others more often and in more impactful ways, ways that help us all shine brighter.

These are just some of my own examples. But maybe they will help you think of areas in your life where you could focus on intentional growth. You don't have to set formal goals in these areas, unless you want to. Just by consciously stating or writing down your intentions, you tap into an invisible flow of energy from Providence that can help make them happen.

The topics that we have covered in this chapter can help us get better as students of life, across every aspect of our lives. They can help us improve our learning curve and increase the joy we experience during our adventures in this metaphorical school. For example, we can always learn to improve how we handle stress. Better yet, we can learn how to change the way we interpret stressful events in our lives and avoid the stress altogether. We can find ways to increase our energy through exercise, diet, sleep, and meditation. Plus, we can learn how to plug energy leaks by getting rid of the clutter in our lives, both the physical clutter we sometimes insist on dragging around and the cognitive clutter of our limiting beliefs, wounds, and unproductive mindsets. And finally, we can open up to an attitude of becoming a growth seeker across the board: in our health habits, our relationships, our careers, and especially in our relationships with ourselves.

No matter where you're starting from, you can always take the next step in your growth and development. You can always find one more way to improve yourself, what you're doing, and how you're doing it. Constantly finding new ways to take on healthy challenges keeps our lives fresh, dynamic, energized, and moving forward. After a while, this pattern turns into a mindset and a habit. It becomes automatic. We move into Unconscious Competence. We don't even have to think about it.

If you set your intention to welcome change and growth into your life, the Universe jumps in to meet you more than halfway. Doors open that might never have budged. Opportunities present themselves in expected and unexpected places. We get to enter a life of exploration and growth that becomes stunningly alive in comparison to where we sat in our complacency. And that growth helps to ensure that when we get to the end of life's journey, we're happy and at peace.

40. *Activities*

Developing a mindset that welcomes change and setting our intention to stretch and grow can propel us forward in surprisingly powerful ways. To get started, answer the following:

1. *What's one intention I can set to become a better student of life?*

2. *I want to stretch and grow in my relationships by*

3. *Here's how I could do a better job of nurturing my gifts and talents:*

4. *Additional areas of my life I want to improve are as follows (think health habits, spiritual growth, career, money matters, and others):*

Keep the answers to these questions in mind when we cover goal setting in the next chapter. You might want to pick one of them and turn it into a specific goal.

Chapter 10
Doing What You Came Here to Do

Finding Your Purpose

I always marvel at the people who find their purpose early in life and use that as a way to earn a living by doing what they love. The child prodigies like pianists, who show extraordinary talent at a young age and flow effortlessly into a passionate career. Children who are gifted like one of their parents, follow in those footsteps, and find similar success.

My eye doctor is a case in point. He knew as a child that he wanted to practice ophthalmology like his dad. After getting his degree, he joined his father in working at a successful eye clinic; he also teaches at a prestigious research university. Plus, he and his dad wrote a book on nutritional aspects of healthy eye care. My doctor gives so much to his patients, students, and profession, and he seems to enjoy every minute of it.

Then there are the young students in high school or college who discover a passion for a particular subject and follow that path throughout their working lifetimes. One of my good friends discovered her love for literature early on, got her college degree in English, and taught creative writing to seventh graders for years. Her students loved her. They would return decades later to thank her for helping them find their own creativity and inner self by writing personal essays in her class.

Another friend of mine found her calling in social work. Her great passion over many years has been working in an oncology unit at a hospital affiliated with a university. My friend also adopts rescue dogs. Her latest? She adopted a rescue beagle that is a cancer survivor and plans to train her as a therapy dog and then take her to work. When you hear stories like this, stories that sound so right, it makes you think every bit of it was surely meant to be.

Most of us know people or know of people who are living their purpose. Even if we're not among them at the time, we can still see them as role models, examples, and teachers for a life well lived.

When I think about these people, I imagine that they feel joyous much of the time, have found a deep sense of inner peace, and get to live a life of wonder and fulfillment by continuing to develop their passions, talents, and gifts. They exude a sense of calm strength, inner power, inspiration, and motivation. The future seems to unfold effortlessly before them, leading them from one success to another. From what I've observed, these fortunate ones continue to work hard—stretching, growing, and finding new and better ways to give their gifts. But because they love what they do, it rarely feels like work to them. They're absorbed in the now, in the joy of each moment. From a distance, it looks like a meditative lifestyle.

The research supports my observations and more. An article by Emily Esfahani Smith states that "having purpose and meaning in life increases overall well-being and life satisfaction, improves mental and physical health, enhances resiliency, enhances self-esteem, and decreases the chances of depression." In another study, having a sense of purpose predicted a longer life for both younger and older adults. In other words, doing what you love works wonders for your health.

Do you remember when we talked about the rules in the school of life? One of those rules is about making greater progress when we align ourselves with the Creative Force in the Universe and become co-creators of our lives. This means going with the natural flow of our authentic selves and honoring our inherent talents by sharing them with the world.

When we do this, it brings a deep sense of meaning and purpose to our lives and helps us transcend our own small, self-centered goals in favor of something that's bigger than us. We get swept up in a way of living that exceeds our loftiest goals and dreams. Our intention becomes laser sharp, and the Universe responds by taking care of all the details, filling in the blanks with resources and opportunities we could never imagine. We get to live the life we were meant to live. And in doing so, we offer our light to help illuminate and support the light and potential in others.

The renowned mythologist Joseph Campbell advised us all to "follow our bliss." When I observe the lives of those who are doing just that, it makes perfect sense. In my own experience, however, it wasn't that simple. Neither was it obvious or straightforward.

Also, most of us know people who have reached the pinnacle of financial or career success. They may have what looks like the perfect formula for living their life purpose. You would think they'd be blissfully happy, and yet they may feel empty and unfulfilled. It's like a part of them realizes they're not honoring their inner need to search for those innate gifts and share them with others. They may have found riches and success in the outside world, but their inner wealth of talents has been ignored. When this happens to us, deep down inside, we know. Our intuition will keep nudging and nagging us through our emptiness and dissatisfaction to dig deeper and dream bigger.

Here's What Happened with Me

My own story includes a combination of intuitive guidance and clueless meandering through life, not even knowing on a conscious level that I needed to be looking for my life purpose. I was well into adulthood before the idea of a calling or mission even registered in my awareness. And at the same time, I had unknowingly been searching all along, especially in looking for jobs that would give me the inner rewards and satisfaction I knew were possible, that would allow me to do what I loved and was naturally good at.

My first real hint came as a freshman in college when I absolutely fell in love with psychology during my first introductory class. But a degree in psych can take you in a lot of different directions, so I started volunteering to get some hands-on experience. First, I volunteered at a private school for children with special needs. Despite feeling like I could make a difference in the children's lives, I felt confined and restless having to work in one room all the time.

Then one day the director of the school *coincidentally* asked if I would like to observe a visiting psychologist administer an individual intelligence test to one of the students. I said "Yes," and a seed was planted. I was fascinated by observing the mental processing of this young child as he went through the various subtests. That fascination later led me to take extra coursework after my master's degree to get certified as an educational examiner. Then *I* became the person who went into the schools and administered individual IQ tests. I loved it.

But after two years of doing the same thing, I was ready to learn something new. I didn't feel intrigued or challenged by the testing anymore, so I went back to school to get my doctorate in counseling. My graduate internships at the university's counseling center helped me realize that I thoroughly enjoyed working with college-age students, those who had mild to moderate dysfunction. Some of my peers wanted to work with people who struggled with more severe symptoms of mental illness, but that never interested me. Finding the right niche came from hands-on experience, an inner knowing, and a lack of interest in other options. Just to make sure, however, I tried volunteering at a state mental hospital for those with serious disorders. It only took one day to know that wasn't the right setting for me.

Out of all my education, training, volunteering, and work experiences, I finally realized that my life purpose involved helping other people. I could fulfill that purpose through a variety of different jobs—which for me have included IQ testing, personal counseling, academic advising, teaching, public speaking, writing, and even administrative work—and I could find lots of ways to help others in my personal life. My purpose also includes helping our animal friends, and I always do what I can for the rescues and other animals that cross my path and need help.

One of my most important life lessons, one of my biggest *aha* moments, came when I realized at a deep level that **I feel happiest when I focus on giving rather than getting**. When I let go of my self-centered needs for money or power or a sense of control or whatever else I come up with, I get to participate in something that's bigger, richer, more meaningful, and makes more of a difference than the focus on me, which eventually leaves me feeling empty and unfulfilled. So my purpose to help others was confirmed by a lesson I learned from my emotions. That's one more reason to pay attention to those extraordinary internal teachers.

Resources to Help You Find Your Purpose

If you're one of those fortunate people who has already found your purpose in life, I applaud you! However, if you're like I was—stumbling along, absorbed in day-to-day goals, not knowing to search for a mission that will lift your life to new heights of joy—you have lots of resources on how to find that hidden treasure.

A number of excellent books have been written on how to find your purpose in life. I'm not providing comprehensive coverage of this topic here; it is already available. This section simply highlights some of the techniques I've found helpful in my own experiences and in working with others. I encourage you to check out other books, materials, and online information if that feels right.

You may also want to take some career exploration tests. In working with university students through personal counseling and academic advising, I often ended up talking with them about selecting a major. And I usually referred them to the career center on campus to meet with a counselor and take the career tests. Almost without exception, they found it helpful.

Even though a job or career is not the same thing as your purpose in life, identifying your values, interests, and abilities through career testing can give you hints about what your calling might be. Maybe you find out you have aptitudes you never knew about, like mathematics or entrepreneurship, or perhaps you discover that your values are similar to people already working in a particular field, like medicine or banking. All that information can help open you up to possibilities you might never explore on your own.

Sometimes jobs give us a chance to express our purpose, even when we don't consciously realize that's what is happening. If you already have a job you love, ask yourself, "What is it about this job that makes me feel alive, happy, and fulfilled?" Maybe you get to be creative, and part of your purpose is to create. Perhaps you get to use your outstanding organizational skills, and sharing those is part of your mission. Pay attention to what makes you lose track of time because you enjoy it so much, especially those areas that come easy for you, where you feel like you're a natural.

I used to work in a wing of a building that was assigned to one particular custodial staff person. Marlene and I ended up having long talks about our families, how we saw the world, the latest happenings in our department. I came to respect her and all the life experiences and support she brought into every conversation with me and others we worked with. We never talked about what we felt were our missions in life. But Marlene did her job with impeccable standards, which supported the overall goals of the university, and she brought joy to those she worked with. The fact that I will never forget her suggests that perhaps at least a part of her purpose was like mine, helping others. Regardless of what you do for a living, it can be done with meaning and purpose.

Sometimes people find their mission lies outside of their work world. Maybe they become enthralled and energized by coaching little league sports, which tells them their purpose might get expressed by working with kids in a sports setting.

I love the arts, especially singing, dancing, and writing. In order to better help my students, I took the career tests myself, the ones I suggested that they take, and here's what I found. It would be extremely difficult for me to earn a steady, solid income through singing and dancing. Even though I love them, my talents in those areas are probably mediocre at best. Lots of people who are much more talented than I am don't even make it to the bottom rung of paying jobs for singing and dancing. So what's the life lesson? Keep those two loves as avocations in my life. Continue to enjoy them, but don't count on them to pay my bills. Most of us prefer and need to get paid for doing what we feel called to do.

That's not to say that if you love skateboarding, you shouldn't try to follow your bliss and find some way to make it pay you a decent income. Some people are able to do that. But all of us need to add an element of realism to our dreams in terms of monetary return. Look at the odds. Do your homework about viable pay for sharing your talent. In this case, maybe you could figure out the income part by giving lessons or working in or owning a skateboarding shop. Maybe you could become a sales representative for one of the major brands, which would still keep you in the field. However, if your passion is for the activity of skateboarding itself, just know you might feel frustrated. Like me, it may need to become an avocation that you enjoy on the side.

But what if you don't have any idea what you're passionate about? What if you don't have the slightest inkling about your talents or gifts or what brings you joy? Then guess. Just off the top of your head, answer this question: "What's my best guess about what I would truly enjoy doing?" And "What do I naturally seem to do well?" In order to help answer these questions, you can also look at how you spend your free time now. What interests you? What are you curious about? Also, identify what you enjoyed doing as a kid. Those answers can give you additional information to go on.

When I've worked with students on how to pick a major or how to develop mission statements for their lives, I've seen lots of them get stuck at the same place. It's like a hazardous zone in discovering your passion and purpose. What happens is that they try to make those decisions out of their heads, out of what they *imagine* they want to do, who they want to be and become, rather than base them on any real-life experiences. Most of the time, finding our purpose comes from engagement, from participating in the activity itself, rather than from a fantasy in our heads about what that would be like.

So, if you have even the slightest idea that you might want to do a particular type of work or activity, try it out. Volunteer. Do an internship if you can find one. Find a summer job or a short-term or part-time position. At the very least, talk with others who work in the field. Offer to take them to lunch and ask questions like "What do you like and not like about your job?" Also ask, "What's a typical day like for you?" Look it up online and see what the average starting salary is and what job settings are available. Do your research. Start getting hands-on and give yourself some real-life information to help make your decision.

If nothing else, your volunteer or job experience may tell you what you *don't* want to do. Sometimes our exploration of options becomes a process of eliminating choices until we get down to the one that's right for us. So finding out what *doesn't* work is valuable information. Then you can cross that option off your list of possibilities. That's what happened to me when I volunteered at the special-needs school and when I spent a day at a mental hospital. I found out those weren't the right options for me.

And here's something else to keep in mind. I've heard that most of us change *careers*—not jobs—at least three times in our working lifetimes. And data shows that the average person will have eleven jobs before the age of forty nine. So if you're looking for a job or career to help fulfill your needs for meaning and purpose, go with your best guess at the time, and know that it will probably become a stepping stone to another job and another, until you get enough experience to figure out what gives you energy, what makes you excited about going to work every morning, and what provides that deep sense of peace and fulfillment. Just like with careers, the way we express our life purpose can, and usually does, change over time.

One of the best-selling books on finding your purpose was written by a pastor, Dr. Rick Warren, and is called *The Purpose Driven Life*. The underlying premise of the book is that instead of asking yourself what *you* want, what *you* would like, what would make *you* happy, ask "What does God want for my life?" This question reframes the issues in a way that includes a Higher Power. If you have religious or spiritual beliefs, you can try praying for guidance about your purpose in life. Even if you're not so inclined, you can always ask the Universe to give you signs about which direction to head. If you do this, watch for coincidences that are too coincidental to be anything other than signs.

Another suggestion: go back to the visual imagery activity from the chapter on intuition, which is in Appendix B. Then pick a question related to your search for your mission. Your question could be as basic as "What's my purpose in life?" Ask that question as you go through the activity, and see what response you get back. These kinds of activities usually help you bypass your conscious thoughts and access more of your subconscious and intuitive wisdom.

You can also pay more attention to the signs the Universe and your intuition may already have given you. Sometimes the answers to our questions are already in plain sight. They're right under our noses. They're so conspicuous we miss them. We haven't yet recognized them as teachers and signs.

I need to add a practical caveat here. A lot of what I've read about finding your life purpose suggests that once you find it, you should make an all-out commitment, right then. As soon as you discover your soul's calling, or at least what you *think* is your calling, dive in. Drop whatever wasn't your mission, and follow your bliss.

But what I've found is that many times, we can't quit our day job. We still have to consider practical considerations of whatever path we choose. We still need to eat, and bills have to be paid. However, many times, instead of making our decision an all-or-none, either/or choice, we can include an option for *both*. Maybe we can keep our day job *and* do what we love on the side. We can volunteer. Or we can work at it part time. Or we can start getting up to speed by studying or going back to school while working at our regular jobs.

I waited until I could retire before launching into my ultimate calling. But until that happened, I read lots of books, went to conferences, attended classes, and regularly wrote in a personal journal, all of which were ways I could exercise the option for *both*. If you want more information on this topic, you might want to read David Howitt's *Heed Your Call*. For practical suggestions on how to weave both into your life, you can check out Barbara Sher's book, *I Could Do Anything If I Only Knew What It Was*.

I never asked my dreams for information about my life purpose. But before I retired from my final university position, I started having these vivid dreams about the next steps in fulfilling my mission. Repeatedly, I would wake up in the night after dreaming about seeing myself on a stage giving a motivational talk, and I would be smiling and happy. That's when I knew what the next phase of my journey would be about. Our dreams are powerful teachers. Ask them for information and guidance on what you're supposed to do. For suggestions, see the section on dreams in chapter 5.

Now I know without a doubt that my purpose in life is to help people learn their life lessons through my writing and speaking. In looking back, I can see that every step along the way, every volunteer experience and dead end, every single time I paid attention to what made me feel joy and peace, as well as boredom and frustration, it all mattered. Even when I wasn't aware of how all the pieces would eventually fit together, of how common threads were woven throughout, or how significant themes would gradually emerge, it mattered. Those coincidences had meaning. And it all culminated in me getting to where I am right now.

Finding your calling, your purpose and mission in life, is one of the most deeply fulfilling experiences we can have as human beings on this planet. We're only here for a short time. Why not give it everything we've got? Why not get to the end after a hard run, used up, filled with peace after completing our mission, and left with no regrets about how we spent our time? Each of us has that option. It's the great invitation to participate in Life at a profoundly meaningful level. To stretch and grow and develop our potential, talents, and gifts. To share those with others and leave this world a better place because we were here. The fact that you're reading this book may be a sign that it's time to say "Yes."

41. <u>Activities</u>

If you already know your mission in this lifetime, good for you. I suggest that you write it down and be open to revisions. Some people write very general mission statements like "I want to be a good person and be happy." You can also include separate statements about your roles in life— for example, friend, husband/wife, mother/father, son/daughter, sister/brother, employer/employee.

I suggest including your talents and gifts in your statement. For example: "I want to use my artistic talents to educate, inspire, and motivate others." And it sometimes helps to think about what you would want people to say about you in your obituary, about what kind of person you were, like "To love deeply, laugh often, and leave the world a better place by sharing my gifts of leadership." Write down your purpose as you understand it today, or simply write down your best guess here:

Remember: lots of information is available in books and other sources to help you develop a mission statement that resonates with you. The goal is to come up with a brief statement of your goals, motivation, and focus which will become your guiding light and basis for making decisions.

If you're still searching for the untapped power of your purpose, here's a list of the resources that were just described:

1. *Check out online information, books, and packaged material. Often those include specific steps on how to create a mission statement.*

2. *Consider career counseling. Find a specialist in your area or look online or in books for ways to assess your values, interests, and abilities. Then develop a plan for career exploration.*

3. *If you already have a job you love, ask yourself, "What is it about this job that makes me feel alive, happy, and fulfilled?"*

4. *Also look outside your job for activities that give you energy and make you eager to learn more (like sports, hobbies, or volunteer work).*

5. *If you don't have any idea about your own passions, talents, or gifts—guess. Ask yourself, "What's my best guess about what I would truly enjoy doing?" and "What do I naturally seem to do well?"*

6. *If you think you might be interested in a particular field, try it out. Volunteer, do an internship, find a summer job or a short-term or part-time position.*

7. *Interview people already working in your field of interest. Ask them questions like "What do you like and not like about your job?" and "What's a typical day like for you?"*

8. *Research your area of interest online to find out basic information like the average starting salary and what job settings are available.*

9. *Ask a Higher Power to help you find your purpose. Pray. Ask the Universe for signs. Watch for coincidences and other signs of teachers who are offering their guidance.*

10. *Do the imagery activity in Appendix B. Ask whatever questions you already have or simply ask "What's my purpose in life?" These activities give your subconscious mind and intuition a chance to speak.*

11. *Reflect on the life lessons you've already learned to see if any of them gives you clues about your life purpose. Many times our purpose is already in plain sight, but it can be so obvious that we miss it.*

Please note that this is not an exhaustive list. Many other excellent resources are available to help you with your search. If you're diligent and persistent, and if you set your intention on finding your answers, the Universe will respond with the information you need.

Setting and Achieving Goals

Out of all the university classes I've taught over the years, goal setting has been one of the most rewarding. By giving people simple guidelines and building in some accountability, they've usually been able to accomplish what they've wanted to do.

It's easy to get caught up in going where circumstances take us, not staying focused on our personal plans. This tendency to drift through life reminds me of a quote by Laurence Peter: "If you don't know where you're going, you will probably end up somewhere else."

Goals keep us focused on our values and priorities. They help mold and shape our future into a future we want to live in.

I first learned about the power of goals when I did a graduate internship at a university counseling center. My responsibilities included helping my supervisor facilitate an eight-week group on assertiveness training. The first time I did the group, I participated as a group member, and my supervisor was the leader. Every week we had homework assignments where we set goals to become more assertive outside the group. Each of us picked a goal, wrote it down, shared it with the group, and then reported to the group the following week on how we did. This provided us with both group support and accountability.

Next, I co-facilitated the group, knowing that if I made mistakes, my supervisor would cover for me. It was an ideal way to learn. Even though I usually didn't talk about them, I continued to set goals for myself outside the group, just like the group members. I worked on all kinds of goals, not just assertiveness.

After co-facilitating twice, I felt comfortable leading the group on my own. By this time I'd had lots of success with my own goals, and I'd seen group members find similar success in surprisingly short amounts of time. To this day, I use the goal-setting steps I learned in those groups to keep myself on track and moving forward.

I can't tell you how much mileage I've gotten over the years from this one technique. After a short time, I internalized the steps. Now I jot down my goals, go through the steps informally, and still get the same positive results. I do it automatically. It's a habit. In this section, I will show you how to do the same. Just remember that as you identify your goals, always allow for the possibility that you can *easily* attain your goals *or something better,* maybe even much better. Allow room for the Universe and your subconscious to create something beyond your grandest dreams.

Finding Motivation

Most goal-setting advice includes many of the same suggestions. An acronym often used to describe this advice is SMART. Make your goals Specific, Manageable, Achievable, Results-focused, and Time-bound. I've been using a variation of the SMART goals over these many years and have been amazed by the results.

However, more recent research into how people succeed with their goals indicates we've been missing a key element, especially for more difficult goals. Author and corporate trainer Mark Murphy conducted a study of over four thousand people and found that those who had a **heartfelt motivator**—a deep emotional reason to achieve their goals—were more likely to weather the obstacles and setbacks that often come when we try to reach them. We need an anchor within ourselves to successfully pull off our harder goals and help us stay the course.

When I look back on the goals I set for myself and *didn't* achieve, I see a pattern. Not always, but the majority of those "no-go" goals were ones I didn't care about enough. Not enough to struggle through changing my habits. Not enough to give up whatever was acting as a reward for my old behavior. Not enough to come up with the energy and focus to make them happen. In other words, I didn't have a strong enough motivation to pull them off. My intention wasn't set on "whatever it takes."

Some goals are easier than others. As we go through the following steps, keep in mind that if you choose to work on difficult goals, you may need a heartfelt motivator to give you the best shot at being successful. Promise yourself a reward after you complete an easy goal, and you can usually manage to succeed without much effort. But for those goals you've longed for over years, those you know will challenge you, be sure before you start that you know *why* you want to achieve them and, for harder goals, that it's a strong, compelling, and deeply felt desire.

I worked with a lot of students who were the first in their families to go to college. They wanted to graduate to make their families proud. Many of them also wanted to be a role model for younger siblings, to be able to say to them, "If I can do it, you can do it." That deeply held emotional reason to succeed helped them overcome all kinds of hardships and frustration along the way. *That* is a heartfelt motivator.

Lifetime Goals

Another way we can find motivation is by identifying the specific goals we want to achieve over our entire lifetime. Some people refer to this as their "bucket list." However, our lifetime goals become more significant when they include more than just external accomplishments. For example, it's more meaningful to include goals in all the major categories of our lives, like family, career, financial, spiritual, and personal growth. We can also add in goals that reflect our values and the kind of person we want to be—like being a good mother or father, being true to our authentic selves, and leaving a legacy.

What are the things that you want to do so that at the end of your life, you have no major regrets? What would you need to accomplish in order to feel your life was a success? Writing down those lifetime goals can show us that with all we want to accomplish, we'll need to be focused and strategic. That's where intention, goal setting, and time management come together.

42. *Activities*

The following activities are similar to those in Alan Lakein's book, How to Get Control of Your Time and Your Life. They have helped thousands of people identify and achieve their goals. So make sure you complete this exercise.

1. *Set aside some time—about twenty minutes. Take a piece of paper, and write at the top "Lifetime Goals." Just off the top of your head, brainstorm for as many lifetime goals as you can think of. Include the categories of goals discussed in the preceding paragraph: family, career, financial, spiritual, and personal growth. Write quickly. Even if a goal seems ridiculous or far-fetched, write it down anyway. You can go back later and evaluate your list. Keep writing until you run out of ideas.*

2. *Next, take a second sheet of paper, and at the top, write "Ten-Year Goals." Do the same thing. Brainstorm for as many ten-year goals as you can think of. Write fast, and don't evaluate your goals. Just get them down.*

3. *Finally, on a third sheet of paper, write "Five-Year Goals." Same deal. Brainstorm for your five-year goals by writing quickly and without judgment.*

4. *After you have identified your goals, take a moment to look over your lists. Add any additional goals that might come to you.*

5. *Obviously, you can't work on all your goals at the same time. You'll need to prioritize which ones are the most important. So go back to each of your lists, and identify your top three goals on each list. You can mark them with one, two, three or A, B, C—whatever works for you.*

6. *You should have identified nine goals. Finally, out of those nine goals, pick your top three. Then prioritize those so you have your most important lifetime goals in order of importance. Write those down.*

Keep this list someplace safe. Go back and review it periodically. You can also repeat this activity to keep your goals relevant. As you change and your life changes, your goals will change. Some you'll accomplish and check off your list. Others will naturally fall off because they're no longer important. Writing down your goals sets the stage for intention to become a part of your accomplishing them. Plus, keeping a current list of lifetime goals can help keep you focused and headed in the right direction.

You can also brainstorm for shorter-term goals, like one-year and one-month goals.

If you're interested in doing more with this goal-setting exercise, I recommend that you read Alan Lakein's book. His exercise includes brainstorming for a list of goals that would be important if you knew you only had six months to live. You can immediately see your values and priorities with that type of list. Sometimes your priorities change if you know your time here will end soon.

Steps to Successful Goal Setting

Making lists of your lifetime goals can help put goal setting in a new perspective. These goals represent how you want to spend your time, what you believe will bring a sense of satisfaction, meaning, and fulfillment to your life. In order to get started on accomplishing your goals, let's first explore the steps involved in goal setting.

The first time you go through the steps, pick an easy goal to work on, one you're 90–95 percent sure you can pull off. You want to set yourself up for success. Save your more challenging goals for later when you're more experienced with the process and when you have more confidence in your skills. I also suggest that you start with a short-term goal, one you can complete within the next week.

The goal you select may or may not be related to any of the goals on your lists. For example, you could pick something simple just to get practice with the steps. Maybe a goal like "Within the next week, I will buy an anniversary card and get it in the mail." A Goal-Setting Form is included in Appendix E so you can write down your goals and the different steps. You may want to make several copies of the form before you write on it.

1. Pick a goal. Every goal needs to be:

- **Attainable:** You believe you can achieve it, and you're strongly motivated.

- **Realistic:** Pick goals that are reasonable and likely to happen. For example, some people set a goal to exercise every day, yet they're not exercising at all right then. That's not realistic. We don't change our behavior that dramatically overnight. So even if you believe it's attainable, even if you *think* you can achieve your goal, be real with yourself.

- **Measurable:** State your goal so you'll know when you reach it. For example, set a goal "to exercise more" rather than "to get in better shape."

- **Specific:** Goal definitions need to answer these questions: What? When? Where? With whom? How often? For example, "Walk for twenty minutes two times during the next week."

- **Controllable:** Sometimes we can't control whether we will achieve our goals because of the way we state them. This often sets us up for failure. I worked with students who wanted to set this goal: "Get my professor to change my grade." The students couldn't control the professor's behavior. So they changed their goal to "*Ask* my professor to change my grade." The students could control how they went about asking for a grade change. Even if their grade remained the same, they could still succeed at their goal by doing their best at making the request.

2. Write down your goal. Putting it down on paper increases the chances you will succeed. Put your written goal somewhere you will see it often.

3. Set a deadline. You need a time frame for when you will complete your goal. Set a realistic deadline to help increase motivation and avoid procrastination. For instance, "By September 23, I will complete my project at work to the best of my ability." However, be careful with this step. Sometimes we try to force goals to happen within a specific time frame, but our choice of timing may make them harder to achieve, if not impossible. For instance, if you're already on overload in your life, unless you have no choice, don't set a major, time-consuming goal that will make you feel even more overwhelmed. Instead, look for windows of time that will support your success, and plug your goals into those slots. You can always do small activities while you're waiting that will move you closer to your goal and start to build momentum for that calculated time when you strategically dive in.

4. Decide exactly *when* you will complete your goal. Scheduling a specific time to complete your goal—or one step toward your goal—makes it a lot more likely to happen. You can either do an informal scheduling in your head, or you can actually schedule it into your calendar. If you need to change the time you have scheduled to work on your goal, be sure to substitute a different time to make sure it gets done.

I like to strengthen this step by also using visualization. The night before I plan to work on my goal, right before I go to sleep, I will visualize the next day and see myself working on my goal, usually in between two other activities I have planned. So I mentally rehearse the timing of when I will work on my goal. It helps.

Sometimes I find that I don't know how long it will take me to complete a certain goal. For instance, with my writing, it may take me an hour to write four pages, or it may take five hours. In situations like this, I don't set ***quantity goals*** on how much I plan to write. I don't set a goal to write four pages a day. Instead, I set ***time goals***—how much time I will spend working on my writing. Maybe my goal is to write two hours a day. When I state my goal like that, I can count my goal as a success if I simply put in the time, no matter how many pages I produce.

5. Create accountability. The assertiveness group I mentioned before had built-in accountability. When participants set a weekly goal, they knew they would have to come back to the group the following week and report on how they did. Motivation was rarely a problem. For your tougher goals, find ways to build in accountability along the way. Touch base with a friend on your progress every week, work with a group of like-minded people and report to each other, or use e-mail or media posts to make your progress public. Find what works for you.

6. Build in support. As I mentioned earlier, one time I set a goal to swim once a week. Even though the outdoor pool was heated, I knew it would be hard for me to show up at 5:30 p.m., in the dead of winter when it was already dark, and swim in a pool that might be colder than usual. So I got a buddy. Melissa and I agreed to swim together every Wednesday evening, right after work. I might have copped out on my promise to myself, but I would never break a promise to a friend. Melissa's support kept me going to the pool every week until it became a habit. When she had to stop swimming, I continued on my own. But I don't think I would have made it that far without her. Another example: I see lots of people walking with someone else during what I assume is their lunch break at work. Find people or other resources in your environment to support you in achieving your goals. It can make all the difference in whether or not you succeed.

7. Break down complex goals into manageable steps. Some goals are simple and don't require much planning. For example, "Pay all my bills before I go out of town." I just watch for an opening, find a small block of time, and get the bills paid. These are straightforward, short-term goals that we can tuck into our schedules as time permits.

Long-term goals are usually more complex and require numerous steps. It's important to break down more complicated, long-term goals into smaller steps or activities. Sometimes it helps to write down all the activities needed to accomplish a goal. Then you can go back, number the steps in the order you'll do them, and set a reasonable deadline for each. So the individual activities would look like this:

Number	Due date	Activity
_____	_____	_____
_____	_____	_____
_____	_____	_____
_____	_____	_____

After you identify all the steps and deadlines, plug those into your calendar. Make an appointment with yourself to complete each one.

8. Use visualization. After you select a doable goal and put all the pieces in place that will help you be successful, then use visualization to increase your chances of success even more. Energy follows thoughts. You can use your thoughts to create a pathway in your brain for your actions to follow suit. Visualizing yourself successfully completing your goal does just that. So turn to Appendix F and do the Goal-Setting Imagery Exercise. This exercise is straight out of sports psychology and is used by world-class athletes to help them achieve their goals. It only takes a few minutes; all the instructions are included. You can use this visualization exercise in addition to that mentioned in step 4, where you visualize the timing of when you'll work on your goal.

A final way to use visualization is what we discussed in the section on intention. Get a picture of what it will look like when you have successfully completed your goal. You can either get a mental picture, just something in your mind, like seeing yourself winning an award. Or you can literally get a photograph of what that will look like and put it on your refrigerator, above your desk, on your bathroom mirror, or any other places where you'll be likely to see it often. I have a picture of me jumping off of a twenty-five foot pole. Even though I was wearing a secured harness, and a safety net was below me, it still scared me—a lot—because I'm afraid of heights. I keep the picture in my kitchen where I see it every day. It reminds me that I can be successful in facing my fears.

9. Reward yourself after completing your goal. My graduate program required a lot of reading. I can remember coming home from a full day of work and classes, only to face a daunting amount of reading and study. But I needed a break. Because music helps me unwind, I would turn on some music as soon as I got home and then get so into the music that it didn't leave enough time for me to study. So I switched things around. I took a short break when I got home, then I did my studying, and *then* I turned on my music. That way, music became my reward for getting my studying done. It was a small change in the sequence of my day, but it made a huge difference in how much I got done.

Find rewards that you enjoy and use them *after* completing your goals. Maybe it's watching your favorite TV program, or spending time on social media, or talking to a friend on the phone. Be careful about using food as a reward or using rewards that cost money, like shopping. Our rewards need to be healthy, or at the very least, not unhealthy. You may need to experiment to find out which ones work for you.

10. Evaluate your success. After you complete your goal, evaluate yourself on how well you did. On a scale of one to one hundred, how successful were you in accomplishing your goal? Seventy-five percent successful? One hundred percent? Be fair to yourself when doing this. Many people rate themselves lower than what they deserve. Go back to how you stated your goal, and use that to decide your degree of success. Be sure to evaluate yourself only on what you did or didn't do and not on the consequences of your goal, like how another person responded to your goal attempts.

Set yourself up for a "no-lose" situation. Even if you don't achieve your goal, you can "win" by learning how you didn't succeed or how maybe you sabotaged your own efforts. These are the lessons we learn from goal setting, and sometimes these lessons are more important than actually accomplishing our goals. Learn from your experiences. Don't lay a guilt trip on yourself if you weren't successful. Write down your lessons on the Goal-Setting Form and save all your forms. If you had trouble achieving a goal, also write down what you need to do differently the next time in order to succeed. You may want to set the same goal again, only this time you can incorporate what you learned from your unsuccessful attempt.

I have found goal setting to be so powerful that no matter what class I'm teaching, I try to find a way to include these ten steps. For example, I used to teach a study skills class to college freshmen. Each week I would ask the class members to come to the front of the room and tell the whole class what their goals would be for the next week. In this case, it had to be an academic goal, like reading three chapters in their history book or finishing a term paper.

Just as with the assertiveness group, the next week the students had to stand and tell the class how they did with their goals. It was amazing how quickly they got better at goal setting. You could see when they started to realize what a useful tool it could be. Many of the students started setting goals to complete their assignments before they were due. For some, it was the first time they had ever finished their assignments early, and it became so empowering.

I got caught up in the magic of my students' success and continued setting personal goals right along with them, including meeting my deadlines early. One time I remember finding an item on a summer clearance sale. I bought several of these items as Christmas gifts and felt this incredible sense of control and well-being, knowing I was one step closer to being prepared for Christmas that year. I even wrote an article about it called "Christmas Shopping in July." If you've never done your Christmas shopping early, I encourage you to try it and see what it feels like. It's so freeing.

We all want to improve our lives. It's a natural urge, a constant desire throughout life. We can take that desire and channel it into goal setting. Once we figure out how to accomplish our goals, we have the power to create the future of our dreams. We have the opportunity—and the tools—to help make our dreams come true.

43. <u>Activities</u>

In order to get good at goal setting, you need to practice. Then practice some more. In Appendix E, you will find the Goal-Setting Form. Make copies of the form before you write on it, and continue to use the form as you set more goals. Save all your forms after you use them.

1. *Pick a goal according to the instructions we just covered in this section.*

2. *Write down your goal in the space provided on the form, including your deadline.*

3. *Visualize your success by doing the Goal-Setting Imagery Exercise in Appendix F.*

4. *Complete your goal within the time frame you have designated.*

5. *Evaluate your success at the bottom of the Goal-Setting Form under "Self-Evaluation."*

6. *Ask yourself, "What did I learn from accomplishing my goal?" Write that down.*

7. *If you had difficulty attaining your goal, then ask, "What do I need to do differently next time in order to successfully reach my goal?" Also write that down.*

If you didn't reach your goal, you may want to set the same goal again. Or you may have learned that it wasn't the right goal or the right time to attempt your goal. Then move on to another goal. As you get more experience working with your goals, you can select more difficult ones.

As long as you use every outcome as a learning experience, you cannot "fail" at this activity. Sometimes what you learn by <u>not</u> attaining your goal is much more valuable than actually achieving it. So put on your student hat, sharpen your awareness, and get good at goal setting. It can literally change the direction and destiny of your life.

Learning to Shine

Something remarkable, almost magical happens when people get good at goal setting. Their self-esteem jumps up at least several notches. You can hear it in the way they talk. From general references of helplessness, frustration, and being stuck to words that reflect a new sense of empowerment. They'll say something like "It's good to know I can change things in my life" or "I felt bad about that for years, and now I don't." Maybe they will start to imagine what it would be like to reach even higher goals and will begin to strategize about how they could get there. Before, those goals seemed like an unlikely possibility in a faraway future.

And their body language will change. They stand up taller. Walk with a firmer stride. You'll notice more self-assurance in their voices. They're more purposeful and confident. And if you look closely, you'll see more of a sparkle in their eyes. Their inner light starts to shine a little brighter.

It's so fun to watch people stretch and grow, master new skills, and know that they deserve their newfound competencies. They take one more step in developing their potential. They feel good about themselves for the right reasons. And in doing so, they inspire others to do the same. Their success motivates those around them, like it's contagious.

Most people learn goal setting because they want to achieve a specific goal. They want to master a new job skill, improve their finances, or find ways to include exercise in their already busy schedules. Once they get the goal-setting steps down, they're often delighted to realize they can use those same steps to accomplish all kinds of goals. They have those skills for the rest of their lives to use whenever and wherever they want.

Some people seem to pick up on goal setting right from the start. They choose realistic goals and don't find it difficult to achieve them. Others struggle more. Most people have one or two areas of their lives where setting goals and achieving them seems like an illusory target they can never quite hit. It's usually one where success always has been and always will be in the future. Often those areas are ones they've wrestled with for a long time, sometimes for years. How many people do you know who have been in a battle to lose weight for most of their lives? Or those of us who have dreamed forever about doing X, Y, or Z, but never seem to get there?

The best way to learn goal setting is to start with easy goals. Get the steps down; then gradually work up to more challenging goals. These include the ones that have eluded us before. Watch the timing, and when it's right, include those goals that support your purpose or calling. Often they challenge us because they're more long term and require many separate steps.

Roy E. Disney, the nephew of Walt Disney, once said, "It's not hard to make decisions when you know what your values are." In other words, when your highest values center around fulfilling your life's purpose, all your other decisions get easier. Everything else falls into place around your priorities. It's like when I was decluttering my house. The most effective question I could ask myself about what to keep and what to toss was, "Does this item support my purpose?"

Some people also find that just the process of getting rid of possessions from their past helps them discover new purpose for their future. Clearing the deck of the old makes room for the new. It gives you a chance to have more clarity and vision for the possibilities that could come next.

Our inner spark of the divine, the part of us that is authentic and true, begins to play a larger role in our lives as we continue to complete goals which support our purpose. In essence, we change into the person we were always meant to be. We grow into our best self. When that happens, it may freak us out. And others may not cheer us on as we had expected or hoped. As Joseph Campbell predicts in his book, *The Hero with a Thousand Faces,* we will be tested and will have to prove that we have the resourcefulness, knowledge, skills, and tenacity to see the journey through.

When I have trouble with my goals, and when I work with others who get stuck, it sometimes helps to go back to the ten steps we covered in the previous section. Often I find that I didn't have a heartfelt motivator or that the goal wasn't realistic to start with. Or maybe what looks like failed goal setting is simply an indication that it will take longer than I thought. Sometimes it's the wrong goal; I need to go in a different direction. For example, maybe my procrastination means I'm not supposed to do something. And sometimes I can't reach my goal because the timing isn't right. That was the case for me for years in writing this book. I knew I wanted to write it, but I was working a full-time job, and I didn't have the time, energy, creativity, or mental focus to write it the way it deserved.

While I was waiting for the right time slot to open up, which for me meant retirement, I worked on preliminary writing goals like attending writers' conferences. I also worked on separate goals, like retirement planning, spiritual growth, and giving everything I could to the job I had. But I knew that writing this book would have to happen in my future, partly because I couldn't stop thinking about it. I started calling it my "Glorious Obsession."

Finally, the day arrived, and I stepped into life as an official retiree. I just knew I would fall into this unending bliss as a writer and motivational speaker. Well, that fantasy got smashed pretty fast. Years earlier, the first draft of this book had flowed out of me with little effort and an exhilaration I'd never known—three hundred pages in two months—and I was done. So, of course I had great expectations of a similar experience when I worked on the second draft.

However, I found that rewriting a book I'd drafted years earlier was much harder than I ever imagined. First of all, I had to find a new writer's voice. Then I had to unlearn my academic writing style, or at least put it aside, and master a whole new set of skills that were better suited for the self-help market. It got easier over time as my writing skills improved. Yes, there were periods of blissed-out, creative euphoria. And the astounding number of coincidences that went along with my writer's journey made it such a kick. I even switched from calling it my "Glorious Obsession" and started referring to it as my "Grand Adventure." But mostly, it was just plain hard work.

I can't tell you how many times I hit the wall while finishing the final draft. Now I'm pretty sure there's a permanent dent in my forehead from repeatedly plowing into a solid object. But I got back up and started writing again. And again. And again.

After a while, another dynamic kicks in. You start to detach from the setbacks, detours, and burnout. You notice and acknowledge that you're feeling overwhelmed, frustrated, annoyed, helpless, inadequate, and more, but those emotions don't cause you to veer off track. They're just part of the deal, and you keep on going. One step at a time. Sometimes one word at a time, trusting that eventually you'll get to where you want to go.

Psychologist Albert Ellis studied this dynamic after noticing how many of the people he worked with experienced what he called **frustration intolerance**. By learning to tolerate greater levels of frustration, they were able to succeed at more challenging goals.

You see a high degree of frustration intolerance in young children when they can't make a toy work the way they want, so they throw it on the floor. They don't get immediate gratification or success, and they give up in anger. You see incredibly well-developed skills in handling frustration in top-notch athletes who are able to transcend resistance from their minds and bodies and pull off some stunning feat.

Psychologist Angela Duckworth studied schoolchildren from horrible backgrounds who nevertheless managed to persevere and succeed. She called the determining factor **grit**. It's the self-control, determination, stick-to-itiveness, and resiliency that make the difference between hanging in there and dropping out. Between making it or not. And that grit is exactly what we all develop when we continue to improve our skills at handling frustration. Goal setting provides an excellent way to deliberately improve our abilities.

Ellis said the way to get better at frustration intolerance is to change your beliefs about the task. And in changing your beliefs, you change your self-talk. For example, instead of telling myself "I should feel ecstatic when I work on my book," now I say, "Sometimes writing is blissful, and many times it's not. It's okay to plug along. Just keep going." When I hit the wall for the umpteenth time, I sometimes say, "You've been here before. You know the only way through this is to keep writing. Take a break if you need to, but don't stop altogether." If you talk to yourself like you might talk to a child or friend who's at the end of their rope, it can help you dig deeper inside yourself and find your own resiliency and grit.

Techniques to Help You Accomplish Your Goals

Besides using self-talk to improve your frustration intolerance, what other techniques can you try when a goal turns out to be unusually difficult to accomplish? Here are the ones I use the most.

1. Learn how to handle fear. I see people get sidelined by fear all the time. It's one of our biggest "stoppers." People can fear failure, and they can fear success. Either way, be aware of when fear becomes an obstacle. Try to identify any beliefs that are underneath the fear. Also look for self-talk that perpetuates the fear. For instance, maybe you're telling yourself "So-and-so won't like me if I'm too successful." That may or may not be true. But are you willing to hold yourself back because of people like that? Chances are good you would resent them if you did, so the relationships would change regardless. Even though they might feel uncomfortable if the balance of power changes between you, over time they could get used to it so that eventually you could be closer than before. Learn to rationally talk through your fear, like with this example.

We need our fear. It warns us of legitimate threats and dangers to be aware of, anticipate, and address. It can also be motivating when we feel the fear of doing something but do it anyway. Just like all of our other emotions, fear is a form of energy. We can learn to ride the energy of our fear to accomplish healthy challenges. We can also learn how to let fear be our teacher and friend. We just can't let it run our lives.

If you're still scared despite your best efforts to work with it, your fear might be trying to give you a message. Try asking:

- What are you trying to help me learn?

- What's the worst thing that could happen if I complete my goal?
- What's the best thing that could happen?
- Can I handle both the worst and the best outcomes? If not, what do I need to do next?

2. Talk with other people. I've had times when I felt so burned out that I wanted to forget I ever wanted to write a book. It helps to know other writers sometimes feel the same way. If you get stuck on a goal, talk to others who are attempting to do the same thing. Sometimes knowing other people experience the same frustrations helps you feel normal and like you're not alone. Or talk with people you trust who will listen as you express your feelings. Maybe they're not doing the same thing, but they can still provide support.

3. Deal with limiting relationships. Sometimes the people around us make it harder to achieve our goals. Many of us are invested in keeping our relationships the way they've always been, so if you start to change, sometimes people will try to pull you back. Be aware of how relationship dynamics might change as you change. We can usually distance ourselves from at least some of the naysayers. But sometimes we need to set boundaries with those people we can't avoid. It's understandable that they might feel threatened by our change, but we can still keep moving forward. For example, many people have told me that if they start to lose weight, a loved one tries to interfere. It's pretty predictable. Just don't let it stop your progress.

4. Remember why you set your goal. One of the most powerful techniques I have in my toolbox of ways to keep going is to remind myself why I'm working on my goal in the first place. It's that heartfelt motivator that Mark Murphy talks about in his book *Hard Goals*. For instance, I go back and remind myself that writing this book is part of my mission, part of why I'm here on Earth to start with.

5. Use projection to anticipate regrets. Sometimes I'll project into the future and imagine I'm near the end of my life and looking back on my choices and experiences. This gives me instant clarity. I imagine that I didn't finish the book. That would mean I couldn't die. In fact, I actually told my family, "If I get close to the edge, tell them to bring me back. I can't leave until this book is done!" I'd have to somehow rally, come back, and get it done, because the book is that important.

Using that imagery of projecting into the future—when you're at the end of your life assessing how you did—works every time for me. There's no way I'm leaving without a finished book. You may find that your goal isn't that important and maybe not worth the time and effort to reach it. That may be okay, too. But we can all learn to imagine our future, then notice if we feel the **anticipated regret** we discussed in chapter 5.

Another version of that projection is that one time I imagined I was at the end of my life looking back. I had tried my best to write a quality book, and it was a total failure. No one wanted to read it, and I basically fell flat on my face. Then I asked, "Could you handle that?" And from deep inside of me came a strong and resounding, "Yes." Failure wasn't the issue. What I couldn't handle was not trying, not giving every ounce of effort I had in me, getting to the end of my life and regretting the fact that I didn't work at it hard enough. That's what I couldn't handle. With that attitude, I knew I'd be fine no matter what happened.

At some point, each of us needs to ask why we're here. So ask yourself: "What am I meant to do with my time and my life? What's my life calling? What's the best way I can use my gifts and talents to find personal happiness and make a difference in the world? What would make my life feel like a success? What will I regret if I don't do it?" Once you get clear on your purpose, you can use the goal-setting steps to make that happen.

Maybe you feel you've already accomplished your mission for this lifetime. If that's the case, it's always possible to extend your reach, to do even more, even better, and make a larger impact. We can always take the next step in our own growth and development. And invariably, we can find more ways to improve our lives and the lives of others.

---

44. *Activities*

As you challenge yourself with goal setting, be sure to build in support for yourself. You will predictably run into obstacles, setbacks, delays and frustrations. Try the following suggestions to keep yourself on track.

1. *Make sure your goals are realistic. If you're at least 75 percent sure you can succeed at your goal but don't, then ask:*

   - *Will my goal take longer than I thought?*
   - *Is it the right goal?*
   - *Is the timing right for me to complete my goal?*

2. *Our more challenging goals usually lead to periods of frustration. When that happens, ask "Do I need to hang in there and develop more frustration tolerance? If so, how can I change my beliefs, expectations, and self-talk?"*

3. *Recognize fear when it shows up, and find ways to deal with it so it doesn't become a "stopper." Also realize that your fear may be trying to tell you something you need to know, so don't dismiss it out of hand.*

4. *Seek support from other people. It's amazing how having someone in your corner can help you move along.*

5. *Remind yourself of why you chose your goal in the first place. If you don't have a heartfelt motivator for what you're attempting, it may be hard to succeed at particularly difficult goals.*

6. *Project yourself into the future. Imagine you're at the end of your life looking back, and you didn't complete your goal. Would that be okay? Or would you regret not having mustered whatever it took to complete it?*

When we set challenging goals, we intentionally create situations that will at times be frustrating. But that feeling of success when you accomplish a particularly difficult goal is like no other. Keep practicing until the steps become automatic and your goals are helping you become your best self, the person you're meant to be, doing what you're here to do.

Chapter 11
Teaching What You Learn

Frank Laubach served as a missionary in the Philippines in 1930. The people he went there to serve didn't show much interest in being saved, but he still felt determined to help. Over time, Laubach became aware of how many of the people couldn't read. He realized they needed to be literate in order to improve their poor living conditions, so he started teaching basic reading skills. Laubach encouraged each person he taught to teach one other person, and his efforts became known as "Each One Teach One." In 1955, he formed an organization called Laubach Literacy International. Today this has become part of a worldwide organization called ProLiteracy, with programs in over one hundred countries. Millions of adults have overcome illiteracy because of one man's actions.

The concept of "Each One Teach One" originally started with the slaves in the U.S. They realized that reading and education could help lead to their emancipation, and as one learned to read, that person taught at least one other person. Knowledge is power, and knowledge and skills together hold a key to freedom for all of us, not just those who are oppressed. The link between education and freedom is written across history, which makes education an incredibly valuable gift to pass on.

Nelson Mandela said, "Education is the most powerful weapon which you can use to change the world." Individual, local, and global change starts with a single thought and a willingness to add your intention to make things happen, for yourself and others. If you want to make a difference in the world, start by changing your own thoughts. When we learn our life lessons, we start to think in different ways. These *aha* moments create a shift in our awareness. By sharing what you've learned from your own education, from the life lessons you've mastered, you can start to become a changemaker.

The Paybacks of Giving

Some of the lessons we learn are unique and apply only to us. For instance, maybe you figure out how your relationship with a parent had a specific dynamic, which contributed to how you are today. By learning that lesson, you may be able to resolve some personal issues and enjoy healthier relationships.

Some of the lessons we learn could also benefit other people. It's natural to want to pass along our knowledge and skills. Parents do it every day as part of how they nurture their children. Friends and relatives share information back and forth in a spirit of giving and affection. As a teacher, I feel joy in helping my students master new concepts and competencies and find it inherently rewarding to watch them learn and grow.

And just look online. YouTube, Pinterest, and other forms of social media allow us to share our latest discoveries, good deals, and skills with people all over the world. Most of this is factual knowledge. But there's a growing trend to also share the "practical wisdom" of the life lessons we have learned. There are now hundreds of books which describe life lessons the authors have either learned themselves or learned from others. Clearly, people value learning their lessons in life. These books indicate that we're learning from lots of different kinds of teachers, including people who are famous or unusually successful, sports figures, those who are dying—even our pets.

When you teach someone else what you've learned, it helps you learn it even better. When you have to explain it and tell about different aspects of what you've figured out, it can help you cement and expand your own understanding. Plus, in any given relationship, we are both student and teacher at the same time. The person you're teaching may turn out to be your teacher as well, and you both increase your learning. I can't tell you how many times I've been talking on some topic, like time management, and one of my students will ask me a question that takes my awareness to a new level. Or maybe students will tell me about a technique they've learned that I might never have thought of on my own.

The lessons we're learning are getting incorporated into places where they didn't use to be. For instance, a colleague of mine wrote a memoir for his family, especially his children and grandchildren. In addition to telling stories about the events in his life, he included the life lessons he learned from his experiences. Sharing these gems of wisdom can make any type of writing more meaningful.

That's exactly what author Sharon Wegscheider-Cruse did in her book *Becoming a Sage: Discovering Life's Lessons, One Story at a Time*. She encourages everyone to write down the lessons drawn from their life experiences and share those often so others can benefit from their sage advice. As the founding chairperson of the National Association for Children of Alcoholics, the author has shared her lessons, wisdom, and purpose in helping millions of children and families of those addicted to alcohol or drugs.

Another example? *The Magnolia Story* by Chip and Joanna Gaines, the couple made famous by their HGTV show called *Fixer Upper*. In their first book, the authors share their inspiring story of success, along with the lessons they have learned. Joanna Gaines also writes about how intuition has guided her at key junctures along the way.

All of us have a story to tell. Why not share it—at least with family and friends? It's easy to include the life lessons that helped you get to where you are today.

We can also teach ourselves and others to be on the lookout for all kinds of new learning, including our lessons in life. As a suggestion, each evening ask yourself what life lessons you learned or relearned that day. Although children may not understand the concept of lessons, you can always help them increase their general awareness of learning. For example, in addition to asking children "What did you *do* today?" ask them "What did you *learn* today?" You may need to give them examples at first to help them get started, but it makes for great dinner conversation, and it's an easy habit to get into. The point is to be more deliberate in sharing your life lessons and value for lifelong learning itself, however you choose to do that.

Giving through Our Life Purpose

One of the most rewarding experiences we can create is when we share with others *while* we are following our own bliss. When we help others meet their needs by fulfilling our own passion and purpose, it can bring us indescribable joy. Most of us need to earn a living while we fulfill our purpose. For many people, getting paid to accomplish their mission is the best of both worlds. Doing what we love and what we came here to do becomes our job, or vocation.

Author Frederick Buechner wrote: "Vocation is the place where our deep gladness meets the world's deep need." What's unbelievably profound is that the Universe is so interconnected and so efficient that a ready-made market already exists for the gifts that come from fulfilling your soul's purpose when they meet others' needs. That means the world is just waiting for you to start sharing your gifts and talents. When you help other people meet their needs, it satisfies a market, and the benefits, including financial ones, then come back to you. Mutual need meeting. Amazing.

Sharing our lessons, passion, and purpose with others *necessarily* means more comes back to us. Imagine that your giving is like an energy stream that goes out from you to others. Then imagine that energy naturally forms a circle so that the gifts you give others return to you. Giving and receiving are part of the same circle, the same cycle—if we don't block the flow.

Earlier in my life, I struggled with what's called codependency. I tended to do for others what they needed to do for themselves. That was because I needed them to need me. Giving to others out of my codependency made me feel like I was in control. Conversely, when I was in a receiver role and other people were giving to me, I felt uneasy, vulnerable, and less in control.

I'm glad I finally learned the lesson about the flow of giving and receiving. Now when good things come back to me because of my giving, I feel grateful instead of uncomfortable. I've also noticed that when I give to others with a pure intention, without any need to be needed or expectations of a payback, I receive even more joy in return. In general, I've found that I'm happier when I focus on *giving* rather than on *getting*. When I give to others in healthy ways, to appropriately help them meet their needs, it simultaneously meets my needs at a deeply gratifying level.

The research on giving shows that we get much more than gratification by helping others. Studies have found that people who help others are healthier and happier. For example, in one study, people who bought gifts for others or made charitable contributions reported being happier than those who spent money on themselves.

Researchers have also found that those who focus on giving to others end up at the top of the success ladder. But that's if—and only if—they also focus on taking care of themselves. If you're a giver who gives and gives without paying attention to self-care, you're likely to just burn out. It's important to set boundaries that allow you to also focus on your own needs. So when you hear the cliché about how "Nice guys finish last," that's only true when those nice guys neglect their own interests and self-care. And when givers can see the impact of their giving and know they're making a difference in the lives of others, they often become motivated and energized to give even more.

One of the best ways to give is by being an example, by being a role model of how to live an authentic life. Children learn more from our behaviors than our words. Others around us do, too. But be prepared. Living your life on purpose by being true to your authenticity will turn you into a more powerful force. That can, and probably will, cause domino effects that change your world.

One of my favorite quotes comes from Marianne Williamson, author of *A Return to Love*. I'm sharing several lines from her piece called "Our Deepest Fear." It's quoted often, but I love it because it highlights the process of answering our calling and what happens when we do.

> *Our deepest fear is not that we are inadequate. Our deepest fear is that we are powerful beyond measure. It is our light not our darkness that*

most frightens us...And as we let our own light shine, we unconsciously give other people permission to do the same. As we are liberated from our own fear, our presence automatically liberates others.

Answering your calling can have tremendous ripple effects on those around you, many of which you can't see or anticipate in advance. The Universe can turn our time, our talents, and our pure intentions into making a positive difference in ways we never could have imagined. Even though you may be scared or feel undeserving of creating such greatness, you can change your thoughts around that.

Maybe it's time to learn the lesson about how to say "Yes" to the joy and passion inside of you. To learn to say "Yes" to that intuitive voice that keeps nudging you to follow your dreams. To trust the light of your authentic self and find ways to let it shine. In doing so, you automatically give others the example and freedom to do the same.

---

45. *Activities*

Sharing the life lessons you've figured out helps you learn them even better. Plus, you're offering your "practical wisdom" to others for their benefit as well. And following your passion and purpose can have untold positive effects. Here are some suggestions.

1. We looked at this earlier in the book, but again, before you go to sleep, ask yourself "What did I learn or relearn today?" This will help you become more aware of your own learning.

   - One thing I learned or relearned today was

2. In addition to asking children (and adults) what they <u>did</u> that day, ask:

   - What did you <u>learn</u> today?

3. As we previously discussed, there's a difference between learning factual knowledge versus life lessons which provide practical wisdom. Here's an idea: keep a life lessons journal. I write in my journal regularly. I don't include all the lessons I'm learning—just the more important ones. And who knows? If you do this, someday you might want to turn your journal into a book for your children, grandchildren, and possibly others. All kinds

of options are available today that make it easy for anyone to self-publish.

4. *At the very least, write one story about a life lesson you learned. Include <u>how</u> you learned your lesson. Take your story, and use it to start your life lessons journal. Then share your story with at least one other person. Print it out and tape it on your refrigerator for family members to read. Or e-mail it to a friend. Or post it on Facebook. Or do all these things and more. By sharing your own life lessons, you encourage others to do the same. Plus, you take one more step in letting your inner light shine.*

5. *Dare to reach for your goals, the ones that will allow you to live out your dreams and complete your purpose. You will then become an example and a light for others to follow. If you're scared or worried about backlash, reread the quote from Marianne Williamson on "Our Deepest Fear." Then find the support you need to feel the fear yet not let it stop you.*

Finding Your Spot

I knew when I retired that I would rewrite the first draft of this book. I wanted to start by visiting some place where I might feel rejuvenated and inspired. That's when I remembered the James Redfield story, about how he went to Sedona, Arizona, and a crow guided him to a certain spot among the vortexes. By sitting in that spot, he received an inspired message on how to write his first book, *The Celestine Prophecy*. Redfield's book touched a chord with readers and became an international best seller. His inspiration was right.

I'd always wanted to visit Sedona, so I decided that's where I would go. But I never made it. I kept stalling. And as it turned out, I didn't need to go. I connected to my intuition, my inner Muse, right in my own home. The inspiration I was looking for wasn't in a physical place. It was already inside of me.

After telling a friend of mine about my experience, she said, "Oh. So you found your inner Sedona." Yes. That was exactly it.

The school of life continually teaches us, anywhere and everywhere we happen to be. However, some places facilitate our next steps in learning better than others. Maybe you need training and life experience before fulfilling your mission, so you head off to school in a different city, or marry and move, or take an out-of-your-area job where you unexpectedly find inspiration to follow a different path in life. All those experiences become opportunities to either learn more about your special calling or take one more step toward completing it.

You may also find that you can better fulfill your purpose in some specific geographic location. I know lots of people who feel an urge to live in a certain physical place, maybe with a group of like-minded people, and that's where they develop and give their gifts.

You may be familiar with a well-known adage that says, "Bloom where you are planted." Adages and clichés usually stick around because they contain a nugget of truth. When you consider the best spot to accomplish your life mission, this adage seems to be true in two ways.

First, I know many people who feel that their life purpose lies in giving their absolute best to their family, through their love, time, and often their financial support. That's what makes them feel the happiest and most fulfilled. Any time they can be with their family or be some place supporting their family, they're in their right spot and able to bloom.

Second, finding the right place to fulfill your life purpose always starts inside. You have to know yourself well enough to learn what brings you joy, what lights your fire, what you naturally gravitate toward, and what sustains you at a deep level. In this sense, our right spot always starts and stays inside of us through the connection we have with our own inner truth. Sometimes our intuition will guide us to go certain places, and those geographic places can help us connect with the wisdom and inspiration within, like the case with Redfield. But the place itself is only a resource for discovering more of our internal intuitive landscape.

Even if you relocate or find that it's better to fulfill your purpose in some other geographic location, that physical spot is secondary to the connection you have to your intuition, that instinctual all-knowing source of creativity and passion. The more you feed the flame of your passion and calling, the more it shines. We become more and more of our authentic selves, living the life our souls want to live. Once your connection to your authentic self is strong enough, you can bloom by sharing your gifts and talents regardless of where you are.

Continuing to Shine

The late Maya Angelou offered us so much wisdom during her time here. I read a story about a talk she gave at a community college in California years ago. As she entered the room and walked toward the podium, she was singing "This Little Light of Mine." That children's song provides a blueprint for living a worthy, authentic, joy-filled life, one that brings happiness and success and leaves the world a better place. The words to the song repeat this line: "This little light of mine, I'm gonna let it shine."

The more we live our purpose, the brighter our inner light becomes. For some people, discovering and fulfilling their purpose seems to be easy. For most of the people I know whose main purpose is loving and nurturing their families, fulfilling their mission seems just as natural as breathing. Even as young children, they knew that's what they wanted to do. They work hard at it, but they enjoy almost every minute. Often, their definition of family expands, and they offer their nurturance to a wider circle, touching the lives of others as well.

Some of us struggle just to figure out what our purpose is. And that purpose may be extremely hard to achieve. In a way, it doesn't matter. We do the best we can with whatever we're called to do, knowing our sincere efforts will eventually result in being our best selves. We do what we came here to do, knowing our intention will summon all Providence to help us along the way.

Sometimes our thinking gets derailed in believing that the goal in life is to be happy all the time. Life naturally brings us highs and lows, with all the accompanying emotions. Our job is to welcome each of those feelings—the negative ones right along with the positive ones—experience them, express them if we need to, and then let them go.

If we're true to our calling, we will inevitably run into external roadblocks, and we often have to deal with obstacles within ourselves as well. Our goals and dreams may be so lofty, they may make us stretch so far, that we're bound to feel frustrated, overwhelmed, discouraged, inadequate, and completely depleted at certain junctures along the way. But if we stick with our goals, that sense of accomplishment at the end becomes a rare jewel, a crowning glory for all our hard work and dogged persistence. Just like in actually climbing an especially challenging mountain, the spectacular view at the top makes it all worthwhile. We may not always feel happy, but even when we're not, we can experience an underlying feeling of inner peace. We know we're doing what we were made to do, and we can feel in our hearts that our efforts are courageous, perhaps even noble.

At the same time, happiness becomes more of an internal state of being rather than a reaction to getting what we want. I knew I'd reached a milestone in my own development when I started feeling happy for no apparent reason. Nothing in my external world had changed, but I felt a deep sense of joy, which led to feeling gratitude, which led to more joy, for which I was grateful. These two emotions build on one another and can make our journey a serendipitous delight.

Some time ago I was cleaning my house, and I took the trash can I normally keep under the kitchen sink over to my dining area. Not ten minutes later, I went to throw something away. Without thinking, I opened the cabinet door where I normally keep the can and dropped a handful of trash right onto the bottom of the cabinet, simply out of habit. Of course, it made a mess.

But what happened next surprised me. Normally when I made silly or careless mistakes, I would say something like "Good move" or "Way to go, Sweetie." Because I have an underlying belief that mistakes are part of growth, my comments were said more as a way to express my frustration than to berate myself. But this time, when I looked at the trash scattered on the floor of my cabinet, I said to myself, "It's okay. You're doing the important things in your life." I didn't feel frustrated, so I had no frustration to express.

My spontaneous change in self-talk told me I'd made a significant shift. I was less likely to get triggered by my mistakes and more likely to be kind and forgiving toward myself. Interestingly, that shift came at exactly the same time I noticed that I was spontaneously becoming less judgmental and more compassionate toward other people as well.

Major change is an inside job. When we change the relationship we have with ourselves—and when we change the way we talk to ourselves—it naturally changes the way we relate to others. As you learn and grow, it changes who you are. As you master more of your own life lessons, you become a different person. Stronger. Braver. More resilient. More filled with kindness, compassion, happiness, and hope.

What still throws me off balance is when I go through long stretches of white water. The stress of lots of challenges and changes in a row, even when they're positive changes, can take a toll. I have to stay extra attentive and focused for long periods of time, which eventually becomes exhausting. If I don't have pools of calm water to help me recoup in between the challenges, I usually don't lose my perspective, but I may make mistakes in areas where I'm normally competent.

So during those long periods of stress, it's even more crucial that I take care of myself by sticking to my basic foundation of diet, sleep, exercise, and meditation. I may still get stressed out and make mistakes, but I can usually minimize the disruptions and stay closer to my optimal stress zone.

For most people, the further they go in the school of life, and the more personal growth they achieve, the more they naturally want to take better care of their minds and bodies. As they learn their lessons from the internal and external teachers in their lives, developing healthy habits gets easier. And when they start to feel better because of those new habits, it provides even more incentive to keep going. Plus, most of us instinctively want to take better care of our health when fulfilling our purpose reaches a certain level of importance.

Many years ago I had a dream. I dreamed that life had become unbearably harsh, sad, and frightening—not just for me but for almost everyone on Earth. None of my usual coping skills worked to bring any relief, and in desperation, I cried out to the Universe for help.

Just when I thought I couldn't stand it any longer, a shockingly intense burst of light exploded around me, illuminating every cell in my body and bringing a profound sense of peace. After that, I was left holding a small candle with a tiny flame, the only evidence of what I'd just experienced.

I wasn't sure what I was supposed to do next. So in my dream, I relaxed, closed my eyes, and asked my intuition what I should do with the candle. Without using words, my intuition told me to use my candle to light the candles that other people were holding. It was only then that I saw hundreds of people around me and that they all had candles in their hands. I reached out and lit the candles of the people closest to me. Then those people did the same. I watched in awe as each person with a lighted candle turned and lit the candles of the people next to them, until every person was carrying the light.

Every single one of us can share our light with others. The more we become our authentic selves, the more we develop our potential and do what we're meant to do, the bolder and brighter our light shines. And as that happens, the more we inspire others to do the same. It's spontaneous. It's contagious. And it's truly awe inspiring.

As you progress through our metaphorical school, passing life's tests and graduating into more advanced classes, the scenery of your life changes. You earn your way into harder classes. You develop the knowledge and skills to be successful because of the tests you had to pass in your previous classes. Your external world starts to look different as your dreams come true. So does your internal landscape. You grow into your authenticity, your best self, the person you always had the potential to become.

It's okay to feel discouraged, sad, and scared by the darkness in the world. But just know that you can take the energy from those emotions and channel it into a worthy cause, which could include fulfilling your purpose in life. Stay focused on what you can do to make things better. Reach out with the love and light that's within you. Regardless of the circumstances around us, our best option is to be our best and do our best. The most we can do is the best we can do. When you add the power of intention to your efforts, you invite all of Providence to join in.

Eventually you'll turn around and realize that you are making a difference, in your life and the lives of others. You matter. Your gifts and talents matter, and it's no coincidence that you're on Earth now, which is the perfect time to share those gifts. And despite the obstacles and setbacks and struggles you may have to go through, in the end, you know—deeply know—that every single one of them has been worth it. You can get to the end of your life without major regrets. Your challenges may bring the worst and the best of experiences. But you stay the course. You keep moving forward, learning your lessons, making your mark. Leaving your legacy. Shining your light.

Appendix A
List of Feelings Words

Pleasant Feelings

Open: understanding, confident, reliable, easy, amazed, free, sympathetic, interested, satisfied, receptive, accepting, kind

Happy: great, gay, joyous, lucky, fortunate, delighted, overjoyed, gleeful, thankful, important, festive, ecstatic, satisfied, glad, cheerful, sunny, merry, elated, jubilant

Alive: playful, courageous, energetic, liberated, optimistic, provocative, impulsive, free, frisky, animated, spirited, thrilled, wonderful

Good: calm, peaceful, at ease, comfortable, pleased, encouraged, clever, surprised, content, quiet, certain, relaxed, serene, free and easy, bright, blessed, reassured

Love: loving, considerate, affectionate, sensitive, tender, devoted, attracted, passionate, admiration, warm, touched, sympathy, close, loved, comforted, drawn toward

Interested: concerned, affected, fascinated, intrigued, absorbed, inquisitive, nosy, snoopy, engrossed, curious

Positive: eager, keen, earnest, intent, anxious, inspired, determined, excited, enthusiastic, bold, brave, daring, challenged, optimistic, reinforced, confident, hopeful

Strong: impulsive, free, sure, certain, rebellious, unique, dynamic, tenacious, hardy, secure

Difficult/Unpleasant Feelings

Angry: irritated, enraged, hostile, insulting, sore, annoyed, upset, hateful, unpleasant, offensive, bitter, aggressive, resentful, inflamed, provoked, incensed, infuriated, cross, worked up, boiling, fuming, indignant

Depressed: lousy, disappointed, discouraged, ashamed, powerless, diminished, guilty, dissatisfied, miserable, detestable, repugnant, despicable, disgusting, abominable, terrible, in despair, sulky, bad, a sense of loss

Confused: upset, doubtful, uncertain, indecisive, perplexed, embarrassed, hesitant, shy, stupefied, disillusioned, unbelieving, skeptical, distrustful, misgiving, lost, unsure, uneasy, pessimistic, tense

Helpless: incapable, alone, paralyzed, fatigued, useless, inferior, vulnerable, empty, forced, hesitant, despair, frustrated, distressed, woeful, pathetic, tragic, in a stew, dominated

Indifferent: insensitive, dull, nonchalant, neutral, reserved, weary, bored, preoccupied, cold, disinterested, lifeless

Afraid: fearful, terrified, suspicious, anxious, alarmed, panic, nervous, scared, worried, frightened, timid, shaky, restless, doubtful, threatened, cowardly, quaking, menaced, wary

Hurt: crushed, tormented, deprived, pained, tortured, dejected, rejected, injured, offended, afflicted, aching, victimized, heartbroken, agonized, appalled, humiliated, wronged, alienated

Sad: tearful, sorrowful, pained, grief, anguish, desolate, desperate, pessimistic, unhappy, lonely, grieved, mournful, dismayed

Source: www.psychpage.com by Richard Niolon, Ph.D. Used by permission.

Appendix B
Inner Guide Imagery Exercise

All of us have an inner guide, a wise being that is always available to share its understanding, vision, and sage advice. Some people think of this guide as their intuition, or their Higher Power, or simply universal energy within them. There are a number of ways to tap into the wisdom of our inner guide. This exercise is one of them.

Please note that some people become concerned if they don't actually see anything when they do imagery exercises. It's fine if you don't get mental images or pictures in your head. We all experience guided imagery in different ways. Just know that whatever you experience is helping you connect with the part of you that has the most wisdom and the best advice.

Start by identifying a question, something you want or need to know. It could be anything. For example, you can ask your inner guide about a decision you need to make or about how to handle a certain situation.

Once you have a question in mind, sit in a comfortable position and breathe normally. Close your eyes and imagine that you are in a forest on a beautiful day. The branches of the tall trees form a canopy of shade, and you feel comfortable and at peace. Even though you are alone, you feel protected and safe.

As you look around, you notice a path leading through the forest and up a small hill. You decide to explore where this goes and walk up the path a short distance to a small opening in the forest. You see two rocks in the opening that are close to each other, and you sit comfortably on one of the rocks.

After a short time, your inner guide comes out of the forest and sits on the other rock, facing you. You greet each other warmly. Notice what your guide looks like. Notice your guide's gentle, all-knowing presence. And also notice that sitting near your guide makes you feel calm, relaxed, and even more at peace.

The two of you sit silently, enjoying each other's presence. When you feel completely relaxed and ready, you decide to ask your guide the question you brought with you. Look at your guide, and ask your question now. Then wait for your guide's response.

Your inner guide's response may come as a direct answer to your question. It may also be more indirect and less obvious, but trust that your guide has given you valuable information about your question. If you need clarification or have more questions, you may ask your guide now. You can stay in this place, communicating back and forth, for as long as you want.

Once you have received the information you asked about, thank your inner guide for sharing its wisdom. Then the two of you get up and return to the forest the ways you came. As you start down the path that led you to this special place, you see a gift on the side of the path. You stop and pick up the gift and then continue walking down the path to where you began. As you walk, you notice that you feel calm, satisfied, and happy.

When you get back to your original starting place, you continue to feel relaxed and grateful for your experience. Then you focus your attention on your breathing. Become aware of how you are sitting. Become aware of where you are sitting. And when you are ready, open your eyes and return to the present. You know you will remember this experience and the feelings of being calm, peaceful, and happy.

After you have completed this imagery exercise, ask yourself the following questions:

1. Did your inner guide look how you expected it to look? If not, what was different?
2. What was your inner guide's response to your question?
3. What did that response mean to you?
4. Did your guide's response fully answer your question?
5. If not, did you ask for additional information? If so, what information did you get back?
6. What is your understanding of what you need to do next in terms of your question?
7. What was your gift?
8. What does the gift mean to you?

It may be helpful to read this exercise out loud and record it. Then you can listen to your recording whenever you want to communicate with your inner guide.

Appendix C
Sensory Modality Checklist

Discover your preferred cognitive style for learning and self-expression. The Sensory Modality Checklist assesses the strengths of each of your major sensory modalities—auditory, visual, and kinesthetic.

There are ten incomplete sentences and three choices for completing each sentence. Some of the choices contain more than one option. If any one of those options seems typical of you, score that answer. All of the options do not have to apply to you.

Score the three choices by rating (3) to the answer most typical of you, (2) to your second choice, and (1) to the last answer.

Sensory Modality Checklist

Score (3) to the answer most typical of you, (2) to your second choice, and (1) to the last answer.

1. **When I want to learn something new, I usually:**
   A ( ) want someone to explain it to me.
   B ( ) want to read about it in a book or magazine.
   C ( ) want to try it out, take notes, or make a model of it.

2. **At a party, most of the time I like to:**
   A ( ) listen and talk to two or three people at once.
   B ( ) see how everyone looks and watch the people.
   C ( ) dance, play games, or take part in some activities.

3. **If I were helping with a musical show, I would most likely:**
   A ( ) write the music, sing the songs, or play the accompaniment.
   B ( ) design the costumes, paint the scenery, or work the lighting effects.
   C ( ) make the costumes, build the sets, or take an acting role.

4. **When I am angry, my first reaction is to:**
   A ( ) tell people off, laugh, joke, or talk it over with someone.
   B ( ) blame myself of someone else, daydream about taking revenge, or keep it inside.
   C ( ) make a fist or tense my muscles, take it out on something else, hit or throw things.

5. A happy event I would like to have is:
A ( ) hearing the thunderous applause for my speech or music.
B ( ) photographing the prized picture of a sensational newspaper story.
C ( ) achieving the fame of being first in a physical activity such as dancing, acting, surfing, or a sports event.

6. I prefer a teacher to:
A ( ) use the lecture method with informative explanations and discussions.
B ( ) write on the chalkboard, use visual aids, and assign readings.
C ( ) require posters, models, or inservice practice, and some activities in class.

7. I know that I talk with:
A ( ) different tones of voice.
B ( ) my eyes and facial expressions.
C ( ) my hands and gestures.

8. If I had to remember an event so that I could record it later, I would choose to:
A ( ) tell it aloud to someone, or hear an audio tape recording or a song about it.
B ( ) see pictures of it or read a description.
C ( ) replay it in some practice rehearsal using movements such as dance, playacting, or drill.

9. When I cook something new, I like to:
A ( ) have someone tell me the directions—a friend or television show.
B ( ) read the recipe and judge by how it looks.
C ( ) use many pots and dishes, stir often, and taste-test.

10. In my free time, I like to:
A ( ) listen to the radio, talk on the telephone, or attend a musical event.
B ( ) go to the movies, watch television, or read a magazine or book.
C ( ) get some exercise, go for a walk, play games, or make things.

Total all *A* choices _____ Auditory
Total all *B* choices _____ Visual
Total all *C* choices _____ Kinesthetic

Look at the three scores you added for
Auditory, Visual, and Kinesthetic
They will range from 10 to 30; together they will total 60.

The **Auditory** score means that you learn and express yourself through sounds and hearing. The **Visual** score means that you enjoy learning and expressing yourself with your eyes, seeing things written, colors, and imageries. The **Kinesthetic** score means that you learn and express yourself through physical, muscular activity and practice.

If the scores are within four points of each other, you have a mixed modality, which means that you process information in any sensory modality with balanced ease.

If there are five points or more between any of the scores, you have a relative strength in that modality as compared to the others. You may have two modalities that seem stronger than the other one. This means that you learn more easily and express yourself more naturally in the modality with the larger score(s).

There are, of course, no right or wrong choices of sensory modalities. This checklist is a criterion-referenced achievement scale, revealing the sensory modalities that you have learned to depend on and enjoy the most. You can practice to improve your skill in any modality with the goal of achieving a mixed and balanced modality of sensory strengths.

Copyright © 1981 Nancy A. Haynie. Used by permission.

Appendix D
Thought-Stopping Form

Most people have five or six negative thoughts about themselves that they think over and over, sometimes without realizing it. Take a few minutes to write down the negative thoughts you have about yourself. These often include thoughts about your body or physical appearance, your intelligence, and your potential. Write counterthoughts in the right-hand column—those that are more positive yet realistic, so you can believe them.

When you catch yourself thinking or saying your negative thoughts, immediately switch and think or say the positive counterthought. Don't let your negative thoughts have the last word.

Negative Thoughts	*Positive Thoughts*
Example A: I'm so fat.	*A. It's true that I'm overweight. But instead of beating myself up about it, I'm going to either accept myself the way I am or find a way to get more fit.*
Example B: I could never do something like that.	*B. I haven't done anything like that in the past. But it doesn't mean I can never do it. If I spend the time and work hard enough, I can probably pull it off, or at least succeed at something close.*

Write your own negative and positive thoughts below.

1.   1.

2.   2.

3.   3.

4.   4.

5.   5.

6.   6.

Practice thinking or saying your positive thoughts long enough for them to replace your negative thoughts and become a consistent habit. Also, visualize a time when your positive thoughts are your new normal, and see yourself happy and successful as you move forward in your life.

Appendix E
Goal-Setting Form

Write down one goal that you will work on during a designated time period. Based on the information in chapter 10, select a goal that is:

- realistic and attainable
- specific and measurable
- controllable

My goal is: _____

Starting date: _____ Ending date/deadline: _____

Self-Evaluation

When you reach the ending date or deadline, evaluate yourself using the following questions.

1. Place an "X" on the line below that best describes your percentage of success in achieving your goal.

0%	25%	50%	75%	100%

2. Explain your rating: _____
_____

3. If you had difficulty achieving your goal and had it to do over again, what would you do differently next time? _____
_____
_____

4. Write down at least one lesson you learned from doing this goal-setting activity:
_____
_____

Appendix F
Goal-Setting Imagery Exercise

Visualizing the successful completion of your goals helps you achieve them. Some people become concerned if they don't actually see or hear anything when they do visualization exercises. It's fine if you don't get sounds or mental images. We all experience guided imagery in different ways. Just know that whatever you experience is helping you take a step toward being successful.

To get started, selected a goal according to the guidelines in the section on goals in chapter 10. Then go through the following exercise.

*Sit comfortably, breathe normally, and close your eyes. Imagine that it is right **before** you attempt your goal. What does that **look like**? See that—not as if you're watching yourself on a stage—but see it like you are in your own body, looking out of your own eyes.*

*And what does it **sound like** right before you attempt your goal? Hear the sounds in your environment. And hear the sounds from inside of you, perhaps a voice inside your head encouraging you to go ahead.*

*And what does it **feel like** right before you attempt your goal? Feel the emotions that go along with your experience right before you succeed at your goal.*

*Now imagine that you are actually completing your goal. You are doing the things that will make it a complete success. What does it **look like** when you are successfully completing your goal? When you are giving 100 percent to accomplishing what you want? What does it **sound like** as your achieve your goal? What are the sounds in your environment? And what are the sounds within you? Maybe you hear a little voice inside supporting you to keep going. And how do you **feel** as you complete your goal? Let yourself feel the good feelings of doing what you want to do.*

*And finally, imagine that you have just finished completing your goal. You gave it your best effort, and you accomplished what you set out to do. Look around you. What does it **look like** after you achieved your goal? What does* it **sound like** after you did what you wanted and found success? What are the sounds in your environment? And what are the sounds within you? Maybe you hear an inner voice congratulating you on your accomplishment. And what does it **feel like** after you have completed your goal? Let yourself experience the good feelings of your success. And understand that you deserve to feel a healthy sense of pride and satisfaction for doing what you set out to do.

After you have had a chance to see, hear, and feel your success at completing your goal, know that you have taken an important step toward making your goal a reality. Also know that you can repeat this exercise whenever you want. Then, become aware of your breathing. Notice how you are sitting. Notice where you are sitting. And when you are ready, you can open your eyes and return to the present, feeling happy and relaxed.

After you complete this imagery exercise, answer these questions:

1. Overall, in general, what was that experience like?
2. Were you able to see or hear or feel yourself successfully completing your goal?
3. How did you feel after you accomplished your goal?
4. What was the most important thing you learned from doing this guided imagery?

This exercise is a surprisingly powerful way to set the stage for actually accomplishing the goals you set. Just like with the Inner Guide Imagery Exercise, you can read this out loud and record it. That way, you have your own voice to guide you through. Plus, once you have done this exercise a couple of times, you can learn to do it on your own without the instructions. All you do is see, hear, and feel successful goal completion before, during, and after you accomplish your goal. Then watch how your success unfolds.

Notes

Chapter 1: Things Happen for a Reason

Page

5   **what they *didn't do* that they regret the most:** Mike Morrison and Neal J. Roese, "Regrets of the Typical American: Findings from a Nationally Representative Sample," *Social Psychological and Personality Science* 2, no. 62 (2011): 576–583.

Chapter 2: Adventures in the School of Life

10   **The research on regrets reveals some surprises:** Ibid.

10   **In one study:** Bronnie Ware, *The Top Five Regrets of the Dying* (Carlsbad, CA: Hay House, Inc., 2012).

12   **Imagine you're an eagle:** Emaho Montoya (American Indian, www.emaho.ws), personal communication, circa 1990.

14   **Short-term sleep loss:** "Consequences of Insufficient Sleep," *Division of Sleep Medicine, Harvard Medical School Online*, accessed October 6, 2016, http://healthysleep.med.harvard.edu/healthy/matters/consequences.

14   **Recent studies indicate that chronic lack of sleep:** Centers for Disease Control and Prevention (CDC), "Did You Get Enough Sleep Last Night?," Press Release, February 16, 2016, http://www.cdc.gov/media/releases/2016/p0215-enough-sleep.html.

16   **in Cherie Carter-Scott's book:** Cherie Carter-Scott, *If Life is a Game, These Are the Rules* (New York: Broadway Books, 1998).

17   **someone who's an *inverse paranoid*:** Jack Canfield, *The Success Principles: How to Get from Where You Are to Where You Want to Be* (New York: Harper, 2005), 46.

19   **Studies on happiness show:** Meg Selig, "Older but Happier? 5 Amazing Findings from Recent Research," *Psychology Today* (blog), January 7, 2015, https://www.psychologytoday.com/blog/changepower/201501/older-happier-5-amazing-findings-recent-research.

21   ***Don't Push the River: It Flows by Itself:*** Barry Stevens, *Don't Push the River: It Flows By Itself* (Berkeley: Celestial Arts, 1970).

23   **The dictionary definition of intention:** *Merriam-Webster Dictionary Online*, s.v. "intention," accessed September 22, 2016, http://www.merriam-webster.com/dictionary/intention.

26   **read the late Wayne Dyer's book:** Wayne Dyer, *The Power of Intention: Learning to Co-create Your World Your Way* (Carlsbad, CA: Hay House, Inc., 2005).

Chapter 3: All about Life Lessons

30 **which refers to them as "practical wisdom":** *Random House Webster's College Dictionary* (New York: Random House Inc., 1995), s.v. "lesson."

Chapter 4: Finding Our Teachers

53 **According to the Merriam-Webster Dictionary definition, coincidence means:** *Merriam-Webster Dictionary Online*, s.v. "coincidence," accessed September 22, 2016, http://www.merriam-webster.com/dictionary/coincidence.

53 **Swiss psychiatrist Carl Jung saw coincidences:** C. G. Jung, *Structure and Dynamics of the Psyche*, Vol. 8, "Synchronicity: An Acausal Connecting Principle" (Princeton, NJ: Princeton University Press, 1972), 417–519.

56 **In his book, *The Teachings of Don Juan*:** Carlos Castaneda, *The Teachings of Don Juan: A Yaqui Way of Knowledge* (New York: Ballantine Books, 1968), 19–25.

58 **During a magazine interview, author James Redfield:** Jean-Noel Bassior, "Prophecies for a New World: An Interview with James Redfield," *Science of Mind Magazine*, December 1994, 35–47.

58 **according to the online Harvard Health Publications:** "Get Healthy, Get a Dog: The Health Benefits of Canine Companionship," *Harvard Health Publications*, accessed September 18, 2016, http://www.health.harvard.edu/staying-healthy/get-healthy-get-a-dog.

Chapter 5: Discovering Our Internal Teachers

66 **a class called *Writing and the Body*:** Lynn Luria-Sukenick, "Writing and the Body: A Course in Creative Writing," University of California Extension, Santa Cruz, March 1990.

69 **referred to as a drunken monkey:** William L. Mikulas, *Taming the Drunken Monkey: The Path to Mindfulness, Meditation, and Increased Concentration* (Woodbury, MN: Llewellyn Publications, 2014), 10.

73 **what Mihaly Csikszentmihalyi calls flow:** Mihaly Csikszentmihalyi, *Flow: The Psychology of Optimal Experience* (New York: HarperPerennial, 1990).

77 **By themselves, emotions are neither good nor bad:** Matthew Hutson, "Beyond Happiness: The Upside of Feeling Down," *Psychology Today*, February 2015, 44–53.

78 **As author Matthew Hutson states:** Matthew Hutson, "Beyond Happiness: The Upside of Feeling Down," *Psychology Today*, February 2015, 53.

78 **In the *Big Book*:** *Alcoholics Anonymous: The Story of How Many Thousands of Men and Women Have Recovered from Alcoholism*, 3rd ed. (New York: Alcoholics Anonymous World Services, Inc., 1983), 64.

83 **I learned that workaholics often have low self-esteem:** Diane Fassel, *Working Ourselves to Death: The High Cost of Workaholism and the Rewards of Recovery* (New York: HarperCollins Publishers, 1990), 31.

83 **it insulates us from intimacy with ourselves and others:** Ibid., 43.

84 **The Japanese even have a word for it:** *karoshi*: Ibid., 44.

86	**The purpose of addictions is to keep us numb:** Anne Wilson Schaef and Diane Fassel, *The Addictive Organization: Why we Overwork, Cover Up, Pick Up the Pieces, Please the Boss, and Perpetuate Sick Organizations* (San Francisco: Harper and Row, 1988), 58.
88	**According to sleep specialists:** "Common Questions about Dreams: Does Everyone Dream?," The International Association for the Study of Dreams, accessed September 21, 2016, http://www.asdreams.org/subidxeduq_and_a.htm.
89	**We can experience all kinds of dreams:** "The Facts About Dreams: What Purpose do Dreams Serve?," *Real Simple,* accessed September 21, 2016, http://www.realsimple.com/health/mind-mood/dreams/facts-about-dreams/nightmares-premonitions.
90	**look at common dreams:** "14 Common Dreams and Symbols and Why They're Important," DreamsCloud, updated December 18, 2015, http://www.huffingtonpost.com/dreamscloud/meaning-of-dreams_b_4504512.html.

Chapter 6: Intuition, the Ultimate Internal Teacher

94	**Gavin de Becker, author of *The Gift of Fear*:** Gavin de Becker, *The Gift of Fear: Survival Signals that Protect Us from Violence* (New York: Dell Publishing, 1997).
94	**Frances Vaughn, the author of *Awakening Intuition*, puts it this way:** Frances Vaughn, *Awakening Intuition* (Garden City, NY: Anchor Books, 1979), 45.
94	**story about Paul McCartney:** Annie Murphy Paul, "The Science of Intuition," *O The Oprah Magazine,* August 2011, 125.
95	**Sometimes our intuition plays the role of a private detective:** Philip Goldberg, *The Intuitive Edge: Understanding and Developing Intuition* (Los Angeles: Jeremy P. Tarcher, Inc., 1983), 46.
95	**Oprah Winfrey credits intuition:** Oprah Winfrey, "What I Know for Sure," *O The Oprah Magazine,* August 2011, 162.
97	**That "still small voice" can speak to us in a number of ways:** Frances E. Vaughan, *Awakening Intuition* (Garden City, NY: Anchor Books, 1979), 66–77.
99	**If I were an animal, what animal would I be:** Frances E. Vaughan, *Awakening Intuition* (Garden City, NY: Anchor Books, 1979), 44.
104	**Research indicates that in our jobs and professions:** Gary Klein, *The Power of Intuition: How to Use Your Gut Feelings to Make Better Decisions at Work* (New York: Doubleday, 2003).
108	**Frances Vaughn, author of *Awakening Intuition*, suggests:** Frances E. Vaughan, *Awakening Intuition* (Garden City, NY: Anchor Books, 1979), 11–32.

Chapter 7: The How-Tos of Learning

109	**One of the most all-encompassing models for learning:** Noel Burch, *Teacher Effectiveness Training (T.E.T.) Instructor Guide* (Solana Beach, CA: Gordon Training International, 1975).
111	**an article about Lupita Nyong'o:** Logan Hill, "Force of Nature," *InStyle Magazine,* April 2016, 255.
113	**In a book about his life, *Did I Win? A Farewell to George Sheehan*:** Joe Henderson, *Did I Win? A Farewell to George Sheenah* (Waco, TX: WRS Publishing, 1995), xiii.

117 **One of the tests Bryan took:** Nancy A. Haynie, "Sensory Modality Checklist," (1981), quoted in George M. Gazda, William C. Childers, and Richard P. Walters, *Interpersonal Communication: A Handbook for Health Professionals* (Rockville, MD: Aspen Systems Corporation, 1982), 257–259.

120 **During an interview several years ago, Underwood said:** Paul McGuire, "'One on One' with Carrie Underwood," CMT Canada, air date June 14, 2012.

Chapter 8: Turning Obstacles into Teachers

127 **comes from social psychology and is called *impression management*:** Anne Wilson Schaef and Diane Fassel, *The Addictive Organization: Why We Overwork, Cover Up, Pick Up the Pieces, Please the Boss, and Perpetuate Sick Organizations* (San Francisco: Harper and Row, 1988), 75.

128 **Psychologist Martin Seligman:** Martin E. P. Seligman, *Learned Optimism: How to Change Your Mind and Your Life* (New York: Vintage Books, 2006).

132 **Recent research on brain dominance:** Daniel Voyer, "The Truth About Being Left-Brained or Right-Brained," *Psychology Today Online* (blog), May 28, 2015, https://www.psychologytoday.com/blog/perceptual-asymmetries/201505/the-truth-about-being-left-brained-or-right-brained.

136 **The research is clear: when we add visualization:** Frank Niles, "How to Use Visualization to Achieve Your Goals," *Huffington Post Online* (blog), updated August 17, 2011, http://www.huffingtonpost.com/frank-niles-phd/visualization-goals_b_878424.html.

137 **what's called the Zeigarnik effect:** Katie Hull-Sypnieski and Larry Ferlazzo, "The Five-by-Five Approach to Differentiation Success," *Education Week Spotlight*, January 17, 2012, 5–6.

142 **coauthors of *Procrastination: Why You Do It, What to Do About It NOW*:** Jane B. Burka and Lenora M. Yuen, *Procrastination: Why You Do It, What to Do About It NOW* (Cambridge, MA: Da Capo Press, 2008).

151 **are called "family rules":** Robert Subby, *Lost in the Shuffle: The Co-Dependent Reality* (Pompano Beach, FL: Health Communications, Inc., 1987), 29–55.

152 **Claudia Black, author of *It Will Never Happen to Me*:** Claudia Black, *It Will Never Happen to Me* (Denver: M.A.C., 1981).

152 **Then there are all the "shoulds" and "musts":** Albert Ellis and Robert A. Harper, *A Guide to Rational Living* (New York: Albert Ellis Institute, Inc., 1997).

Chapter 9: Continuing to Grow

162 **Each of us has what is called an optimal level of stress:** Dan Goldman, "The Sweet Spot for Achievement," *Psychology Today* (blog), March 29, 2012, https://www.psychologytoday.com/blog/the-brain-and-emotional-intelligence/201203/the-sweet-spot-achievement.

163 **Optimal Stress Zone (graph):** adapted from Mark A. Staal, "Stress, Cognition, and Human Performance: A Literature Review and Conceptual Framework," NASA Ames Research Center, August 2004, http://human-factors.arc.nasa.gov/flightcognition/Publications/IH_054_Staal.pdf, 4.

168 **75 to 90 percent of all doctor visits:** Joseph Goldberg, "The Effects of Stress on Your

Body," *WebMD Online*, reviewed June 12, 2016, accessed October 9, 2016, http://www.webmd.com/balance/stress management/effects-of-stress-on-your-body.

177 **Recent research from the Centers for Disease Control:** Centers for Disease Control and Prevention (CDC), "Did You Get Enough Sleep Last Night?," Press Release, February 16, 2016, http://www.cdc.gov/media/releases/2016/p0215-enough-sleep.html.

177 **studies show, that even one night:** "Consequences of Insufficient Sleep," *Division of Sleep Medicine, Harvard Medical School Online*, accessed October 6, 2016, http://healthysleep.med.harvard.edu/healthy/matters/consequences.

177 **the benefits of a quick daytime siesta:** Sarah Klein, "6 Convincing Reasons to Take a Nap Today," *Huffington Post*, updated August 11, 2014, http://www.huffingtonpost.com/2013/03/11/nap-benefits-national-napping-day_n_2830952.html.

177 **also been found to help prevent heart disease:** Lisa Stein, "Napping May Be Good for Your Heart," *Scientific American*, February 12, 2007, https://www.scientificamerican.com/article/napping-good-for-heart/Scientific American.

178 **especially as more research shows its benefits:** Emma Seppala, "20 Scientific Reasons to Start Meditating Today," *Psychology Today Online* (blog), September 11, 2013, https://www.psychologytoday.com/blog/feeling-it/201309/20-scientific-reasons-start-meditating-today.

178 **especially as more research shows its benefits:** Kristine Crane, "8 Ways Meditation Can Improve Your Life," *Huffington Post Online*, updated September 19, 2014, http://www.huffingtonpost.com/2014/09/19/meditation-benefits_n_5842870.html.

179 **Taking that time actually increases your productivity:** Peter Bregman, "If You're Too Busy to Meditate, Read This," *Forbes Online*, October 13, 2012, http://www.forbes.com/sites/peterbregman/2012/10/13/if-youre-too-busy-to-meditate-read-this/#6af0051a4ea5.

179 **people like Oprah Winfrey, Jerry Seinfeld, Arianna Huffington:** Sasha Bronner, "How 5 Mega-Famous People Make Time for Daily Meditation," *Huffington Post Online*, updated March 14, 2015, http://www.huffingtonpost.com/2015/03/14/famous-people-who-meditate_n_6850088.html.

179 **Paul McCartney:** Frances Dumlao, "14 Famous People Who Meditate," American Grandparents Association, *Grandparents.com Online*, accessed September 24, 2016, http://www.grandparents.com/food-and-leisure/celebrity/famous-people-meditate.

179 **Steve Jobs swore by it:** Geoffrey James, "How Steve Jobs Trained His Own Brain," *Inc. Online*, March 19, 2015, http://www.inc.com/geoffrey-james/how-steve-jobs-trained-his-own-brain.html.

181 **meditation increases our neurotransmitters, including endorphins:** Jane L. Harte, George H. Eifert, and Roger Smith, "The Effects of Running and Meditation on Beta-Endorphin, Corticotropin-Releasing Hormone and Cortisol in Plasma, and on Mood," *Biological Psychology*, June 1995, 251–265.

192 **the number one source of stress in this country is money:** "2015 Stress in America Survey," American Psychological Association, accessed September 21, 2016, http://www.apa.org/news/press/releases/stress/2015/impact-of-discrimination.pdf.

195 **Research shows this cycle gives your body:** Martin J. Gibala, Jonathan P. Little, Maureen J. MacDonald, and John A. Hawley, "Physiological Adaptations to Low-Volume, High-Intensity Interval Training in Health and Disease," *The Journal of Physiology* 590, no. 5 (March 2012): 1077–1084, doi:10.1113/jphysiol.2011.224725.

Chapter 10: Doing What You Came Here to Do

202 **The research supports my observations:** Emily Esfahani Smith, "There's More to Life Than Being Happy," *The Atlantic Online*, January 9, 2013, http://www.theatlantic.com/health/archive/2013/01/theres-more-to-life-than-being-happy/266805/.

202 **In another study, having a sense of purpose:** Patrick Hill and Nicholas Turiano, "Having a Sense of Purpose May Add Years to Your Life," *Psychological Science Online News*, May 12, 2014, http://www.psychologicalscience.org/index.php/news/releases/having-a-sense-of-purpose-in-life-may-add-years-to-your-life.html.

207 **data shows that the average person:** "Number of Jobs Held, Labor Market Activity, and Earnings Growth Among the Youngest Baby Boomers: Results From a Longitudinal Survey," *Online Economic News Release*, Bureau of Labor Statistics, U.S. Department of Labor, March 31, 2015, http://www.bls.gov/news.release/nlsoy.nr0.htm.

207 **One of the bestselling books on finding your purpose:** Rick Warren, *The Purpose Driven Life: What on Earth Am I Here For?* (Grand Rapids, MI: Zondervan, 2002).

208 **David Howitt's *Heed Your Call*:** David Howitt, *Heed Your Call: Integrating Myth, Science, Spirituality, and Business* (New York: Atria Books, 2014).

208 **you can check out Barbara Sher's book, *I Could Do Anything If Only I Knew What It Was*:** Barbara Sher, *I Could Do Anything If Only I Knew What It Was: How to Discover What You Really Want and How to Get It* (New York: Dell Publishing, 1994).

212 **Mark Murphy conducted a study of over four thousand people:** Mark Murphy, *Hard Goals: The Secret to Getting from Where You Are to Where You Want to Be* (New York: McGraw-Hill, 2011).

213 **similar to those in Alan Lakein's book, *How to Get Control of Your Time and Your Life*:** Alan Lakein, *How to Get Control of Your Time and Your Life* (New York: David McKay Co., Inc., 1973), 31–36.

214 **I recommend that you read Alan Lakein's book:** Ibid.

215 **A Goal-Setting Form:** Catherine M. Steel and Janice M. Hochman, *Assertion Skill Training: A Group Procedure for High School Women* (Washington: American Personnel and Guidance Association, 1976).

218 **straight out of sports psychology:** Jim Taylor, "Sport Imagery: Athletes' Most Powerful Mental Tool," *Psychology Today Online* (blog), November 6, 2012, https://www.psychologytoday.com/blog/the-power-prime/201211/sport-imagery-athletes-most-powerful-mental-tool.

222 **predicts in his book, *The Hero with a Thousand Faces*:** Joseph Campbell, *The Hero with a Thousand Faces*, 2nd ed. (Princeton, NJ: Princeton University Press, 1973).

223 **what he called *frustration intolerance*:** Albert Ellis and Kristene A. Doyle, *How to Control Your Anxiety before It Controls You* (New York: Kensington Publishing Corp., 1998), 89, 217.

223 **Angela Duckworth studied school children:** Angela Duckworth, *Grit: The Power of Passion and Perseverance* (New York: Scribner, 2016).

224 **Ellis said the way to get better at frustration intolerance:** Albert Ellis and Kristene A. Doyle, *How to Control Your Anxiety before It Controls You* (New York: Kensington Publishing Corp., 1998), 217–225.

Chapter 11: Teaching What You Learn

229 **Frank Laubach served as a missionary:** Frank C. Laubach, *Letters by a Modern Mystic: Excerpts from Letters Written to His Father* (Colorado Springs: Purposeful Design Publications, 2007).

229 **part of a worldwide organization called ProLiteracy:** "Our History," ProLiteracy Organization, accessed September 24, 2016, https://proliteracy.org/About-Us/Mission-History.

229 **The concept of "Each One Teach One" originally started:** "Each One Teach One," Each One Teach One Organization, accessed September 24, 2016, http://www.eachoneteachone.org.uk/about/About.

230 **what author Sharon Wegscheider-Cruse did in her book, *Becoming a Sage*:** Sharon Wegscheider-Cruse, *Becoming a Sage: Discovering Life's Lessons, One Story at a Time* (Deerfield Beach, FL: Health Communications, Inc., 2016).

231 ***The Magnolia Story*:** Chip and Joanna Gaines, *The Magnolia Story* (Nashville, TN: W Publishing, 2016).

232 **people who help others are healthier and happier:** Emily Esfahani Smith, "There's More to Life Than Being Happy," *The Atlantic Magazine Online*, January 9, 2013, http://www.theatlantic.com/health/archive/2013/01/theres-more-to-life-than-being-happy/266805/.

232 **people who bought gifts for others:** Kira M. Newman, "Six Ways to Get More Happiness for Your Money," *Greater Good Science Center Online*, October 4, 2016, http://greatergood.berkeley.edu/article/item/six_ways_to_get_more_happiness_for_your_money.

232 **Researchers have also found that those who focus on giving:** Adam Grant, *Give and Take: Why Helping Others Drives Our Success* (New York: Penguin Books, 2013), 155–185.

232 **her piece called "Our Deepest Fear":** Marianne Williamson, *A Return to Love: Reflections on the Principles of a Course in Miracles* (New York: HarperCollins Publishers, 1992), 165.

234 **the James Redfield story:** Jean-Noel Bassior, "Prophecies for a New World: An Interview with James Redfield," *Science of Mind Magazine*, December 1994, 35–47.

235 **I read a story about a talk she gave at a community college:** Janice Stevens, "When Angelou Lit Up the Room," Valley Voices, *Fresno (CA) Bee*, June 7, 2014.

Index

Major discussions of a topic are indicated by page numbers in **bold**. Activities 1–45 and assessments in the Appendices are indicated by pages in *italics*.

A
abstinence, 88
addiction, **82–88**
    to activities, 126
    assessment of, *87–88*
    to aversion/avoidance, 86, 145
    characteristics of, 85–87
    ignored feelings and, 128
    as internal teacher, 3, 46
    lessons from, 33
    negative emotions and, 78
    recovery from, 84, 87
    self-perpetuation of, 84, 86–87
    unsuspected, 3
    vulnerability to, 86
    wake-up calls from, 19
    See also workaholism
adrenaline rush
    addiction to, 61, 124
    procrastination, 144
    See also addiction
affirmations. *See* self-talk
Al-Anon, 82–83
alarm system, 95
Angelou, Maya, 235–236
animals, 3, 46, 58–60, 93
anticipated regret, 78, 115, 226. *See also* regret
anxiety
    in clearing clutter, 186
    discomfort of, 47
    disorder, 193
    in dreams, 90
    effects of, 8
    emotional generation of, 141
    intuitive messages and, 103
    as motivation, 166
    negative emotions and, 78
    panic attacks and, 102
    relieving, 72–73, 141
    in stress reaction, 167, 169, 173
    substitute behaviors and, 75
    thoughts and, 80
    worry and, 70, 191
    See also coping mechanisms; procrastination; stress management
aspirations (dreams)
    authentic self and, 238
    behaviors for achieving, 75–76
    clutter and, 186, 188
    effects of fear on, 126
    frustration in achieving, 236
    intention and, 202
    intuition and, 233
    life lessons for, 4–5
    life purpose and, 73
    lifestyle for achievement, 162
    procrastination and, 141
    realism in, 205–206
    unconscious beliefs and, 126, 189–190
    See also goal setting; life purpose
attitude
    for achieving goals, 24
    can-do, 170, 181
    changing negative, 192–193
    exercise effects on, 175
    glass-half-empty, 77, 191–192
    improvement of, *194*
    with intention, 23
    inverse paranoid, 17
    laid-back, 39
    observational learning of, 49, 128
    positive, 171
    punitive, 18
    seeking growth, *194*, 198
    stress management, 170
    towards intuition, 103
    Universe response to, 193
    whatever-it-takes, 24–25, 41
auditory learning. *See* learning style
authentic self
    fulfilling purpose and, 235
    harmony with, 21
    lifetime goals and, 212

limiting beliefs and, 157
natural flow and, 202
sharing light as, 238
Awakening Intuition, 94, 108
awareness
    actions and conscious, 105–106
    of body, 65–69
    for change, *158*, 192
    of coincidences, *55*
    competence/incompetence, 114
    dreams and, *90–91*, 93
    happiness and, 97
    intuition in, 94, 103, *107*
    for learning, 110, 113–115
    of life purpose, 203
    meditation for, *71–72*, 178
    of needs, 18–19
    of procrastination, 142–143
    self-observation for, 65, *87–88*
    from teaching, 230–231
    unconscious messages for, 31
    See also addiction; beliefs; meditation; procrastination

B
Becoming a Sage: Discovering Life's Lessons, One Story at a Time, 230
behavior as teacher, **72–76**
behavior change
    insight for, 114–116, 129
    intention and, 229
beliefs, **148–159**
    aspirations and, 126, 189–190
    authentic self and, 157
    changing limiting, **155–159**
    core, 150–151
    identifying limiting, 126, 153–*155*
    intention and, 150, 193
    questioning with logic, 155
    self-perception and, 49
    unconscious, 126
Big Book, 78
Black, Claudia, 152
bodies as teachers, **65–69**
boredom, 62, 103, 144, 163, 168, 208
boundaries, 126–127, *130*, 225, 232
breathing
    in imagery exercise, *244*, *254*
    in meditation, 72, 177, 180–181, *182*
    with physical activity, 195
    stress lowering with, *166–167*, 172
Buechner, Frederick, 231
Burka, Jane, 142
burn-out, 7–8, 117, 166, 178

C
Campbell, Joseph, 202, 222
Canfield, Jack, 17
Carter-Scott, Cherie, 16
Castaneda, Carlos, 56
Celestine Prophecy, The, 58, 234
Chicken Soup, 17
cognitive clutter, **188–194**
    cognitive dissonance, 189
    limiting beliefs, 189
    unproductive mindsets, 191–192
    wounds, 189–191
    See also anxiety; energy
cognitive dissonance, 189
coincidence, **51–55**
    awareness of, 53–54, *55*
    intention and, 24, 54
    life lesson instruction by, 31
    life purpose and, 4, 11, 20, 239
    personal meaning of, 53
    Providence and, 54
comfortable procrastination. *See* procrastination
commitment
    for healing, 87
    to intention, 25, 26, 41
    life purpose and, 207
    as motivation, 133
common lessons, 2, 30
competence/incompetence
    conscious and unconscious, 109–110
    for empowerment, 110
    feelings of incompetence, 18
    in life lessons, 17–18
    progression in, 111–114, 198
    stages of, 109–110
compulsion to closure, 136–137
Conscious Competence Learning Model, 109–112
contingent behaviors, 141
coping mechanisms
    anxiety and, 143
    failure of, 238
    individuality of, 172
    unconscious feelings and, 161
    See also addiction; stress management; workaholism
core beliefs. *See* beliefs
Covey Steven, 78
Creative Force, 21, 202. *See also* Universe
critical thinking skills, 94
Csikszentmihalyi, Mihaly, 73

D

de Becker, Gavin, 94
decision making
    dreams in, 89
    sleep deprivation and, 177
    strategy for, 78
    See also goal setting; priorities
déjà vu experiences, 95, 100
detachment
    approval/disapproval of others, 83, 84
    from feelings, 80
    from inner experience, 65
    observer role, 13
    practice of, *87, 168*
    from thoughts, 70, 80, 154
    See also meditation
Did I Win? A Farewell to George Sheehan, 113
diet, 176. *See also* personal health
divine energy. *See* Universe
divine intelligence, 93. *See also* Universe
divine protection/intervention, 32, 95. *See also* Universe
Don't Push the River: It Flows by Itself., 21
"Don't Worry, Be Happy," 48
dreaming, **88–90**
    common, 90
    interpretation of, 89–*92*
    intuitive communication by, 98, 106
    messages from recurring, 31
    nightmares, 89, 92
    as teacher, 3, 46, 65, 89
dreams. *See* aspirations (dreams)
Duckworth, Angela, 223
Dyer, Wayne, 26
dysfunctional behavior
    changing, 4
    learning and unlearning of, 39, 152
    limiting beliefs in, 189
    using detachment with, 83
    See also addiction

E

Each One Teach One, 229
Edison, Thomas, 62
Einstein, Albert, 94
Ellis, Albert, 223, 224
Emerson, Ralph Waldo, 107
emotions, **76–81**
    denial of, 77
    experiencing, *81–82*
    expression of, 81, 128
    intuitive communication by, 97–98
    music for expression of, 173
    as teachers, 81
    words for describing feelings, *241–242*
    See also negative emotions
empowerment
    conscious competence for, 110
    expressions of, 221
    as healthy reward, 131
    life lessons for, 2–3
    vs. power/control over others, 124
endorphins, 181
energy
    cornerstones of, 183
    leaks, 183–184
    See also meditation; personal health
enjoyment
    body as teacher for, 68
    growth and, 19
    loss of, 21
environmental stressors, 7–8, 164–165, 169
excitement, 124, 144, 166
exercising, **245–247**
    benefits of, 77, 175–176, 181, 183, 198
    goal setting for, 129, 215
    for healthy lifestyle, 15, 17, 18, 171, 173, 176, 179
    maintaining programs for, 111, 125, 175, 195, 196
    moderation in, 115
    in stress management, 237
    workouts, 195
    See also addiction; physical activity
experiences, **47–48**
external teachers, **47–63**, 106–107

F

failure
    childhood experiences and, 190
    fear of, 224
    procrastination and, 143–144
    unrealistic goals in, 129, 145, 215
    See also goal setting; success
fear
    of failure, 143
    recognition of, *227*
    self-talk and perpetuation of, 224
    of success, 144
feelings. *See* emotions
Field of Dreams, 106
flow. *See* natural flow of life
frustration
    assessment of, *227*
    expression of, 237
    manifestations of, 221
    sources of, 83, 125, 169
    See also goal setting
frustration intolerance, 223–224

G

Gaines, Chip, 231
Gaines, Joanna, 231
Gift of Fear, The, 94
gifts. *See* talents and gifts
goal setting, **211–228**
    form for, 251
    imagery exercise, *253*
    procrastination management, 147
    setting deadlines, 135, 217
    in stress management, 174
    See also failure; life purpose; motivation; success
Goethe, Johann Wolfgang von, 25, 54
Goldberg, Philip, 95
gratitude
    addiction recovery and, 87
    contrast to negative feelings, 77
    happiness and, 22, 236
    intuition and, 106
    practice of, 170–171
    to teachers, 272
grit, 223–224
growth/progress, **161–199**
    childhood learning, 49–50
    experience, 47–49
    goal setting for, 38–39, *226–227*
    inner issues in, 161–162
    intentional, 22, 196–198, *199*
    learning from body, 65–69
    lesson priorities for, 33
    life purpose and, 226
    meditation for, *71*
    natural flow for, 21–22
    optimistic attitude for, 17–22
    priorities in, 39–40
    school rules for, 22
    self-care for, 13–15, 66, 237–238
    skill learning in, 109–110
    unlearning and letting go for, 38–39, 153, 196
    See also intention; life lessons
guided imagery
    activities, *58, 181*
    anticipated regret, 78, 115, 225–226
    belief change with, 154
    in finding life purpose, 207, *210*
    goal-setting, 217–218, *220*
    inner guide, 243–244
    meditation, 178, 181, *181*
    sensory modalities and, 18
    unconscious information from, 104
    visualization with intention, 34, 219

H

happiness
    aging and, 19
    awareness of intuition and, 97
    giving and, 232
    internal state of being, 236–237
    life circumstances and, 48–49
    life purpose and, 226, 235–236
    negative emotions and, 77
    responsibility for, 8, 51
    using talents for, 19
"Happy" (song), 173
hazardous zone signs, **125–130**
heartfelt motivator, 212
Heed Your Call, 208
helplessness
    observational learning of, 128–129
    stress symptoms, 128, 169
Higher Power. *See* Universe
Howitt, David, 208
Huffington, Arianna, 179
Hutson, Matthew, 78

I

If Life Is a Game, These Are the Rules, 16
imagery. *See* guided imagery
immediate gratification, 223–224
impression management, 127
incompetence. *See* competence/incompetence
incomplete tasks. *See* energy
individual lessons. *See* unique lessons
innate intelligence, 93
insight
    in behavior change, 114–116, 129
    goal setting and, 129
    intuitive, 106
    right brain and, 138
    wound healing and, 190–191
    See also awareness; intuition
insomnia, 70–71, 167. *See also* sleep
instinctual wisdom, 93
intelligence, 12, 93
intention, **22–27**
    achieving goals with, 134
    behavioral change with, 74, 198
    coincidences with, 54
    commitment to, 25, 41, 134
    Conscious Competence with, 112
    Creative Force and, 202
    defined, 23
    giving, 232
    global changes from, 229
    intuition and, 132
    mental focus of, 71

in mental/behavioral change, 63, 192, 197
motivation and, 133, 212
negative beliefs and, 150, 193
power of, 22, 25, 63
right-brain technique and, 133, 137
setting for growth, 199
stress management with, 170
time distortion and, 73
Universe response to, 25, 236, 239
using, **22–27**, 41–42
visualization with, 26, 219
whatever-it-takes attitude for, 24
See also goal setting
internal teachers, **65–90**, 106–107
intuition, **93–108**
  acting on, 105–106
  aspirations and, 203, 207
  benefits of, 94–96
  guidance from, 234–235, 238
  guided imagery for, 103, *108*, 134, *243*
  intention and, 132
  as internal teacher, 3, 46
  listening to, 46, 96–*100*, 101–104, 129
  strengthening, *107–108*
  time management, 132–133
  worry as message, 98
  See also procrastination; thoughts
Intuitive Edge, The, 95
inverse paranoid, 17. *See also* attitude
It Will Never Happen to Me, 152

J
Jobs, Steve, 179
Jung, Carl, 73

K
karoshi, 84
kinesthetic learning. *See* learning style

L
Lakein, Alan, 213–214
Law, Vernon Sanders, 48
learned helplessness. *See* helplessness
Learned Optimism: How to Change Your Mind and Your Life, 128
learning curve
  changes to increase, 162
  personal health and, 179, 198
  See also learning model; learning style
learning how-tos, **109–121**
learning model, 109–112
learning style, **117–120**
  activities for assessment of, 120–121
  assessment of, 245–247
  meditation focus and, 178
  sensory modality checklist, 1–5
left brain. *See* right-brain, left-brain activity
left-brain/right-brain techniques, 132, 137
life as school for learning, 13, 15
Life Code, 95
life events
  coincidences, 53–54
  interpretation of, 169, 171, 198
  intuition and, 98–99
  meaningfulness of, 16–17
  as stimulus-response pattern, 31
life lessons, **31–44**
  changing, 29–30, 38–39, 196
  characteristics of, 31–35
  effectiveness of, 1–2
  growth-producing, 37–38
  guidance from, 10
  learning of, 15, 176, 179, 198
  permanent, 38–39, 40
  recognition of, 3–4, 40, *43*
  teachers for, 3–4, *51*
  See also external teachers; internal teachers; school of life
life purpose, **201–227**
  changes in, 207
  commitment to, 207–208
  discovery of, 4, *209–210*
  fulfilling, 9, 234–235
  giving in, 231–232
  happiness and, 21
  information from dreaming, 208
  inner needs and, 202
  as motivation, 212–213
  need for, 203–204
  overview, 1–5
  possessions and, 186–187
  See also aspirations (dreams); goal setting
lifestyle, **161–200**
  excitement in, 124
  issues in, 4
  for learning and growth, 162
  priority of health in, 15
  procrastination in, 124–125
  workaholism, 62
limiting beliefs. *See* beliefs
logic, 94, 96, 155
long-term goals. *See* goal setting

M
Magnolia Story, The, 231
mañana syndrome, 139
Mandela, Nelson, 229

McCartney, Paul, 94, 179
McFerrin, Bobby, 48
McGraw, Phil, 95
meditation
    attitude change by, 192
    changing beliefs through, 155
    for concentration, *108*
    detachment with, 70
    energy increase with, 183
    goals of, 69, 177–178
    observer role during, 70–71
    physiological effects of, 181
    stress management, 172–173, 237
    techniques for, *71–72*, 179–180, 181, *182–183*
    workout exercise as, 177, 195
mental images, 98, 99. *See also* guided imagery; intuition
mood-altering substances/activities. *See* addiction
motivation
    deadlines as, 144
    heartfelt motivator, 212, 225
    intention and, 133
    intuition for, 134
    regret as, 134, 179, *227*
    stress as, 166
movement meditation, 181. *See also* meditation
Murphy, Mark, 212, 225
music
    attitude shift from, 192, 195
    as creative expression, 172
    de-stressing technique, 173
    as escape activity, 171
    meditation, 181–182
    as reward, 218

N
natural flow of life
    authentic self and, 202
    consequences of, 19
    Creative Force and, 21–22
    time distortion with, 73
negative emotions
    experiencing, *80–81*
    expressing, 78–79, 80, 128
    identification of, 79
    physical sensations with, 79–80
    See also addiction
neurotransmitters, 181
nightmares/night terrors, 85–86. *See also* dreaming
nutrition, 176. *See also* personal health

O
observer role/position
    during meditation, 70–71
    thought observation with, 80
    See also detachment
obsessive-compulsive relationships, 85–86
obstacles as teachers, **123–159**
    hazardous zones, 125–129, *130–131*
    lessons from, 9–10
"Our Deepest Fear," 232–234
Outlaw, Frank, 75
overcommitment, 140, 143, 147. *See also* workaholism

P
paradoxical intention, 170
paralysis by analysis, 193
Peck, M. Scott, 102
people as teachers, **49–51**
perception
    conscious shift of, 192
    experienced reality and, 150
    life lessons and, 31–32
    of others, 161
    reinterpretation stressors, 170–171
    of self by others, 150
    of teachers, 46, 49
    in wound healing, 190–191
    See also beliefs
perfectionism, 86, 143–144, 164
personal health
    cornerstones of, 176–179, 183, *184*
    energy levels, *184*
    improving, 173, 184
    prolonged stress and, 237
    in stress management, 171
personal lessons. *See* unique lessons
physical activity
    in emotional expression, 80–81, *82*
    focus during, 181
    for kinesthetic learners, 117
    in time management, 63
    See also exercising
physical clutter, *188*. *See also* energy
physical sensations
    with emotions, 79–80, *82*
    as intuitive communication, 97
    in meditation exercises,
physiological changes
    with addiction, 86
    in intuitive communication, 97
physiological stressors, 164. *See also* personal health; stress; stress management
places as teachers, **55–58**
Power of Intention, The, 26

practical wisdom, 2, 30
priorities
    to-do list items, 135
    goal setting and, 63, 136, *213–214*
    health, 14, 15
    setting, 40, 42
    strategic delays with, 140
    See also goal setting; procrastination
procrastination, **139–147**
    effects on psyche, 167
    fear and, 126
    fear of failure in, 143–144
    forms of, 123, 139
    management techniques, 142–*148*, 188
    as message, 147, 222
    rewards of, 61–62, 124–125, 130, 146
    setting deadlines, 216
    as teacher, 124
    See also stressors
Procrastination: Why You Do It, What to Do about It NOW, 142
Providence, 54, 63. *See also* Universe
Purpose Driven Life, The, 207

R

recurring dreams. *See* dreaming
Redfield, James, 58, 234–235
regret
    avoiding, 5, 78, 98, 190
    goal-setting and, 226
    intuition and, 105
    in life, 10
    as motivation, 134, 179, *227*
    vulnerability to, 74
relationships
    attitudes in, 39
    boundaries in, 127, 225
    energy drain from, 184
    family learning effects on, 50–51
    growth in, 197, *199*
    limiting beliefs in, 150–151
    problems in, *184–185*
    See also addiction
relativity, 34–35
relaxation
    guided-imagery for, 57–58, *181*
    for intuitive communication, *108*
    See also meditation
reward
    for behaviors, 73–74
    excitement as, 124
    music as, 218
    for procrastination, 61–62, 124–125, 130, 146

    in procrastination management, 143–145
    sequencing with tasks, 218
right-brain, left-brain activity, 132–133, 137–138, *139*. *See also* intuition
Road Less Traveled, The, 102
Robbins, Tony, 193
Runner's World, 113

S

school of life
    adventures, 10–28
    empowerment in, 1–5
    external teachers, 45–64
    internal teachers, 65–92
    intuition, 93–108
    learning how-tos, 109–122
    lifestyle development, 161–200
    making progress in, 12–14
    obstacles as teachers, 123–159
    purpose and goals, 201–228
    recognizing adventures in, 7–12
    rules of, 16–22
    teaching, 229–240
    See also life lessons; school rules
school rules, **16–22**
    developing unique talent, 21
    fulfilling your purpose in life, 20
    increasing awareness, 19
    learning and testing, 17
    meaning and purpose of events, 16–17
    opportunities to learn, 16
    promotion, 17–18
    repeating classes, 8, 18
    resisting natural flow, 19
    resources and support in, 20
Seinfeld, Jerry, 179
self-awareness. *See* awareness
self-care
    burn-out, 178, 232
    for growth/progress, 13–15, 66, 237–238
    See also personal health
self-esteem
    core and limiting beliefs, 150, 157
    effects of procrastination on, 141, 146
    goal setting and, 221
    life lessons and, 30
    with life purpose, 202
    self-criticism and, 116
    thought stressors, 164
    time management for, 61, 172
    workaholism and, 83, 84
    wounds and, 190
self-observation, 142–143
self-talk
    for attitude and behavior change, 224, 227

frustration intolerance and, 237
perpetuation of fear, 224
punitive, 18
in stress management, 170
Seligman, Martin, 128–129
Service, Robert, 33
Sheehan, George, 113
short-term goals. *See* goal setting
skill development. *See* competence/incompetence
sleep
   deprivation effects, 13–15, 19, 32, *174*, 177
   disturbance as stressor, 164
   dreaming during, 88, *90–92*
   energy levels with, 176, 183, 198
   as hazardous zone, *130*
   insomnia, 70
   peak performance and, 164
   for personal health, 114–115, 171, 177
   in stress management, 173, 174
   time management and, 131, 137
   in workaholism, 84
   See also dreams
Smith, Emily Esfahani, 202
soul, 69, *71*, 93
sources of stress. *See* stressors
spontaneous knowledge. *See* intuition
stimulus-response pattern, 31, 106–107
strategic plans
   contingency procrastination, 140–141
   procrastination as message in, 147, 222
stress
   assessment of, *163–164*
   cumulative nature of, 169
   experiencing, *168*
   negative interpretation of, 166
   optimal level of, 4, 166, 168
   from procrastination, 123
   reactions to, 172
   symptoms of, 167, 168
stress management, **162–174**
   cornerstones of, 173, 176, 179, 183
   developing a plan for, 172–173, *174*
   with intention, 170
   interpretation of events for, 166
   meditation, 172–173
   mental health days, 8
   mental shift/mindset for, 10–11, 166
   recognizing stress symptoms, 167
   techniques for, 170–172
stressors
   cognitive, 168
   emotional, 167
   environmental, 165, 169
   perfectionism, 164
   physical, 167
   spiritual, 168
subconscious/unconscious
   dreams from, 31, 89
   incompetence and competence, 109, 110, *112*, 198
   intuition, *210*
   limiting/core beliefs, 126, 148–149, 151, 153, 157
   use of imagery, 104, 207
substitute behavior, 75. *See also* anxiety
success
   fear of, 144
   fear of failure in, 149
   using imagery for, *220*
   See also failure
Success Principles, The, 17
synchronicities, 53

T

talents and gifts, 8, 226. *See also* life purpose
teachers, **45–108**
   addictions, 82–87
   animals, 58–60
   behaviors, 72–76
   bodies, 65–68
   coincidences, 51–55
   dreams, 88–90
   emotions, 76–81
   experience, 47–49
   intuition, 93–108
   people, 49–51
   places, 55–57
   thoughts, 69–71
   time, 60–63
teaching, 229–239
Teachings of don Juan, The, 56
thoughts, **69–71**
   assessing validity of, 70
   intuitive communication through, 98
   self-fulfilling of, 71
   as stressors, 164
   See also meditation
thought-stopping, form for, 249–250
time as teacher, 60–64
time management, **131–138**
   meditation techniques in, 179–180, 182–183
   physical activity in, 63
   procrastination management, 147
   techniques for, 134–137, *138–139*
   See also goal setting; priorities
time on task, 62, 135
time-out periods, 61, 137–138

to-do lists, 134
Twain, Mark, 191

U
unconscious. *See* subconscious/unconscious
unconscious competence. *See* competence/incompetence
unique lessons, 2, 4, 30
Universe
    answering your calling, 19–21, 233
    assistance from, 25, 44–45, 63, 106, 193, 198, 202
    attention to lessons from, 41–42
    coincidences as signs from, 52–54, 207
    Creative Force in, 202
    dreams as guidance from, 90
    energy from, 24
    getting our attention, 10, 114
    intention and, 134
    internal clock synchronization, 33
    intuition and, 106–107
    real-life lessons from, 11, 31
    response to attitude, 193
    signs/messages from, 17–18, 31, 43, 49, 106
    speaking through people, 49
    teachers from, 107, 109, 197
    wake-up calls from, 13, 19–20, 32–33

V
Vaughn, Francis, 94, 108
victim-to-student move, 11, 191
visual imagery. *See* guided imagery
visual learning. *See* learning style
visualization. *See* guided imagery

W
wake-up calls, 13–14, 19–20, 32–33
Warren, Rick, 207
Wegscheider-Cruse, Sharon, 230
Williams, Pharrell, 173
Williamson, Marianne, 232, 234
Wilson, Bill, 78
Winfrey, Oprah, 95–96, 179
witness position, 69–70, 72–73, 80
workaholism, **82–85**
    effects of, 83–85
    limiting/core beliefs for, 152
    purpose of, 161, insight
    as teachers, 85
    time management and, 137
working out. *See* exercising

Y
Yeats, William Butler, vii
Yuen, Lenora, 142

Z
Zeigarnik, B., 137
Zeigarnik effect, 137, 146

Acknowledgments

Sometimes the school of life gives us individual assignments that we need to complete alone, and at other times, the task requires a group effort. The making of this book definitely happened through a group. It's astounding how many resources the Universe pulled together along the way. I'm so grateful for getting to be a part of this "Grand Adventure" and for the following people who joined me on this path.

My heartfelt appreciation to the university students I had the joy of working with. Thank you for sharing your struggles and successes with such courage and sincerity. Your efforts were a constant source of inspiration, and you taught me invaluable life lessons.

I offer my sincere thanks to Janice Stevens, the leader of my writers' critique group, for her boundless enthusiasm and unwavering support. Janice believed in me and my potential from the get-go, just as she does with all of her students. Thank you for being such a bright light for so many.

A huge thanks to the members of my Writing for Publication critique group, who listened to me read every word of this book and offered their feedback with honesty and caring: Richard Bailey, Jim Benelli, Robert Eiland, David Elkin, Mary Eurgubian, Don Farris, Veronica Giolli, Lucia Hammar, Earlene Holguin, Beverly Horsley, Gus Knittel, Sue Bonner Martin, Terry Meehan, Jim Mobley, Tom Morton, Linda Robertson, Pat Shanley, the late Chuck Soley, Fran Thomas, and Franz Weinschenk. A special thanks to Hank Palmer for affirming my efforts and reminding me to share personal stories. And especially to CJ Collins, my heartfelt thanks for your friendship, your support as a fellow writer, and for consistently questioning the content of my book. Your honesty has been such a gift.

In the early stages of developing this book, I needed ways to field-test the concepts. I'm so grateful to the Department of Counselor Education and Rehabilitation at California State University, Fresno (CSUF) for approving me to teach the material as graduate coursework, which allowed me to refine my ideas and get crucial, in-the-trenches feedback. I also want to thank Susan Hawksworth, Tracy Bessey, and other staff from the Division of Continuing and Global Education at CSUF for so generously supporting my weekend classes. And sincere thanks to my content editor, Jana Price-Sharps, Ed.D., licensed psychologist, for reviewing my writing with the seasoned perspective of her extensive experiences in teaching and individual therapy.

My family gave me the foundation to write this kind of book. I so deeply appreciate my parents, Sarah and Jim Gannaway, for their unconditional love, for supporting me in everything I ever wanted to do, and for constantly showing me how to live a life filled with faith, purpose, kindness, and joy. Many thanks to my sister, Sharon Gannaway, for our shared history, for always being there, and for helping me learn so much. And my heartfelt appreciation goes to my sister, Vivian (VS) Gannaway Walker, Ph.D. Thank you for listening to endless tales of my writing and for supporting me with intuitive input, perfectly-timed edits, understanding, enthusiasm, and encouragement.

Many thanks to John Eggen and the talented staff at The Mission Marketing Mentors, especially my coach, Janet Tingwald. You helped me shape and publish a better book than what I would have done on my own. My sincere thanks to Hobie and Kathi Dunn of Dunn and Associates for your professional guidance and creative cover design. I also appreciate Anne Fifer, D.O., Ph.D., for doing such a great job on the index. And a big thanks to Chris Estep with TheChatterBox Guys for stepping in to help with the interior book design and typesetting.

Finally, my sincere thanks to the following people who provided essential support through the many facets of my writing process: Arlene Bireline; Kathy Winter; Gena Gechter, Ph.D.; John Campise, D.C.; Abbas Bazzy, N.D.; Minnie Loftus; Fabienne Buckle; Gary Funk; Scott Swarthout, D.C.; Janeil Swarthout, Ph.D.; Cleo Bauer-Papagni; David Schelzel, J.D.; Beth Bridges; Darryl Dote; Wayne Everett; and Tom Milne. Your support has helped me more than you could know. I'm so grateful we could share parts of this incredible journey.

Invitation

An Invitation to Book Clubs and Other Groups

Most of the material in this book was first taught in university courses. I appreciate my students' honesty and candor in providing me with feedback about the material and the way I taught it. Their input contributed to the book as it is presented here.

The activities at the end of most sections of this book were tested and refined in those courses. Some of the benefits students got out of the activities were because of the discussion with other members of the class. One person's questions, answers, or comments helped other students further explore how the material applied to their own lives. Working with this material in a small-group setting seemed to help all the students get more out of the class and our time together.

If you are a member of a book club or other group that reads and discusses books, I hope you will consider reading this book in your group. You already have an ideal situation for exploring and discussing the activities and your responses.

Even if you're not involved with a book club or similar group, I encourage you to find at least one other person to work with. Perhaps you have a friend who would be interested in doing the activities together and comparing answers. At the very least, you might be able to talk with a trusted family member or friend about what you're learning as you work through the activities on your own. The more you put into your reading and active involvement, the more you'll get out of it.

Also, keep me in mind if you need a speaker for your conference, organization or university event. I love to talk about the topics in this book and my experiences as a writer. I also offer one-on-one coaching for people who want support to achieve their goals. For more information, visit my website at www.lindagannaway.com.

About the Author

Linda Gannaway has always been fascinated with learning. She received her doctorate in education, an Ed.D. in counselor education, from the University of Arkansas, Fayetteville. She also completed a predoctoral internship in counseling and clinical psychology from the University of Texas at Austin.

Certified as an educational examiner, Dr. Gannaway tested students in the public schools who had learning difficulties and identified ways they could improve. That experience gave her a hands-on, in-depth understanding of how we learn and how we get stuck in the learning process.

Linda also worked more than twenty-five years at several universities as a personal counselor, administrator, and instructor. She taught classes to thousands of students on basic life skills such as time management, procrastination, stress management, and learning life's lessons. In addition, she has extensive experience in the areas of goal setting, relaxation, guided imagery, and sports improvement.

Linda currently enjoys writing, speaking, and consulting. She lives in California's Central Valley with two rescue cats, a rescue turtle, and a delightful talking parrot named McKee.

Publisher's Cataloging-In-Publication Data

(Prepared by The Donohue Group, Inc.)

Names: Gannaway, Linda.

Title: The power of life lessons : how to learn your lessons and create the life you want / Linda Gannaway, Ed.D.

Description: First edition. | Fresno, CA : Keaton Publishing, a division of TCS Communications, LCC, [2017] | Includes bibliographical references and index.

Identifiers: LCCN 2016910732 | ISBN 978-0-9985066-0-9 | ISBN 0-9985066-0-5 | ISBN 978-0-9985066-9-2 (ebook)

Subjects: LCSH: Life skills. | Conduct of life. | Self-actualization (Psychology) | Time management. | BISAC: SELF-HELP / Motivational & Inspirational.

Classification: LCC HQ2037 .G36 2017 (print) | LCC HQ2037 (ebook) | DDC 646.7--dc23

www.ingramcontent.com/pod-product-compliance
Lightning Source LLC
Chambersburg PA
CBHW070555300426
44113CB00010B/1258